JOURNAL FOR THE STUDY OF THE OLD TESTAMENT
SUPPLEMENT SERIES
301

Editors
David J.A. Clines
Philip R. Davies

Executive Editor
John Jarick

Editorial Board
Robert P. Carroll, Richard J. Coggins, Alan Cooper, J. Cheryl Exum,
John Goldingay, Robert P. Gordon, Norman K. Gottwald,
Andrew D.H. Mayes, Carol Meyers, Patrick D. Miller

Sheffield Academic Press

Away from the Father's House

The Social Location of na'ar and na'arah in Ancient Israel

Carolyn S. Leeb

Journal for the Study of the Old Testament
Supplement Series 301

To my daughters

May you never encounter locked gates
on the pathway to your dreams

Copyright © 2000 Sheffield Academic Press

Published by
Sheffield Academic Press Ltd
Mansion House
19 Kingfield Road
Sheffield S11 9AS
England

Typeset by Sheffield Academic Press
and
Printed on acid-free paper in Great Britain
by Biddles Ltd
Guildford, Surrey

British Library Cataloguing in Publication Data

A catalogue record for this book is available
from the British Library

ISBN 1-84127-105-5

CONTENTS

ACKNOWLEDGMENTS

The publication of this book based on my doctoral dissertation finds me indebted to so many people that I could never mention them all. I thank the editors at Sheffield Academic Press for including my work in this series and for their guidance through the publication process. A few people need to be thanked individually, beginning with the late Professor Robert Boling, a fellow Presbyterian who steered me to the doctoral program in Biblical Studies at the Lutheran School of Theology at Chicago. Special thanks must also go to Professor Wesley Fuerst, who found a spot in that program for a 'walk-on' student, and to the institution for its financial support. The help of Professor David Rhoads in alerting me to the bibliographical resources that are the methodological basis for this book was critical; I thank him for his willingness to work with someone in the 'other testament'. I am at a loss for words to express my gratitude to Dean Ralph Klein, who not only directed my dissertation but also baptized my youngest daughters, Natalie and Magdalen. He has been a teacher and mentor, pastor and friend.

Others whose support has been less obvious but just as necessary need also to be acknowledged. For their help with myriad details involved in navigating the institutional process, I wish to thank LaVerne Berry, Irene Connor and Magdalen Ypparila, three women of wit, wisdom and warmth, who provided not only assistance but also words of humor and cheer in the darkest moments of this process. My thanks go to friends, and to two especially: to Mercedes Garcia-Bachmann, for many conversations that helped to convince me that I was not alone in the ways I viewed the texts, and to Peggy Hall for her unfailing belief in me.

Finally, and especially, I thank my husband David, who periodically beat my computer into submission. Without his monumental assistance in ways too numerous to list, this journey could not have been completed. Without his love, the trip would not have been worthwhile.

ABBREVIATIONS

AB	Anchor Bible
ABD	David Noel Freedman (ed.), *The Anchor Bible Dictionary* (New York: Doubleday, 1992)
AEO	Alan H. Gardiner, *Ancient Egyptian Onamastica*. I. *Text* (Oxford: Oxford University Press, 1947)
AfO	*Archiv für Orientforschung*
AnBib	Analecta biblica
ANET	James B. Pritchard (ed.), *Ancient Near Eastern Texts Relating to the Old Testament* (Princeton: Princeton University Press, 1950)
AnOr	Analecta orientalia
AOAT	*Alter Orient und Altes Testament*
BA	*Biblical Archaeologist*
BASOR	*Bulletin of the American Schools of Oriental Research*
BDB	Francis Brown, S.R. Driver and Charles A. Briggs, *A Hebrew and English Lexicon of the Old Testament* (Oxford: Clarendon Press, 1907)
Bib	*Biblica*
BibOr	Biblica et orientalia
BIOSCS	*Bulletin of the International Organization for Septuagint and Cognate Studies*
BN	*Biblische Notizen*
BTB	*Biblical Theology Bulletin*
BZAW	Beihefte zur *ZAW*
ETL	*Ephemerides theologicae lovanienses*
FF	Foundations and Facets
FOTL	Forms of the Old Testament Literature
FRLANT	Forschungen zur Religion und Literatur des Alten und Neuen Testaments
HS	*Hebrew Studies*
HSM	Harvard Semitic Monographs
HUCA	*Hebrew Union College Annual*
IBC	*Interpretation: A Bible Commentary for Teaching and Preaching*
ICC	International Critical Commentary
IDBSup	*IDB*, Supplementary Volume

IEJ	*Israel Exploration Journal*
JAAR	*Journal of the American Academy of Religion*
JANESCU	*Journal of the Ancient Near Eastern Society*
JAOS	*Journal of the American Oriental Society*
JARCE	*Journal of the American Research Center in Egypt*
JBL	*Journal of Biblical Literature*
JNES	*Journal of Near Eastern Studies*
JNSL	*Journal of Northwest Semitic Languages*
JSOTSup	*Journal for the Study of the Old Testament*, Supplement Series
KRI	*Ramesside Inscriptions*, K.A. Kitchen (ed.) (London: Blackwell, 1969)
NCB	New Century Bible
NICOT	New International Commentary on the Old Testament
OBT	Overtures to Biblical Theology
OTL	Old Testament Library
ResQ	*Restoration Quarterly*
RSP	L.R. Fisher *et al.* (eds.), *Ras Shamra Parallels* (AnOr, 49-51; 3 vols.; Rome: Pontifical Biblical Institute, 1972–81)
SAT	H. Gunkel, W. Stärck, P. Volz, H. Gressmann, H. Schmidt and M. Haller (eds.), *Die Schriften des Alten Testaments* (Göttingen: Vandenhoeck & Ruprecht, 2nd rev. edn, 1921)
SBL	Society of Biblical Literature
SBLDS	SBL Dissertation Series
SWBA	Social World of Biblical Antiquity
ThWAT	G.J. Botterweck and H. Ringgren (eds.), *Theologisches Wörterbuch zum Alten Testament* (Stuttgart: W. Kohlhammer, 1970–)
UF	*Ugarit-Forschungen*
UT	C.H. Gordon, *Ugaritic Textbook* (AnOr, 38; Rome: Pontifical Biblical Institute, 1969)
VTSup	*Vetus Testamentum*, Supplements
WAS	Adolph Erman and Hermann Grapow, *Wörterbuch der aegyptischen Sprache* (Berlin: Akademie-Verlag, 1971)
ZAW	*Zeitschrift für die alttestamentliche Wissenschaft*

Chapter 1

INTRODUCTION

Understanding the Word נער in the Hebrew Bible

The Hebrew noun נער appears 239 times in the Hebrew Bible; its feminine equivalent נערה occurs 61 times.[1] The words are most at home in
prose narrative, prominently in the Former Prophets and in the stories
of the ancestors in Genesis.[2] Nearly any beginning student of the Hebrew language knows the meanings of these two words as 'boy' and
'girl', or 'lad' and 'maiden', or similar terms. The understanding is
widespread that these nouns have somehow come to mean 'servant' in a
majority of cases. The terms are generally believed to apply to persons
who are youthful, if not actually children. However, these time-honored
definitions are simply inadequate. A few examples will serve to illus-
trate the sorts of narratives in which these words appear, as well as the
range of circumstances which they address.

Function

In a large number of cases, the נער is without question an individual in
service to another. This service could be performed in one of several
areas. 2 Kings 4 clearly illustrates the נער in household or domestic service. Gehazi, one of the few servant נערים who are named, is Elisha's
personal attendant (2 Kgs 4.12, 25; 5.20; 8.4).[3] A prosperous couple
from Shunem have a נער in their service (2 Kgs 4.22), probably the
same one who is referred to as *her* נער and accompanies the woman on

---

1.   Exact count varies, depending on whether certain instances are viewed as
the noun under study, another (related) noun, or a verbal form. All occurrences of
the feminine in the Pentateuch are with the *defectiva* spelling (e.g. Gen. 24.12, הנער);
elsewhere it is spelled *plene*.

2.   Neither word appears in biblical Aramaic.

3.   For a complete listing of נערים who are given names, see Appendix A.
Among נערות only Rebekah, Dinah, Esther, Ruth and Abishag are named.

a journey (2 Kgs 4.24). Elisha's servant is asked to prepare a pot of stew (2 Kgs 4.38), while Abraham's נער prepares meat in Gen. 18.7, both clearly domestic functions.

In other cases, the service performed seems to be agricultural. Nabal's נערים are working as shepherds for his flocks (1 Sam. 25.8, 14, 19). In performance of the task of tending sheep, both Joseph (Gen. 37.2) and David (1 Sam. 16.11) are also referred to as נער, although neither is a servant at the time.[4] In all likelihood, the נער who accompanies Saul in searching for Kish's lost asses (1 Sam. 9.3) is also serving as an agricultural worker, perhaps specifically in caring for livestock. Boaz employs both נערים and נערות as reapers or as supervisor to reapers (Ruth 2.5, 6, 9, 15, 21).

Many, many נערים serve in military capacities, frequently either as personal assistants to a warrior or perhaps as mercenaries in battle themselves. We see the word used in reference to Jonathan's armor-bearer[5] (1 Sam. 14.1, 6) and to the fellow who fetches his arrows, during practice if not also in combat (1 Sam. 20.21, 21, 35, 36, 37, 38, 39, 40, 41). The men of David's entourage are called נערים, both in the incident in which they stave off hunger by eating the 'shewbread' (1 Sam. 21.3, 5, 6) and in the encounter with Nabal (1 Sam. 25.5, 9, 12, 25, 27). The men who kill the sons of Rimmon in 2 Sam. 4.12 are נערים, as are the men who perform ritual combat in the presence of Abner and Joab (2 Sam. 2.12-17). The servants in Nehemiah (4.10, 16, 17; 5.10, 16; 13.19) are armed (and thus fill a military role), while also working on the rebuilding of the wall of Jerusalem. The king's ministers in Esther (2.2; 6.3, 5) are governmental advisors, as well as having, no doubt, domestic or military responsibilities.

Age and Marital Status
The standard lexica reflect this broad range of meanings. BDB[6] suggests the following definitions for נער: boy, lad, youth, servant, retainer (i.e. personal attendant, household servant, follower); for נערה: girl,

---

4.   Both Joseph and David are in the countryside at some distance from home, however. Joseph is evidently under the supervision of the sons of Bilhah and Zilpah, his older half-brothers, when he is referred to in this way. At this point, he is 17 years old and probably considered a young adult, not a child.

5.   Other armor-bearers serve Joab (2 Sam. 18.15) and Abimelech (Judg. 9.54).

6.   F. Brown, S.R. Driver and C.A. Briggs, *A Hebrew and English Lexicon of the Old Testament* (Oxford: Clarendon Press, 1952), p. 654.

damsel, female attendants, maid. Cited examples, for the masculine form, rule out the possibility that age is the determinative criterion: an unborn child (Judg 13.5, 7, 8, 12), an infant (Exod. 2.6), a just-weaned child (1 Sam. 1.24), a youth of 17 (Gen. 37.2), a young man of marriageable age (Gen. 34.19) or of an age to be a seasoned warrior (2 Sam. 18.5, 12). Ziba, long-time servant to the house of Saul (2 Sam. 9.9, 16.1-4), remains a נער through many years of his adult life, and other נערים are conspicuously adult as well.

The examples for the feminine form likewise cover a wide age span, and include both single and married females: young daughters (Job 40.29); marriageable young women (Gen. 24.14, 16, 28, 55, 57); betrothed girls [*sic*] (Deut. 22.25, 27); young widows (Ruth 2.6; 4.12); a concubine (Judg. 19.3, 4, 5, 6, 8, 9); even a prostitute (Amos 2.7).[7] When a servant is indicated, no specificity with respect to age can be inferred (Gen. 24.61; Exod. 2.5, 1 Sam. 25.42; Prov. 9.3; 27.27; 31.15; Esth. 2.9; 4.4, 16; Ruth 2.5, 8, 22, 23). In each case, the נערה is arguably a woman, not a child.[8]

Root

BDB distinguishes three roots: נער I, meaning to growl or bray; נער II, meaning to shake or shake out or off; and נער III, where the nouns under study are listed, for which it reports that the meaning of the root is unknown. The definitions given, as mentioned above, range so widely that only maleness (or femaleness) seems to be a uniting factor. Cognates in other languages have not settled the question. BDB, while suggesting an Arabic root connected to the root for נער I, mentions only a single Phoenician inscription relating to נער III, and declines to offer a meaning for that one. The translation of related words in Ugaritic has, of course, been influenced by the commonly accepted meanings of the Hebrew words.[9] For Ugaritic *n'r*, Cyrus Gordon suggested 'boy, unmarried son'. He adds that

7.   Although not all scholars believe that this נערה is a prostitute. This remains one of the most disputed verses of Hebrew scripture.

8.   Only the נערה קטנה of 2 Kgs 5 seems to be a girl. This phrase is discussed in more detail in Chapter 7.

9.   Cf. Koehler: 'The discovery of cognate languages affected Hebrew lexico-graphy in a double way. It has enriched the Hebrew lexicon with many supporting statements, with a heap of parallels. On the other side what we know today of the Akkadian and Ugaritic lexicon would be impossible to a great extent without Heb-

in 2068 *n'r* (.3, 25) is distinguished from *bn* (.6, 19, 26, 27), though both
are members of households (‖ *att*), so that *n'r* has some other meaning
such as 'servant'…m.pl. *n'rm* (113.60; 169.12): members of a certain
guild, perhaps 'servitors' or 'soldiers'

He goes on to compare them to the 'New Egyptian *n'rn* == *na'arûna*'.[10]
Evidently he was cognizant of some range and variability, even in its
limited occurrences in the Ugaritic texts. Clearly, the traditional under-
standings lack specificity and consistency.

Each of the possible English terms that have been suggested as definitions could be rendered by other well-known Hebrew words: עבד or
אמה for servants, עלם or עלמה (young man or young woman), איש or
אישה (man or woman), ילד or ילדה (boy or girl), even בתולה (traditionally rendered 'virgin') or זונה (prostitute). The choice of the term נער (or
נערה) by various biblical authors suggests that the term carries connotations that these other words do not. The intent of the proposed
investigation is to discover what common threads connect this word in
all its varied uses in the Hebrew Bible.

The contribution of an adequate definition for these words is clear.
Broad, flexible, generic definitions for נער and נערה conceal the social
realities that the stories can reveal. Alongside the historical/critical task
of discovering the political situation of the biblical narratives (the rulers,
the geography, the dates) is the sociological/anthropological task of discovering the social world of pre-exilic Israel, the society's structure and
the identity, that is, social location, of the various 'ordinary folk' of the
biblical narrative. Both set the stage for the story and fill in the details
that bring the story to life.

The planned research will contribute an understanding for these terms
that explains the social location of the נער and נערה, suggesting why
these words and not one of the others available were used in each specific case. The final product will be a definition that coheres, encompass-
ing all (or most) of the occasions when it is used in the Hebrew
scriptures. The result will be a more nuanced understanding of some

rew' (L. Koehler, 'Preface to the Hebrew Part', Introduction, in Koehler and
W. Baumgartner, *The Hebrew and Aramaic Lexicon of the Old Testament* [revised
by W. Baumgartner and J.J. Stamm; Leiden: E.J. Brill, 1995], pp. lxviii-lxxii [lxx]).

    10. *UT*, p. 445, no. 1666. See Chapter 8 for a discussion of the Egyptian evi-
dence and how misunderstanding it has introduced misperceptions into our understanding of the Hebrew, both directly and *via* the Ugaritic evidence.

well-known narratives and a more nearly adequate comprehension of certain problematic passages.

Review of Recent Research

Two major studies of the Hebrew word נער have appeared in the last two decades. A number of lexica have been updated in recent years, and their entries on this word rely heavily on these two studies.[11] Additionally, a brief treatment of the word in Stager's seminal article on the ancient Israelite family has drawn the attention of the wide readership of that article to the meaning and significance of the term.[12] Aspects of each of these three works will be covered briefly.

Hans-Peter Stähli

Twenty years ago, Hans-Peter Stähli published his dissertation on the Hebrew word נער. This is a masterpiece of philological study, and his attention to the history of scholarship on each pericope is quite thorough.[13] In the final analysis, Stähli distinguishes two semantic domains for the word. For neither of these is the principal distinguishing feature 'young-ness', since he proposes that they represent legal or social states rather than phases of life. One is a category of 'servant' in which he includes cultic functionaries and 'Elitekämpfern' along with more ordinary servants.[14] The other is a category of dependent persons whose common characteristic (at least in the case of the males) is the fact of being unmarried and thus under the power of the head of the family, whom Stähli refers to as the *paterfamilias*.[15] (The females, in his view, remain נערות after marriage owing to their generally more dependent

11. See, for instance Koehler and Baumgartner, *Lexicon of the Old Testament*, s.v. נער.

12. L.E. Stager, 'The Archaeology of the Family in Ancient Israel', *BASOR* 260 (1985), pp. 1-35.

13. The present study has not attempted to duplicate Stähli's work in this area, but rather to explore what newer methods offer in the way of insight into the meaning of this word. For the history of the study of נער using traditional methods, especially for source-critical analysis, the reader is referred to Stähli's excellent footnotes.

14. Stähli, *Knabe-Jüngling-Knecht: Untersuchungen zum Begriff Na'ar im Alten Testament* (ed. Jürgen Becker and Henning Graf Reventlow; BBET, 7; Frankfurt: Peter Lang, 1978), pp. 135-217.

15. Stähli, *Knabe*, pp. 96-100.

status in Israelite society.) This dependency (and the status of נער) ends, according to Stähli, upon marriage. This conclusion perhaps accords more with late-twentieth-century European and American expectations of achieving independence upon marriage than it does with a world in which each nuclear family cell of an extended family remained under the control and oversight of the family's head. Stähli fails to discover a common thread that links these two different uses of the word (servant and unmarried male), nor does he offer any explanation of the fact that some biblical authors use the word with both meanings in close proximity in the texts.[16]

John Macdonald

In contrast to the methodical approach of Stähli, John Macdonald (in some cases in collaboration with B. Cutler) has taken an eclectic approach to the investigation of the terms, inspired by his work with the Mari letters:

> When I first realised that the traditional rendering of the term *ṣuḫārū* 'young men, servants' frequently did not meet the requirements of the various contexts, my thoughts immediately turned to the term *ne'arim* (*ne'ārîm*) in the Israelite literature. After a careful study of this latter term I realised that the Israelite *na'ar* (young man) was a very different figure from that normally understood.[17]

Having been captivated by the happenstance that this etymologically unrelated word from the Mari correspondence is conveyed in translation by the same two English terms, Macdonald goes on to investigate the *n'r* of both ancient Israel and of Ugarit. His conclusions owe more to Mari, perhaps, than to Israel:

> *Na'ar* undoubtedly means a young male, whether he is a babe-in-arms or a young man. What seems not to have been realized till now is that he is a young male of high birth.[18]

---

16. Stähli, *Knabe*, pp. 275-76.

17. J. Macdonald, 'The Role and Status of the Suharu in the Mari Correspondence', *JAOS* 96.1 (1976), pp. 57-68 (57). A comprehensive analysis, using sociological methods, has not to my knowledge been done for this word in its Mari contexts. Such an investigation is beyond the scope of the present study, but would clearly add a great deal to our knowledge of the ancient world. In general, social science methodologies have not been systematically applied to the other Semitic literatures.

18. J. Macdonald, 'The Status and Role of the Na'ar in Israelite Society', *JNES*

He focuses principally on military contexts, and eventually settles on a definition of 'squire' or 'young knight'.[19] The examples he suggests as evidence of 'high birth'—for instance, Ishmael (Gen. 21.12, 17, 18, 20; 22.12), Esau and Jacob (Gen. 25.27), Joseph (Gen. 37.2), Shechem (Gen. 34.19), Manasseh and Ephraim (Gen. 48.16), Moses (Exod. 2.6), Samson (Judg. 13.5-7, 12, 24), Ichabod (1 Sam. 4.21), Samuel (1 Sam. 1.22, 24-25)—are, with the exception of Joseph, *not* in positions of service, either military or domestic. Whenever persons are referred to as the נערים *of* someone, the reference is to the individual whom they serve, not to their father. By combining the 'noble' status of the individuals named above with the occupational roles of others referred to in the Hebrew scriptures as נערים, he creates a far-reaching, but ultimately untenable, definition.[20]

Lawrence Stager

Citing both of these authors, Stager connects the נער to

> firstborn males waiting for the *pater familias* to 'pass on' or of younger
> sons who had difficulties establishing themselves as heads of household,

35.3 (1976), pp. 147-70 (147). The notion that the word נער denotes some sort of elite status can be traced back ultimately to Meyer's handling of the Egyptian cognate, for which see Chapter 8. Macdonald repeatedly uses the adjective 'high' without any systematic study of status and values in the societies to which he applies the term.

19. Macdonald, 'Status and Role of the Na'ar', pp. 169-70. Even in a European context, 'high birth' might be an inappropriate designation for a knight. 'The *nobiles* were wealthy hereditary landholders exercising broad jurisdictional powers. The knights were their military retainers, usually of humble means, defined by their military vocation rather than their lineage'. C. Warren Hollister, 'Knights and Knight Service', in American Council of Learned Societies', *Dictionary of the Middle Ages*. VII. *Italian Renaissance-Mabinogi* (Joseph R. Strayer ed. in Chief; New York: Charles Scribner's Sons, 1986), pp. 276-79 (276).

20. In his expositions of this definition, Macdonald includes outdated assumptions as well as errors of fact. He assigns a date (and presumably therefore historical authenticity) to Abraham: 'no later than the 18th century'. He identifies 'the Israelite *na'ar* Jeroboam, son of Solomon' in 1 Kgs 11.28, although v. 26 clearly states that Jeroboam was the son of Nebat, Solomon's servant (עבד), whose mother was now a widow. Obviously, whether this נער can be subsumed under the category of 'high-born males' is more tenuous if he is a servant's son than had he been the king's son (B. Cutler, 'Identification of the Na'ar in the Ugaritic Texts' [collaborator J. Macdonald], *UF* 8 [1976], pp. 27-36 [31]; Macdonald, 'Role and Status of the Suharu', pp. 57-68 [58]).

with sufficient land and wealth. In ancient Israel, as in medieval Europe and many other cultures, this 'safety valve' for young, unmarried males involved careers in the military, government, or priesthood.[21]

Stager goes further by making specific comparisons to the aristocratic 'youth' of twelfth-century France:

> This was a stage in the life of the noble male, beginning when he became a knight and ending when he put down roots, married, became head of a household, and started to rear a family. It was a turbulent period of knight errantry, when fighting in battles, competing in tournaments, and courting fair maidens were the primary concerns.[22]

Stager's suggestion that the נערים were unable to establish themselves as heads of households is probably quite accurate, although the servanthood in which most of them are found can hardly be understood as a 'career path', but rather as hiring themselves out. Most often the נערים are found in the humbler roles, tending livestock and carrying weapons. Only occasionally do we see them in any real governmental role, and only one נער *chooses* the priesthood.[23] None of the biblical נערים can be identified as first-born sons; most are later-born sons who may never achieve the status of 'head of household'. Furthermore, the social structures of pre-exilic Israel (especially early monarchic Israel) were not identical with those of an ancient Canaanite city-state nor of medieval Europe. The aristocratic French youth shared with the נערים of early Israel a penchant for 'getting into trouble' when they were away from home, but the carefree high jinks of knighthood are probably not the best analogy for the hard physical labor that most of the נערים endured. Conditions favoring knighthood, with its complicated code of chivalry (or some roughly equivalent institution), require a highly organized, highly stratified society, a situation that obtained least during the pre-monarchic and early monarchic periods, when the majority of the narratives containing the נערים are set.[24]

---

21. Stager, 'Archaeology of the Family', p. 25.
22. Stager, 'Archaeology of the Family', p. 25.
23. I.e., the Levite of Judg. 17–18. Samuel and Samson are both dedicated to the Nazirate prior to birth.
24. The distinction is clearly drawn by C.J.H. Wright: 'Palestine before Israel was a city-state culture, with a very stratified social and economic hierarchy, topped by the local kings and their elites, supported by the mass of taxpaying tenant peasants... By contrast, Israel emerged as a social system based on a broad equality of kinship groups, initially without a centralized, elite power base' (C.J.H. Wright,

The principal shortcoming of all three of these approaches is their adoption, with little examination, of the notion that נער was a term that carried 'high status' or 'high position'. In order to assign high status to a role within a society, we must first examine the values of that society to determine what attributes it considers important.[25] Such a value-laden assessment must be couched in terms of those elements that the society in question most values. In the case of early Israel, the values most cherished by society included possession of land, male progeny and respect within the community. From the beginning of its existence, these were the things that brought a man status.[26] These were also manifestly out of the reach of the individuals in the Hebrew texts who are called נערים. Serving in the court of the king, working in another man's fields or household, fighting the battles of a chieftain—all of these are ways to build up another man's 'house', not one's own. A few of these individuals (the minority whose names are provided by the narrator) may have come initially from high-status families, but in the case of the majority, we know nothing of their father's houses except that the individuals referred to as נערים were away from them.

Walter Mayer and R. Mayer-Opificius
More recently, these two authors have completely rejected this notion of 'noble birth' for the נער, demonstrating from the Egyptian evidence of the accounts of the Battle of Qadesh that the *na'aruna* (as well as the *n'r* of the Ugaritic materials) are better understood as servants and camp followers.[27] While these authors do not explore the ramifications of their work for understanding the social location of the נערים of early Israel, their research is vital to our understanding of the way in which a

'Family', *ABD*, II, pp. 761-69 (762). Cf. also N.K. Gottwald, *The Tribes of Yahweh: A Sociology of the Religion of Liberated Israel, 1250–1050 B.C.* (Maryknoll, NY: Orbis Books, 1979), pp. 321-23.

25. 'Values are shared ideas about what is socially desirable.' Our own society, for instance, values affluence and material comfort. Thus, to *us*, a bureaucratic position in close attendance on those in power might be highly valued (W.E. Thompson and J.V. Hickey, *Society in Focus: An Introduction to Sociology* [New York: HarperCollins College Publishers, 1994], p. 72).

26. Cf., e.g., the Call of Abraham (Gen. 12) and the Covenant with Abraham (Gen. 15) in which progeny, land and 'name' are clearly the highest rewards for faithfulness.

27. W. Mayer and R. Mayer-Opificius, 'Die Schlacht bei Qadeš: der Versuch einer neuen Rekonstruktion', *UF* 26 (1994), pp. 321-68.

misreading of the Egyptian evidence has encouraged the proliferation of analyses that suggest a 'high-born' status for the נער. Accordingly, their work will be covered at length in Chapter 8.

Distribution of the Words

Pentateuch and Former Prophets

With two arguable exceptions, the appearances in the Tetrateuch (נער 31 times, נערה 9 times) all come from material which is 'non-P'.[28] The words are not found in Leviticus at all. Within the Former Prophets (נער 142 times, נערה 14 times), the words occur exclusively in material drawn from Dtr's sources rather than from apparent expansions and insertions by the editor(s) themselves. Deuteronomy 28.50, which is the sole appearance of נער in Deuteronomy itself, is drawn from the blessings and curses section of old treaty material, while נערה shows up 13 times in a block of legal material in Deuteronomy 22. The masculine and feminine terms frequently occur together,[29] both exhibiting 'clusters' in Ruth, Esther and the Elijah–Elisha stories, as well as in Judges and in stories about Saul and David. The pattern of distribution leads to the conclusion that these words were used by the earliest 'tellers of tales' rather than by compilers and editors.

Postexilic Writings

Neither word appears in Daniel or Ezra, and their occurrence in other indisputably postexilic writing is scarce. The feminine occurs in postexilic writings only in Esther (13 times). The masculine, in addition to its 4 uses in Esther, appears 5 times in Chronicles and 8 times in Nehe-

---

28. As delineated in M. Noth, *A History of Pentateuchal Traditions* (trans. B.W. Anderson; Chico, CA: Scholars Press, 1981), translator's Supplement, pp. 261-76. Noth considers Gen. 37.1-2 to be P. However, Gottwald places these two verses in question in 'non-P' material. I will avoid wading into the scholarly fray regarding the boundaries and existence of 'E', but the interested reader should see Stähli for discussion of this topic using traditional categories (N.K. Gottwald, *The Hebrew Bible: A Socio-Literary Introduction* [Philadelphia: Fortress Press, 1985], pp. 151-53, 182-87).

29. For example, נער in Gen. 34.19, נערה in 34.3, 12; נער in Exod. 2.6, נערה in 2.5; נער in Judg. 19.3, 9, 11, 13, 19; נערה in 19.3, 4, 5, 6, 8, 9; נער in 1 Sam. 9.3, 5, 7, 8, 10, 22, 27; נערה in 9.11; נער in 1 Sam. 25.5, 8, 9, 12, 14, 19, 25, 27; נערה in 1 Sam. 25.42; נער in 2 Kgs 5.14; נערה in 2 Kgs 5.2, 4; נער in Ruth 2.5, 6, 9, 15, 21; נערה in Ruth 2.5, 6, 8, 22, 23; נער in Est. 2.2; נערה in 2.2, 3, 4, 7, 8, 9, 12, 13.

miah. Clearly, late in Israel's history נער and נערה were words that were not in vogue, either because the social reality they indicated was no longer extant or because other words had been taken over to describe it.

Poetry

Non-prophetic poetic materials contain נער a mere 15 times (excluding, for the moment, the 7 in the aphorisms of Proverbs). Of these, fully 9 reflect the stereotyped pairing of נער–זקן. The words are rare in Psalms, Proverbs and Job: the Psalmists use the masculine 3 times, the feminine not at all. נערה appears in 3 places in Proverbs, while נער appears 7 times. Job accounts for one example of the feminine, 7 of the masculine, but 4 of those occur in the prose prologue. Lamentations uses נער just twice. For the feminine form, then, we find only a single poetic occurrence (in Job 40.29), in addition to 3 mentions in Proverbs.

Prophets

The entire corpus of the writing prophets contains the word נער only 16 times, and 1 of those is a verbatim parallel with an occurrence in the Former Prophets (Isa. 37.6, 2 Kgs 19.6). The celebrated 'girl' of Amos 2.7 is the cameo prophetic appearance for the feminine form, although this may well be a verbal form.[30] The meanings that these texts appear to reflect are consistent with, but less differentiated than, those that are apparent from the narrative texts.[31]

The general pattern seems to be that the words designate a quite precise social location in the oldest material, while in later, especially poetic, texts a more generalized youthfulness seems to be designated. This 'semantic drift' over time may well have occurred by means of a kind of *pars pro toto* mechanism. The role and status of נער was indeed

---

30. See Chapter 6 for Marvin Chaney's suggested solution to this *crux*.

31. In fact, the situation is quite analogous to that found by Katharine D. Sakenfeld in her study of חסד: 'The understanding of *ḥesed* which can be gleaned from the texts to be discussed here [Psalms, Proverbs, Job, and hymnic passages from other books] accords well with what has been said of *ḥesed* in the foregoing chapters [on narrative materials] and the picture is enhanced and enriched. Yet, because of the difficulty of dating and absence of concrete contexts, these examples cannot in themselves provide an independent basis for establishing the parameters of *ḥesed*. There are additional difficulties. Many of these passages do not in themselves give any clue as to the content of the word' (K.D. Sakenfeld, *The Meaning of Hesed in the Hebrew Bible: A New Inquiry* [ed. F.M. Cross; HSM, 17; Missoula, MT: Scholars Press, 1978], p. 214).

most often occupied by a person who was relatively young, and in time the word came to connote that general young-ness rather than the more specific features of being a נער. In particular, it would be easy to see how the specificity might be lost if the social realties changed in such a way that most males, upon reaching adulthood, had to leave their ancestral lands and indenture themselves or seek employment away from home. An inescapable situation for young adults might become synonymous with that stage of life. Certainly, what is known about the economic life of ancient Israel, beginning with the demands of the indigenous monarchy and continuing through the period of domination by the Assyrian, Babylonian, Persian, Greek and Roman empires, suggests that the security of tenure of the patrimonies became steadily more tenuous.

Chapter 2

METHODS

Methodological Considerations

Lexicographical Method

The principal method to be employed in this investigation will be a close reading of the Hebrew texts, resulting in what could be called 'argued lexicography', or perhaps 'definitions from within narrative'. The contexts in which the words appear will be examined for the elements that are consistent between one pericope and the next. Those threads will then be woven into a definition that will fit the full range of the situations in which the words are used. Although it is tempting to believe that it is possible to get 'behind' the texts in order to discover some pure definition that is not tainted by the inherently circular reasoning of contextual studies, the reality is that all study of language is contextual.

Some studies by researchers from prior generations of biblical scholars have exhibited keen enthusiasm about the information provided by etymological studies, an enthusiasm that Barr considered overblown:

> Etymology...is concerned with the derivation of words from previous forms. It must be emphasized that this is a historical study. It studies the past of a word, but understands that the past of a word is no infallible guide to its present meaning. Etymology is not, and does not profess to be, a guide to the semantic value of words in their current usage, and such value has to be determined from the current usage and not from the derivation... Nevertheless there is a normative strain in the thought of many people about language, and they feel that in some sense the 'original', the 'etymological meaning', should be a guide to the usage of words, that the words are used 'properly' when they coincide in sense with the sense of the earliest known form from which their derivation can be traced; and that when a word becomes in some way difficult or

ambiguous, an appeal to the etymology will lead to a 'proper meaning' from which at any rate to begin.[1]

In laying out the present study, Barr's caveat has been duly noted. No attempt will be made to delve as far back in time as possible to find some sort of original meaning for נער and נערה. Rather, meaning will be sought in the context of the biblical materials themselves, especially those from earliest Israel, supplemented but not overridden by whatever information is available from Israel's *nearest* neighbors. Words that describe a social location may be expected to vary somewhat more than more concrete words, given the differences in social structure among the various societies whose written records contain these words. Thus caution in the way in which data about cognates is used is particularly appropriate in such an investigation as this one.

This commitment to privilege context over cognates is reflected in the design of the present study. In contrast to most studies of Hebrew words, which place comparative and etymological speculation at the beginning, we will begin with an examination of the word in its narrative use.[2] Similarly, among the extrabiblical sources greatest weight will be given to those which are nearest in time and geography to early Israel. Thus, the Ugaritic and Egyptian documents and inscriptions will be carefully noted, since they come from very close by and near to the time of Israel's origins. Documents from several centuries prior to the beginning of the Iron Age will be considered less pertinent.[3] In light of the semantic drift that words exhibit over time (and which will be demonstrated for נער in Chapter 7), and in light of the diminishing frequency of occurrence of the word in late biblical Hebrew (and its gradual shift toward an age-related meaning) as well as its absence from biblical Aramaic, post-biblical sources will not be treated.

Narrative Method
A variety of tools exists for looking at the literary artistry that has been employed in creating a text. The failure to make use of these methods

---

1.   J. Barr, *The Semantics of Biblical Language* (Oxford: Oxford University Press, 1961), p. 107.

2.   Cf., e.g., the Tables of Contents in Sakenfeld, *The Meaning of Hesed*; W.B. Barrick, 'The Word BMH in the Old Testament' (unpublished PhD dissertation; Chicago: University of Chicago, 1977).

3.   In point of fact, however, this is a theoretical consideration only, since no form of *n'r* has been identified in, for example, the Mari collection.

can result not only in missing the full aesthetic value of a composition, but also in misunderstanding its meaning, as for instance when we read a text without knowledge of its genre or without understanding that an author intends something ironically rather than straightforwardly.[4] In the words of Eskenazi, 'Put simply, literary criticism analyzes *what* is said by looking at *how* it is said.'[5] Literary methods are not a substitute for sociological methods, nor is the reverse the case. Techniques from both literary criticism and the social sciences must be used in tandem in order to reveal the full import of a text.

In ascertaining such information as social location, the social scientist would like to have a broad database resulting from controlled scientific observation. Needless to say, in studying the ancient Near Eastern world, and the biblical world in particular, this ideal is never closely approximated. Narratology can be employed to gain the maximum useful information from the data that are available. Stories can be scrutinized for the details, as well as the silences, that give clues to the world of the writer. Evidence of power within the narrative can be used to determine the possibilities for power for such characters within the worlds that could be imagined by the storytellers and their hearers, although we must be on guard for the possibility that the intent of the story is to portray a world in which power is reordered. In Darr's words, 'Bringing, as best we are able, the ancient audience's extratextual repertoire to bear enables us to recover the meaning and import of poems for its earliest audiences.'[6]

Beyond the use of narrative analysis for evidence of social structures, societal values, and expected roles and relationships, narrative analysis

---

4. This last mistake is often made, for example, in the traditional readings of the story of the breaking of the Aramean siege of Samaria, accomplished by the נערים of the district governors', in 1 Kgs 20.13-21, as will be discussed further in Chapter 8, in the discussion of Egyptian cognates.

5. T.C. Eskenazi, 'Torah as Narrative and Narrative as Torah', in J.L. Mays, D.L. Petersen and K.H. Richards, *Old Testament Interpretation: Past, Present, and Future: Essays in Honor of Gene M. Tucker* (Nashville: Abingdon Press, 1995), pp. 13-30 (15).

6. K.P. Darr, 'Literary Perspectives on Prophetic Literature', in J.L. Mays, D.L. Retanen and K.H. Richards, *Old Testament Interpretation: Past, Present, and Future: Essays in Honor of Gene M. Tucker* (Nashville: Abingdon Press, 1995), pp. 127-43 (141).

can also provide clues (and protect against false assumptions) concerning the boundaries, the provenance, and the redaction history of a tale. The use of repetition, for instance, may be seen as a tool of the artist and not everywhere and inevitably a sign of compositeness or the use of sources. Such information can help to identify the time and place in history when the tale was told, when the story was written down, when the text was edited. By relating these things to what we do know of the social and political changes in the ancient Near East, we are provided with additional information with which to describe a social world.

A number of authors have proposed methodologies for exploring aspects of narrative artistry in Hebrew texts.[7] In each case, they have used those tools to look at one or more representative passages. The present study will use the categories developed by Berlin, as well as her appropriation of the work of William Labov, as a lens through which to look closely at the biblical passages containing the word נער, because they have proved to be relatively simple to apply and because they have yielded fruitful results.[8] Simplicity is an important consideration, given the large number of texts to be considered, but this cursory application of narrative methods is far from exhausting the potential. A number of these narratives could be examined more closely and would produce very interesting, although lengthy, results.

Berlin observes three sorts of characters in biblical narrative. First is 'the agent, about whom nothing is known except what is necessary for the plot'. This is the character who is, so to speak, part of the background rather than foreground. Second is 'the type, who has a limited and stereotyped range of traits, and who represents the class of people with these traits'. Finally, the most fully developed is 'the character, who has a broader range of traits (not all belonging to the same class of people), and about whom we know more than is necessary for the plot'.[9] In other words, only this last sort of character has individuality and distinctiveness. Characterization is achieved through a combination

---

7.　See, e.g., R. Alter, *The Art of Biblical Narrative* (New York: Basic Books, 1981); M. Sternberg, *The Poetics of Biblical Narrative* (Bloomington: Indiana University Press, 1985); P. Trible, *Rhetorical Criticism: Context, Method, and the Book of Jonah* (Philadelphia: Fortress Press, 1994).

8.　A. Berlin, *Poetics and Interpretation of Biblical Narrative* (Sheffield: Almond Press, 1983).

9.　Berlin, *Poetics and Interpretation*, p. 32.

of description, inner life, speech and actions, and contrast with another character (or with an earlier self or an expected norm).[10] The degree of character development establishes a character's power or status or importance in the narrative world and may provide clues to the sort of position that a similar personage might be expected to hold in the real world as well. In particular, a *pattern* of minimal character development for a particular class of persons may suggest that they are not highly valued in the social context of the hearers of the tales.

For her examination of narrative structure, Berlin makes good use of William Labov's socio-linguistic studies of inner-city speech and narrative patterns, and I, in turn, have borrowed her outline of his work.[11] In schematic form, Labov's sequence of well-formed narrative includes:

1. Abstract
2. Orientation
3. Complicating Action
4. Evaluation
5. Result or Resolution
6. Coda

The Abstract (which is not always present) is a summary that introduces the narrative. The Orientation sets the time, place and cast of characters of the story. The Complicating Action provides the heart of the tale, while the Evaluation gives its point, its *raison d'être*. The Resolution informs the hearer of what finally happened, the ultimate outcome. The Coda is the narrator's way of signalling that the narrative has come to an end. It is a way of returning the hearers (or readers) to the real world after their stay in the world of the story. Berlin suggests that many biblical etiologies function as Codas: some phrase on the order of 'and it is there to this day' takes the audience out of the story world, while establishing the link between that world and their present one.[12] These then are the basic tools that will be used to examine the biblical narratives in which the word נער (or נערה) appears.

---

10. Berlin, *Poetics and Interpretation*, pp. 34-42.

11. W. Labov, *Language in the Inner City: Studies in the Black English Vernacular* (Philadelphia: University of Pennsylvania Press, 1972), quoted in Berlin, *Poetics and Interpretation*, pp. 101-10.

12. Berlin, *Poetics and Interpretation*, pp. 107-109, 154.

Sociological Method

Use of Models. The use of models in a study of the social structure of an ancient world is not optional; the question is only whether we will make our models explicit so that they can be discussed and examined.[13] Anthropologists have studied a number of agricultural cultures in the Mediterranean basin and formed an understanding of the ways those societies function.[14] New Testament scholars have very productively examined the world that gave birth to the Christian Testament in light of those models. Certain social roles and relationships that seem strange to twentieth-century European and American readers make sense in light of these simplified pictures of the way some of these cultures function. The objection is frequently raised that these cultures are many centuries removed from the New Testament world, and that even the New Testament world was very different from the world of ancient Israel. Without question, these observations are accurate. Nevertheless, preindustrial societies on the rim of the Mediterranean are demonstrably closer in many respects to the world from which the Hebrew narratives came than is our own industrialized society.

Whenever we refuse to develop a conscious model, using the best data that is available to us, the model that we employ is drawn from our own experiences. Thus, when we say that a character was a 'youth', we are apt to imagine the rather carefree, somewhat rebellious, decidedly extended period in the life of modern 'youths' instead of the considerably harsher realities of life in an agrarian society. The final test of a model, of course, is whether it helps to make sense of the data. An increasing number of Hebrew Bible scholars have been putting various social-scientific models, especially those growing out of the field of Mediterranean anthropology, to use in examining the world that produced these texts and to the meaning of the texts themselves.

---

13. For a useful (and entertaining!) introduction to the use of models in social-scientific inquiry, see T.F. Carney, *The Shape of the Past: Models and Antiquity* (Lawrence, KS: Coronado Press, 1975), esp. Ch. 1, pp. 1-43.

14. Important studies include J. Pitt-Rivers, *The Fate of Shechem, or the Politics of Sex: Essays in the Anthropology of the Mediterranean* (Cambridge Studies in Social Anthropology, 19; Cambridge: Cambridge University Press, 1977); J. Peristiany (ed.), *Honour and Shame: The Values of Mediterranean Society* (London: Weidenfeld & Nicolson, 1965); J. Davis, *The People of the Mediterranean: An Essay in Comparative Social Anthropology* (London: Routledge & Kegan Paul, 1977).

The Social World in which the Word Was Used

Ancient Israel as an Agrarian Society[15]

Premonarchic Israel emerged in the hill country of Judah and Samaria at the beginning of the Iron Age, sometime after about 1100–1050 BCE.[16] The mechanism by which this 'emergence' occurred—whether by conquest, revolt or infiltration—is still disputed among scholars.[17] Whatever the mechanism, the new entity was an agrarian society pioneering virgin sites. The ability to exploit the hill country for agriculture was dependent on finding means to collect rain water, slow run-off and store crop surpluses, since the rainfall (and hence also harvest size) on which survival depended is notoriously capricious in this part of the world. This was accomplished by building terraces, hewing cisterns and creating jars, pits, silos and buildings devoted to storage of surpluses.

15. That is, one which 'depends for its subsistence on crops raised with the help of plows, draft animals, and intensive agricultural methods' (Thompson and Hickey, *Society in Focus*, p. 106).

16. To understand the importance of the development of iron tool use, see P.M. McNutt, *The Forging of Israel: Iron Technology, Symbolism, and Tradition in Ancient Society* (JSOTSup, 108; Sheffield: Almond Press, 1990); J.C. Waldbaum, *From Bronze to Iron: The Transition from the Bronze Age to the Iron Age in the Eastern Mediterranean* (Studies in Mediterranean Archaeology, 54; Göteburg: Paul Aström, 1978).

For a very helpful study of the factors involved with settlement of the hill country, see D.C. Hopkins, *The Highlands of Canaan: Agricultural Life in the Early Iron Age* (SWBA; Sheffield: Sheffield Almond Press, 1985).

For the challenges of exploiting the highlands for agricultural production, see O. Borowski, *Agriculture in Iron Age Israel* (Winona Lake, IN: Eisenbrauns, 1987).

For a readable comprehensive survey of issues in ancient Israel's social world, see V.H. Matthews and D.C. Benjamin, *Social World of Ancient Israel: 1250–587 BCE* (Peabody, MA: Hendrickson, 1993).

17. For some of the now-classic formulations of these arguments, see G.E. Wright, *Biblical Archaeology* (Philadelphia: Westminster Press, rev. edn, 1962); G.E. Mendenhall, *The Tenth Generation: The Origins of the Biblical Tradition* (Baltimore: The Johns Hopkins University Press, 1973); M. Noth, *The History of Israel* (New York: Harper & Row, 1958); Gottwald, *The Tribes of Yahweh*. For overview and critiques of various aspects of these arguments, see G.W. Ramsey, *The Quest for the Historical Israel* (Atlanta: John Knox Press, 1981); M.L. Chaney, 'Ancient Palestinian Peasant Movements and the Formation of Premonarchic Israel', in D.N. Freedman and D.F. Graf (eds.), *Palestine in Transition: The Emergence of Ancient Israel* (SWBA, 2; Sheffield: Almond Press, 1983).

These activities placed a high labor demand on the community that in
turn caused reproductions that produced additional laborers, to be
especially valued.[18]

The structure of this collection of communities seems to have been
grossly egalitarian across families.[19] Small villages were comprised of
several extended families (בתי אבות) that were in turn made up of several nuclear family units. Apparently each nuclear family lived in its
own dwelling, but the cells of an extended family might be clustered
loosely into a compound.[20] Each extended family worked a portion of
land, referred to as a נחלה or patrimony, which it controlled and from
which it retained any surplus. Whether the נחלה was periodically redis-
tributed or not is not certain. Community expectations backed by religious injunction dictated a system of mutual aid by which families who
were experiencing abundance provided assistance to those who were in
difficulty.

The crops produced were principally those of the 'Mediterranean triangle': grain, olives and grapes, minimally supplemented by legumes,
fruits and vegetables. Integral to the success of this agricultural enterprise was a pastoral component, wherein flocks of small animals, principally sheep and goats, were tended for their milk, manure, fiber and
draft potential. Meat was not a frequent dietary component, but was
valued for ritual/festive observances as well as its potential as an emer-
gency food source in times of crop failure. The wide range of animal
and agricultural products raised allowed the labor needs of the community to be spread across all segments of the population and throughout
the year.

Prosperity and even survival depended on acquiring and retaining
land and the labor necessary to make it productive. The need for community cooperation and mutual aid made it essential to maintain the
high regard and trust of one's neighbors. Accordingly, the highest val-

18. C.L. Meyers, 'Procreation, Production, and Protection: Male–Female Balance in Early Israel', *JAAR* 51.4 (1983), pp. 569-93.

19. Meyers provides a description of both families and the communities in which
they lived in C.L. Meyers, 'The Family in Early Israel', in L.G. Perdue,
J. Blenkinsopp, J.J. Collins and C. Meyers (eds.), *Families in Ancient Israel* (The
Family, Religion, and Culture; Louisville, KY: Westminster/John Knox Press,
1997), pp. 1-47.

20. Y. Shiloh, 'The Four-Room House: Its Situation and Function in the Israelite
City', *IEJ* 20 (1970), pp. 180-90; Stager, 'The Archaeology of the Family', pp. 1-35.

ues of this society were land, sons and honor. The witness of the entire biblical corpus affirms this evaluation.[21]

Urbanization. With the establishment of the monarchy, a layer of control and obligation was superimposed on top of this society that siphoned off both agricultural products and labor for the support of the royal family and administration, for military campaigns of both expansion and defense, and for trade and traffic in luxury goods.[22] Somewhat later this society, which was in many ways a counter-formation to the Late Bronze Canaanite cities, saw the development of its own incipient urban centers, supported of course by the population on the land. Indeed, one of the most common ways of defining a settlement as a 'city' is its non-self-sufficiency with regard to food, fiber and raw materials.[23] Still, compared with the Hellenistic and Roman periods, Israel in the early years of the monarchy had only a few modest urban centers, with the bulk of the population living in villages and towns.[24]

Foreign Domination. In time yet another burdensome layer was added, this time in the form of foreign empirical powers and their bureaucracies. These impositions were sometimes quite harsh, other times somewhat less so. Throughout, however, the basic structure of the *peasant* social order and its values remained conservative and therefore largely unchanged.[25] Bendor's careful survey of Israel's social structure has confirmed this observation.

> We have found that society in Israel and in Judah, despite the changes it underwent, despite the burden of the monarchy and the system of monarchial adminstration, and despite the tempestuous developments in the course of its history, remained in principle a society of free farmers settled on their land and among their kinsmen.

21. Consider, e.g., the Call of Abraham (Gen. 12) and the Covenant with Abraham (Gen. 15), which emphasize land, progeny and name.

22. For a comprehensive examination of the changes in social and political structure that accompanied the change from filiated tribes to statehood, see F.S. Frick, *The Formation of the State in Ancient Israel: A Survey of Models and Theories* (SWBA, 4; Sheffield: Almond Press, 1985).

23. G. Lenski and J. Lenski, *Human Societies: An Introduction to Macrosociology* (New York: McGraw–Hill, 1978), p. 488.

24. Lenski and Lenski, *Human Societies*; L. Perdue *et al.* (eds.), *Families in Ancient Israel* (Family, Religion, and Culture; Louisville, KY: Westminster/John Knox Press, 1997), p. 6.

25. 'Peasant' here as defined by the Lenskis as a member of the agrarian society who actually works the land (Lenski and Lenski, *Human Societies*, p. 486).

It would appear that during the period in question no changes took place in the mode of production that would undermine the efficiency of the kinship structure. Thus the structure of *batei 'ab* and *mišpaḥot* was able to persist and contribute to the stability of a free productive society, through a dynamic balance—faltering and renewing itself—between trends of unity and of conflict.[26]

Values of Pre-exilic Israel

The categories of honor and shame in Mediterranean societies have been studied by anthropologists and their findings have been applied with enlightening results to New Testament texts.[27] Because of the slow rate of change in preindustrial social systems, these observations about first-century Palestine provide a helpful model in regard to the phenomena of honor and shame for the earlier Iron Age and Exilic culture of the area as well.[28] More recently, scholars have made use of these studies for shedding new light on the Hebrew Bible.[29] The precise outline of

26. S. Bendor, *The Social Structure of Ancient Israel: The Institution of the Family (Beit 'Ab) from the Settlement to the End of the Monarchy* (Jerusalem Biblical Series, 7; Jerusalem: Simor, 1996), p. 280.

27. Books that have been foundational in the field are B.J. Malina, *The New Testament World: Insights from Cultural Anthropology* (Louisville, KY: Westminster/John Knox Press, 1981), and more recently B. Malina and R. Rohrbaugh, *Social-Science Commentary on the Synoptic Gospels* (Philadelphia: Fortress Press, 1992). The vocabulary of this field of growing importance is conveniently collected in J.J. Pilch and B.J. Malina, *Biblical Social Values and their Meaning: A Handbook* (Peabody, MA: Hendrickson, 1993). For a current bibliographical survey of the field, see R. Rohrbaugh (ed.), *The Social Sciences and New Testament Interpretation* (Peabody, MA: Hendrickson, 1996). An excellent brief treatment is H. Moxnes, 'Honor and Shame', BTB Readers Guide, *BTB* 23 (1993), pp. 167-76.

28. On the slow rate of change over time of family forms and social structures, see K.C. Hanson, 'Kinship', BTB Reader's Guide, *BTB* 24 (1994), pp. 183-94 (187).

29. G. Stansell, 'Honor and Shame in the David Narratives', in F. Crüsemann, Christof Hardmeier and Ranier Kessler (eds.), *'Was ist der Mensch?' Beiträge zur Anthropologie des Alten Testaments* (Munich: Chr. KaiserVerlag, 1992), pp. 94-114; T. Laniak, 'Esther—A Tale of Honor and Shame', Paper presented at SBL Annual Meeting, Chicago, IL, 1994;; K.A. Stone, 'Gender and Homosexuality in Judges 19: Subject-Honor, Object-Shame?', *JSOT* 67 (1995), pp. 87-107; V.H. Matthews and D.C. Benjamin, 'Social Sciences and Biblical Studies', in *Honor and Shame in the World of the Bible* (Semeia, 68; Atlanta: Scholars Press, 1996), pp. 7-21; R. Simkins, ' "Return to Yahweh": Honor and Shame in Joel', in Matthews and Benjamin (eds.), *Honor and Shame*, pp. 41-54; K.A. Stone, *Sex, Honor and Power in the Deuteronomistic History* (JSOTSup, 234; Sheffield: Sheffield Academic Press, 1996).

the ways these values functioned was not constant, either through time or from place to place, but certain common features mark these cultures off as related to one another in certain features and as quite different from our own with respect to these values.

A definition of honor in this context comes from Pitt-Rivers:

> Honor is the value of a person in his own eyes, but also in the eyes of his society. It is his estimation of his own worth, his *claim* to pride, but it is also the acknowledgement of that claim, his excellence recognised by society, his *right* to pride.'[30]

The ancient Mediterranean villager viewed all people as possessing two kinds of honor. Ascribed honor resulted from one's birth into a particular family, nation, religious group, village, and of course gender. It was essentially an hereditary property.

Acquired honor, on the other hand, results from the villager's success or failure at meeting the duties and expectations of his community. Honor is acquired at the expense of another's honor. First-century Palestine has been described as an 'agonistic' society, and pre-exilic Israel could probably be described in the same terms. Just as members of an agrarian community universally experienced *tangible* valuables in their world as being in limited supply, they also experienced intangibles such as honor as being limited goods. This perception leads to never-ending competition to acquire honor at the expense of one's neighbors, a competition that plays out by the issuing of challenges and responses to challenges.

> The challenge is a claim to enter the social space of another. This claim may be positive or negative. A positive reason for entering the social space of another would be to gain some share in that space or to gain a cooperative, mutuallly beneficial foothold. A negative reason would be to dislodge another from that person's social space, either temporarily or permanently.[31]

Challenges could be either negative (an insult, a threat) or positive (a gift, a word of praise). Both alike required a response, if honor was not to be lost.

The parrying of challenges and responses was an interchange that could only take place between equals. Thus every challenge presented a dilemma of whether to respond or whether to ignore it. To be unwilling

---

30. Pitt-Rivers, *Fate of Shechem*, p. 1.
31. Malina, *The New Testament World*, pp. 34-35.

or unable to meet a challenge with an effective response caused a loss
of honor, but to respond to an inferior as if to an equal also caused such
a loss. Every social interaction outside the immediate family was
loaded in this way and required a careful evaluation of the other actors.

Both ascribed and acquired honor were inextricably bound up with
the honor of the groupings of which the individual was a part, especially the family. The honor of one's parents, siblings, children, even
servants determined one's own honor. This explains a great deal about
preoccupation with lineage and legitimacy. Unfamiliar persons had to
be carefully assessed to discover their place in the social hierarchy. A
visitor to the village could expect almost continual challenging until his
relative status was ascertained. In determining the visitor's level of
honor, as well as in finding the weak points to exploit in order to diminish it, information was essential. All of this assessing of relative position was possible in the face-to-face social world of the village in a way
that would be impossible in our own contemporary setting.

Expectations for men were different from those for women. Men were
expected to advance their own honor and protect the women of their
family. Women were to exhibit 'shame', that is to say, not shameful-
ness or shamelessness but a sense of shame, a sensitivity to shame. They
were to exhibit modesty and deference. In sexual matters, men were to
show virility, women to give no cause to question their chastity.

> The honour of a man and of a woman therefore imply quite different
> modes of conduct. This is so in any society. A woman is dishonoured,
> loses her *vergenza*, with the tainting of her sexual purity, but a man does
> not. While certain conduct is honourable for both sexes, honour = shame
> requires conduct in other spheres, which is exclusively a virtue of one
> sex or the other. It obliges a man to defend his honour and that of his
> family, a woman to conserve her purity.[32]

More about gender differences in this value system (as also about other
aspects of the concepts of honor and shame) will be introduced in the
sections in which they are used in examining the biblical texts.

Social Institutions
The Family: Kinship by Birth or by Residency in the בית־אב. The family, or בית אב, was the basic unit of production, and cooperation and
mutual assistance among families was imperative for the survival of

---

32. Pitt-Rivers, *Fate of Shechem*, p. 20.

communities pioneering the hill country.[33] Furthermore, a man's ability to exercise power and leadership within the community, and to have a say in the administration of justice, was conditioned on his being recognized as a member in good standing of the village assembly. Therefore, how a family was regarded by its neighbors—whether it was considered to possess 'honor' or not—was an issue with ramifications far beyond the psychological realm. The categories of honor and shame were operative in all relational interactions, and this honor or shame was 'corporate' as much as individual.

> Since first-century societies did not consider individualism a pivotal value as we do…collective or corporate honor was one of their focuses. Social groups, like the family, village, or region, possess a collective honor in which the members participate… Depending upon the dimensions of the group, which can run a replicating range from individual, nuclear family, to kingdom or region, the *head* of the group is responsible for the honor of the group with reference to outsiders, and symbolized the group's honor as well. Hence members of the group owe loyalty, respect, and obedience of a kind which commits their individual honor without limit and without compromise.[34]

Although the evidence indicates that the household of residence was limited to a nuclear family, an individual's identity and honor were connected to the extended family (בית אב),[35] which may have lived in a collection of connected or closely situated dwellings constituting the

---

33. 'In its core usage as a term for the household unit in ancient Israel [בית־אב], it included both biologically related individuals as well as those with affinal or other ties. It was in effect a living group as much as a kinship group. The "father's house" achieved its basic configuration in the rural communities in which it functioned at the time of Israelite beginnings and probably throughout much of the succeeding centuries; and its importance was integrally related to its role as the basic economic unit, producing virtually all of what was needed for the subsistence of its members' (C.L. Meyers, 'To Her Mother's House: Considering a Counterpart to the Israelite Bēt 'Ab', in D. Jobling (ed.), *The Bible and the Politics of Exegesis: Essays in Honor of Norman K. Gottwald on His Sixty-Sixth Birthday* (Cleveland: Pilgrim, 1991), pp. 39-52 (41). See also Gottwald, *Tribes of Yahweh*, pp. 248, 285-92.

34. B.J. Malina, *The New Testament World: Insights from Cultural Anthropology* (Louisville, KY: Westminster/John Knox Press, rev. edn, 1993).

35. This term came to indicate descent from a common ancestor (real or fictive), thus designating the patriline. In general, the extended family is indicated when the text refers to the 'house' of a living individual, whereas speaking of the 'house' of an individual long dead indicates that genealogy rather than residence is the issue.

family 'compound'.[36] The household, or 'family', was comprised of individuals who were related by birth or marriage ('kin') and those who were associated with the family through the operation of various other social or ritual means ('fictive kin'). Servants or slaves, for example, were members of the household.

Leadership in Family and Community: Patriarchs and Elders. Ancient Israel (as indeed most of the ancient Near East) was a typical agrarian society, organized socially along patriarchal lines, and the senior male of the extended family (the *paterfamilias*) had broad power to decide issues that affected the functioning of the family. In particular, he was responsible for retaining and advancing the family's honor (and guarding against occasions for shame) by oversight and protection[37] of the other members of the household. The conduct of both types of family members, relatives and dependents, contributed to the assessment of honor (or shame) by which other villagers evaluated the family. Accordingly, the patriarch could be expected to exercise vigorous supervision and discipline over family members, whether related to or merely dependent upon the household.

For males, honor equals precedence, and the father's task was to provide training and resources that allowed a son to 'get on in the world'. Included in this task seems to have been teaching work habits and self-control and keeping the young man out of trouble. For females, honor meant avoidance of occasions for shame, especially in the sexual realm, where exposure even to the possibility of impropriety was a scandalous thing. In the case of daughters, the father's principal task was to guard against sexual impurity. This could be accomplished most easily and most convincingly by keeping the daughter 'cloistered' in the private spaces of the home.

Decisions that affected more than one family were reached and carried out by the community's elders.[38] These appear to have been the

36.	Stager, 'Archaeology of the Family', pp. 17-18.

37.	Which is to say that in the proper course of events, the *paterfamilias* is the 'patron' and his dependent family members are his 'clients'. When a person becomes a *na'ar(ah)*, he is forced to become dependent on another patron.

38.	For full discussions of the role of 'elder' in early Israel, see J.L. McKenzie, 'The Elders in the Old Testament', *Bib* 40 (1959), pp. 522-40; V.H. Matthews and D.C. Benjamin, 'The Elder', *Bible Today* 30 (1992), pp. 170-74; H. Reviv, *The*

heads of the various families, quite likely the senior male or patriarch of each extended family. To become an elder was the highest status to which one could aspire in early Israel, since these were the men to whom the well-being of the community was entrusted. Conversely, to have no hope of attaining this status was a condition to be avoided. In most cases, only one surviving son (generally the oldest) of one of the component nuclear families became the new 'father' of the 'father's house' when the patriarch died. In the process, he likely also became an elder in his community.

When Kinship Fails: Patronage in Early Israel. The ideal of independent subsistence of the extended family required hard work and cooperation from all family members, but when external factors made survival difficult, the family sometimes had to resort to outside help. The משפחה was the next more inclusive level of societal organization, and apparently it existed in part as a 'protective association of families' to provide such assistance.[39] Mutual aid also occurred at the level of the שבט or tribe.

Another strategy for dealing with adversity was to seek help from someone with more resources, more power, more status than oneself, which is to say to seek a patron and become a client.[40] Even this was conceived in terms of family imagery:

> The patron–client relationship is a social, institutional arrangement by means of which economic, political, or religious institutional relationships are outfitted with an overarching quality of kinship or family feeling. The word 'patron' derives from the Greek and Latin word for father, *patēr*. In the Bible, anytime anyone is called a 'father' who is not a biological father, the title refers to the role and status of a patron... The patron is like a father, and clients are like loving and grateful children, no matter what their age. The client relates to his patron according to the social norms of child relations to actual parents, while the patron is expected to relate to clients as a parent would to his...actual children.[41]

Elders in Ancient Israel: A Study of a Biblical Institution (trans. L. Plitmann; Jerusalem: Magnes Press, 1989).

39. Gottwald, *Tribes of Yahweh*, pp. 315-18.

40. 'Patronage provides an alternative or a supplement to reciprocity within kinship groups and between status equals. In fact, it is hard to imagine a peasant society surviving without both lateral and vertical support systems' (A. Wallace-Hadrill [ed.], *Patronage in Ancient Society* [London: Routledge, 1989], p. 157).

41. Pilch and Malina, *Biblical Social Values*, pp. 133-34.

Two things about such a relationship should be obvious. The first is that the client in such an arrangement suffers a loss of autonomy and honor in taking on what is essentially the role of a child. The second is that such relationships are facilitated by stratification within a society, whereby there is a class of potential patrons with excess resources that they offer in exchange for power over other persons. The complex systems of patronage that existed in the Roman empire had not yet developed in early Israel, but as we examine biblical passages, we will see many in which the dynamic which is described can best be understood in terms of client–patron relationships.[42]

Slavery and Wage Labor. At times, the family's survival might depend on goods or money which various family members could bring in by work as day laborers. This was a fateful step to take, however, because the diversion of labor away from the primary agricultural operation placed a burden on the whole enterprise from which it might be difficult to recover. The family with high reproductive success might be in a position to take advantage of opportunities for paid labor, but most would be hard pressed to lose productive hands. A more severe crisis might require taking steps more binding (and more humiliating) than placing oneself under another's patronage or hiring out oneself (or one's children). A family member might become an actual dependent of

---

42. For background on client–patron relationships as they developed in various parts of the Mediterranean world, see R.P. Saller, *Imperial Patronage under the Early Empire* (Cambridge: Cambridge University Press, 1982); D. Chinchen, 'The Patron–Client System: A Model of Indigenous Discipleship', *Evangelical Missions Quarterly* 31 (October 1995), pp. 446-51; J.K. Campbell, *Honour, Family and Patronage: A Study of Institutions and Moral Values in a Greek Mountain Community* (Oxford: Clarendon Press, 1967); H. Moxnes, 'Patron–Client Relations and the New Community in Luke–Acts', in J. Neyrey (ed.), *Social World of Luke–Acts* (Peabody, MA: Hendrickson, 1991), pp. 241-68; P. Garnsey and R. Saller, *The Roman Empire: Economy, Society and Culture* (Berkeley: University of California Press, 1987); J.K. Chow, *Patronage and Power: A Study of Social Networks in Corinth* (JSNTSup, 75; Sheffield: JSOT Press, 1992); S.N. Eisenstadt and L. Roniger, 'Patron–Client Relations as a Model of Structuring Social Exchange', *Comparative Studies in Society and History* 22 (1980), pp. 42-77; B.J. Malina, 'Patron and Client: The Analogy behind Synoptic Theology', *FF* 4.1 (March 1988), pp. 2-31; L. Roniger, 'Modern Patron–Client Relations and Historical Clientelism: Some Clues from Ancient Republican Rome', *Archives of European Sociology* 24 (1983), pp. 63-95; J.H. Elliott, 'Patronage and Clientism in Early Christian Society: A Short Reading Guide', *FF* 3.4 (December 1987), pp. 39-48.

another household, as an 'indentured servant' or 'supplementary worker'.[43]

> Dependency and clientage are not the same thing, although there are obvious points of contact and real similarity. Dependency relations are links between members of different status groups, but unlike clientage they are not entered into voluntarily and are backed up by legal and extra-legal sanctions.[44]

The commonest mechanisms for the establishment of dependency relations was the pledging (as surety for a loan) or the outright sale of persons from the family.

> Debt slavery, one of the many forms of slavery, has various facets. Debts or crop failure or other factors leading to naked hunger can drive the free man, stripped of his possessions, to indenture himself as a last resort, simply to survive. The creditor can try, by distraining the debtor, to extract the debt from his clan as 'ransom.'… The creditor can exploit the debtor's manpower but also has the option of selling him to another as a slave.[45]

The end result was the same in either case: slavery or servanthood, as part of another's household.

> At every level, the master–servant relationship evinces identical characteristics: regulation under law and custom, with mutual rights and responsibilities. Service and unconditional allegiance are demanded of the servant. The master provides sustenance and protection. He replaces the *bayit* (the clan, the family) as the source and focus of the servant's life.[46]

Israel's earliest history was marked by various structures that worked to prevent social stratification, but with the development of the monarchy, they proved less and less effective.[47] As the economic demands on

43. G. Chirichigno, *Debt–Slavery in Israel and the Ancient Near East* (JSOTSup, 141; Sheffield: JSOT Press, 1993), p. 51; Meyers, 'Family in Early Israel', p. 17.

44. Wallace-Hadrill, *Patronage*, p. 158.

45. K. Baltzer, 'Liberation from Debt Slavery after the Exile in Second Isaiah and Nehemiah', in P.D. Miller Jr, P.D. Hanson and S.D. McBride (eds.), *Ancient Israelite Religion: Essays in Honor of Frank Moore Cross* (Philadelphia: Fortress Press, 1987), pp. 477-84 (481).

46. Baltzer, 'Liberation from Debt Slavery', p. 478.

47. '[W]ith the advent of the monarchy and its respective state-controlled economy social stratification increased, particularly during the eighth century BCE and

families became greater in response to the needs of the monarchy, more households became indebted and slid into clientship or dependency. This increased the gap between rich and poor and further accelerated the loss of the potential for independent subsistence.

> From an economic point of view, therefore, social stratification can be seen as the result of a process by which free citizens eventually lost control over their means of production, on account of their growing dependency upon the large landowners (and merchants) and state for resources. Once this dependency was established the small landowners were often forced into procuring loans which often included high interest rates. If their crop(s) failed or was below expectation, then the debtor would be hardpressed to pay back the loan. Therefore, many of these small landowners were likely to become insolvent, since they were able to engage only in subsistence farming. As a result of their insolvency farmers were forced to sell or surrender dependents into debt-slavery. Furthermore, they would eventually be forced to sell their land (means of production), themselves and their families.[48]

The process was a self-perpetuating spiral, which the ethical demands of the prophets were not able to slow.

Social Location

Status means 'a socially defined position in a social structure', whereas a role 'is a set of expectations, rights, and duties that are attached to a particular status'.[49] As the sociologist Linton has observed, we occupy statuses, but we play roles.[50] Depending on an individual's status and role in a society, he or she will have more or less power to accomplish goals, whether those goals include simple survival or ruling the world.

later... However, during the early Monarchic period there was an active suppression of social stratification by both the secular and sacral league authorities, who continued to exert pressure on the king throughout the period (cf. 1 Sam. 8; 10.17-27; 11.12). Nevertheless, the history of Israel is characterized by various periods of increased social stratification, although it is likely that Israel did not develop into as highly a stratified society as those in the states of Mesopotamia and Canaan (Coote and Whitelam 154-9; de Vaux, Ancient Israel 164-5). Therefore, only two social classes can be clearly distinguished in Israel: (1) free citizens; (2) chattel-slaves. However, it is likely that some segments of the foreign population that were used as labour by the Israelite kings occupied a social position equivalent to that of semi-free citizens' (Chirichigno, *Debt Slavery in Israel*, pp. 139-40).

48. Chirichigno, *Debt-Slavery in Israel*, pp. 50-51.
49. Thompson and Hickey, *Society*, pp. 72, 94.
50. R. Linton, *The Study of Man* (New York: Appleton–Century–Crofts, 1936).

These three, then—power, status, role—must be considered in assessing an individual's social location. In our efforts to discover the social location of the נער and נערה in early Israel, we will examine these three attributes, to the extent that the text gives information about them, being careful to consider the indigenous values of the society that created and preserved the narratives.

Working Hypothesis
This study will demonstrate that the common social location that these characters all share is neither age nor marital status nor 'social class' (i.e. 'high-born' or noble). Their function or role is not always as a servant, whether domestic, military, agricultural or governmental. Rather, what these characters share is the situation of being 'away from their father's house', beyond the protection and control of their fathers, while not yet master or mistress of their own households. Most often this results from being literally 'away from home', but the orphan and the 'virtual orphan' are also called נער or נערה by the biblical writer when the normal relationship between them and their fathers is severed in some other way, as for instance by the father's death or absence or by grave illness, from which the father is powerless to protect them. Frequently the stories will show נערים seeking a substitute father in the form of a 'master' or patron.

Chapter 3

SPECIFIC TEXTS IN THE HEBREW BIBLE:
HOUSE BOYS AND FIELD HANDS

General Considerations

By far the most frequent role in which to find the נער (or נערה) in the biblical texts is that of a servant of some sort. The overall impression is of a retainer or personal attendant, serving in domestic, agricultural or even cultic contexts. The various roles are, in fact, not distinct, with individual נערים apparently functioning in more than one capacity. These functions are also closely associated with the military roles for נערים which will be treated in Chapter 4.

Several interesting observations can be made about נערים as servants generally. Perhaps the most important is how seldom the biblical text actually reports them *doing* anything. The most prominent feature of their activities seems to be their presence: they are 'with' other characters, they are taken along, they are sent and left behind, they speak and are spoken to, but often the real work of the narrative is performed by other characters. A most conspicuous example of this phenomenon is the two נערים whom Abraham takes along on the journey to Mount Moriah in Genesis 22. Abraham cuts the wood and saddles the donkey (v. 3), while the servants are simply 'taken' (לקח) on the trip. Once they have reached the mountain, the servants stand by, presumably tending the donkey (v. 5), until the drama has unfolded and our two principal characters return (שוב, v. 19). Then all arise (קום) and go (הלך) together (v. 19). This narrative is one of the best known in which נערים appear and the fact that these servants have no obvious function in the story is significant, but it is by no means exceptional in this regard. Compare, for instance, the episode in 1 Sam. 25 when Abigail loads her donkeys with gifts and sends her נער ahead of her when she sets out. The narrative gives us no further clue to the importance of this individual. In fact, a survey of the places where נערים appear reveals that this lack of specified activity is the rule rather than the exception.

The narratives of the Hebrew Bible are generally compact and well-crafted, and the presence of characters who seem not to play a role in the action of the stories suggests that they serve some other function. One way that they enrich the narratives is as 'status indicators': any character who is shown by the writer to possess one or more נערים is clearly a person of some substance.[1] These are persons with land and power, whom other characters, not just נערים, frequently address with the deferential term עבדך, 'your servant'.

From the point of view of narrative art, the נערים often serve as foils for monologue, without requiring that the author depict a character talking to himself. Not infrequently, the only apparent job of a נער is to be someone for the main character to talk to: an offended Ahasuerus (Est. 2.2), a sleepless Ahasuerus (Est. 6.3, 5), a tormented Saul (1 Sam. 16.18). These troubled characters find just the person to use as a sounding board or informant in the נער who happens to be 'standing by' at the critical moment. Within this category of נערים who are servants, the verbs used most commonly are those of address: they are called (קרא, 2 Sam. 13.17; 2 Kgs 9.4), commanded (צוה, 2 Sam. 13.28; Ruth 2.9, 15), told (ספר, Gen. 41.12) or asked (שאל, 1 Sam. 25.8), but mostly spoken to (אמר, Gen 22.5; 2 Sam. 13.17; 1 Kgs 18.43; 2 Kgs 9.4; Est. 6.3; 1 Sam. 9.7, 10, 27; 25.19; Judg. 19.11; Ruth 2.5). What is said to them is only occasionally imperative, requiring action. More often, they answer (ענה, 1 Sam. 9.8; 16.18; Ruth 2.6), report (נגר, 1 Sam. 25.14; Num. 11.27), or say (אמר, 1 Kgs 18.43; 2 Kgs 9.4; 1 Sam. 2.15, 16; 9.6; 16.18; 25.14; Judg. 19.11; Est. 2.2; 6.3, 5). Thus the pre-eminent verb of which the נערים are both subjects and indirect objects is אמר.

They often function as 'anchor points' for the point of view of the narrative, allowing the scene of the story to be viewed from a distance (as, for instance, in Gen. 22), or carrying the eye of the reader back and forth between characters (2 Kgs 4.2, 6; 1 Kgs 18.43), giving a sense of distance and of time. They are taken, left, returned to, functioning almost like a camera left running on a tripod that records a scene from close up or from far away as the characters move in and out of its range (1 Kgs 19.3).

---

1.   Some of the characters who have a נער are Abraham, the brothers of Joseph, Pharaoh, Moses, the 'sons of Israel', Elijah, the priest (Eli), Elisha, the wealthy Shunammite, Nabal and Abigail, Amnon, Absalom, Kish, the king, Saul, the Levite, Micah (Micaiah), David, Boaz and Job.

Notwithstanding the fact that the main actions of the biblical narratives are most frequently carried on by characters other than the נערים,
these servants function in certain specific contexts. We will look at each
of these contexts individually, including a detailed examination of a few
of the more fully developed characterizations in each type.

Domestic Servants

In a number of cases, נערים seem to function in the domestic sphere,
whether as household servants or valets or in other forms of personal
service. We can assign them to the domestic sphere more by the location in which the narratives place them than by the tasks that they perform. Abraham's servant, one of the few specifically involved in food
preparation, is near or in the tent of Abraham (Gen 18.7). Another cook
is the unnamed נער of Elisha (2 Kgs 4.38, probably *not* Gehazi), who is
directed to put the kettle on to make stew for the 'sons of the prophets'.
Joseph, in Genesis 39, serves in the house of Potiphar (v. 4) after he has
been imprisoned, although he is not identified as נער until 41.12. The
נערים who respond to Saul (1 Sam. 16.18) and Ahasuerus (Est. 6.3) in
their insomnia are working in the sleeping quarters of the royal household. In 1 Sam. 9.22, Samuel brings both Saul and his נער into the dining hall at the shrine, thus presumably allowing the servant to continue
to attend Saul during the meal. A word used frequently in connection
with these נערים is משרת, a participle often translated as minister or ministering, which conveys a sense of the breadth of the services performed. (Thus, for example, Joseph is called both נער [Gen. 37.2;
41.12] and משרת [Gen. 39.4; 40.4]. Similarly, both terms are used for
Amnon's servant [2 Sam. 13.17], King Ahasuerus's servants [Est. 2.2;
6.3] and Joshua [Exod. 33.11, *inter alia*]. Even a נערה can be both, as is
the case with Abishag [1 Kgs 1.4, 15]).

These characters also serve as conduits for information about the local
scene. In all servant-holding societies, information is shared between
resident servants or slaves and visitors of the same status when they
share meals and quarters, while their masters attend to whatever busi-
ness has required travel. Often this gossip is useful later to the masters,
whose own conversations may have been more circumspect. A servant
can increase his value to his master by giving him reports on the local
state of affairs. So, for instance, Boaz expects his נערים to know
the identity of the young woman who is new in the 'neighborhood'

(Ruth 2.5), and Saul's נער knows of the presence of a 'man of God' in the vicinity and is able to suggest the appropriate 'gift' to be offered in exchange for a consultation (1 Sam. 9.6, 7). These characters serve as messengers, go-betweens, even informants or tattle-tales. Joseph carries a report on his half-brothers to his father (Gen. 37.2). A נער reports to Moses that Eldad and Medad are prophesying (Num. 11.27). Elijah sent his נער back and forth to provide weather updates when he was demon-strating for Ahab his ability to bring an end to the drought (1 Kgs 18.43).

Dialogue between the Levite and his נער (Judg. 19) allows us to 'listen in' on the master's thoughts as he ponders the lateness of the hour and the various options for insuring his party's safety overnight. The נער's suggestions, which reveal that he has some knowledge of the local scene, are ultimately rejected. The נער is mentioned once more when the Levite assures the old man that he will not need to provide anything except a roof for the travelers. After that he serves no further purpose for the narrator, and he disappears, playing no part in the per-ilous events of that night or of the next few days.

Frequently, the נער serves at the margin of the domestic sphere, at the threshold of the tent, house or palace, as something of a doorkeeper (Joshua in Exod. 33.11; Amnon's נער in 2 Sam. 13.17). They are also the persons who traverse the threshold, functioning both within and out-side of the household. They are, for instance, sometimes the individuals who are drawers of water (Gen. 24.20; Ruth 2.9; 1 Sam. 9.11), which would involve a daily trip to the community water source, at least in those places where families did not have individual cisterns. Their pres-ence at these community gathering spots allows them, even when not traveling abroad, to gather the information that so often is valuable to their masters.

Many of these facets of the role of the נערים can be illustrated by looking at a few of the texts that feature them in narratives of some length. Two in particular, Gehazi and Ziba, are not only given names, which is somewhat unusual, but also play featured roles in the narra-tives of which they are a part.

Gehazi

One of the most extensive portraits of a נער in the Hebrew Bible is that of Gehazi in 2 Kings. An extended narrative (2 Kgs 4.8-37; 5.1-27; 8.1-6) follows this character through Elisha's encounter with the wealthy woman of Shunem; the birth, death and resuscitation of her son; the healing and bilking of Naaman; and the restoration of land to the Shunammite woman after her absence during a famine. This narrative is intertwined with other stories of Elisha, including many which include reference to a נער[2] serving the prophet (2 Kgs 4.38; 6.15, 17), but we will focus on the story that names Gehazi explicitly. Most נערים are not given names; of those that are, only a few, such as Gehazi, Ziba and Joseph, for example, function in servant capacities.[3] These then might be expected to be more fully characterized, and thus their portraits may give us important information about what it means to be a servant נער.

Within 2 Kings, three types of narrative can be discerned in which Elisha is involved: stories of Elisha and the company of prophets, stories of Elisha and the great leaders of his time, and stories of Elisha and his servant Gehazi. The possibility of one or more collections of traditional stories about Elisha is acknowledged by most commentators.

> This unit [Elisha's succession of Elijah, 2 Kgs 2.1-25] stands at the head of what may have originally been one or more cycles of Elisha traditions (H.-Chr. Schmitt), or even part of a pre-Dtr 'prophetic record' still visible in 1 Sam. 1.2-2, Kgs 10.28... Now intertwined with accounts of various royal affairs in 2 Kings 3–13, the prophetic career of Elisha lives in material of diverse character, genre, and age—including brief legends of the prophet's miracles (e.g., 2 Kgs 2.19-22, 23-25; 4.1-7, 38-45), and more artistically developed but hardly less legendary narratives (2 Kgs 3.4-27; 4.8-37; 5.1-27...).[4]

Although most scholars agree that these stories are older than the material into which they have been incorporated, little headway has been made into discovery of their earlier history, other than to acknowledge the 'obscure origins and history of this prophetical tradition'.[5] The occasion for the events of the narratives seems to have been the reigns of

2.   Indeed, 2 Kgs 4–6 contain examples of almost all types of נערים and נערות.

3.   Most נערים who are given names by the narrator, such as Absalom, David, Ichabod, Esther, are not servants at all. Rather they are at risk or in danger in some way, and they become נערים by virtue of their imperilment. This phenomenon is the subject of Chapter 5. (Joseph, too, falls into this category.) For a complete list of named נערים and נערות, see the Appendix.

4.   B.O. Long, *2 Kings* (FOTL, 10; Grand Rapids: Eerdmans, 1991), p. 19. See also A.F. Campbell, SJ, *Of Prophets and Kings: A Late Ninth-Century Document (1 Samuel 1–2 Kings 10)* (CBQMS, 17; Washington: Catholic Biblical Association, 1986).

5.   Long, *2 Kings*, p. 19.

Jehoram, Jehu, Jehoahaz and Jehoash, but they were written down in the form we have them by the 'Deuteronomistic historian' at a time near the exile.[6]

Past scholarship on Elisha traditions has valued principally accounts of historic personages and been less interested in the social world depicted in them. Montgomery divides this Elisha material into two portions: political narratives, which he praises for 'authentic details'[7] or for being 'stories of early origin, historically authentic',[8] and the stories of the prophets, which encounter a much more mixed reception. 'For the North the political history was embalmed in lengthy narratives proceeding from the schools of the Sons of the Prophets'[9] (of which Elisha is the head).[10] 'The most striking story in this cycle is that of Jehu's revolt (II. 9, 10), a brilliant political narrative, in which Elisha appears only in the preface as inceptor of the uprising. Within this complex are inserted, with historical justification, two brilliant stories, connected with otherwise unknown prophets',[11] namely the defeat of Ben-Hadad at Aphek, and the story of Micaiah and of Ahab's death. 'The remaining Prophetical Stories of the North are midrash in the current sense of the word, of dubious historical value.'[12] These stories he dismisses by merely enumerating them.

Gray, likewise, contrasts the material in which Elisha deals with the great men of history and the remaining portions of the prophetic narrative:

> Together with this matter, which is of real historical value, there is included in the record of the times, solely on grounds of contemporaneity, a mass of prophetic tradition concerning Elijah and Elisha of quite a different order... Most of these incidents are quite trivial and indicate an authority of little discrimination. They are, in the case of Elisha, associated for the most part with prophetic, or dervish, communities of various localities, and it is possible to see a certain local rivalry in claiming association with the great prophet. This is the breeding-ground of

6. Long, *2 Kings*, p. 19.
7. J.A. Montgomery, *A Critical and Exegetical Commentary on the Books of Kings* (ICC; New York: Charles Scribner's Sons, 1951), p. 38.
8. Montgomery, *Kings*, p. 39.
9. Montgomery, *Kings*, p. 36.
10. Montgomery, *Kings*, p. 47.
11. Montgomery, *Kings*, p. 41.
12. Montgomery, *Kings*, p. 41.

miracle,[13] and it is noteworthy that here, in contrast to the first group of traditions of the prophets, miracles abound. The conclusion is, then, suggested that in the second group of traditions concerning Elijah and particularly Elisha the source is a concatenation of local hagiology, or folklore of the prophets.[14]

This concern, then, with what appears to be historiography and with a rationalist elimination of anything that smacks of the miraculous has, among other things, obscured the fact that the Elisha material is some of the oldest narrative in the book of Kings and can be, on the basis of the cast of characters present, divided into the three types of narrative mentioned above.[15] On that basis, the existence of an extended 'Gehazi narrative'[16] is not so difficult to see, interbraided as it is with material of the other two types. The intent of this weaving of strands is no doubt to try to give some chronological coherence, while preserving all of the (then) extant traditions.

The plot of the Gehazi story is masterful, and interest is maintained by the contrasting actions of a series of characters whose statuses occur in pairs of opposites. In fact, it can be viewed as a drama in three acts, each with four episodes, plus a final epilogue or coda. Act One concerns the Shunammite woman (2 Kgs 4.8-37), Act Two is about Naaman (5.1-14), Act Three centers on reward and punishment (5.15-27), and the Epilogue restores all characters to their proper places (8.1-6).

13. Note the assumption that stories of the miraculous are a pestilence to be eradicated.

14. J. Gray, *I & II Kings: A Commentary* (OTL; Philadelphia: Westminster Press, 1963), pp. 32-33.

15. See p. 46 above.

16. The attempt by Rofé to eliminate 8.1-6 as secondary is misguided, in my view. He cites the king's request of Gehazi to *tell* him about Elisha's great deeds as evidence that this pericope is 'still within the *oral* stage of the *legenda*'. In this, he mistakes orality in the narrative for the oral stage of the composition. As we saw above, it is this telling and being told that characterize the role of a נער in the biblical narrative (A. Rofé, 'The Classification of the Prophetical Stories', *JBL* 89 [1970], pp. 427-40 [434]).

Nor is it necessary, contra Gressmann (H. Gressmann, *Die älteste Geschichtsschreibung und Prophetie Israels* [SAT; Göttingen: Vandenhoeck & Ruprecht, 1921]), to call this a literary secondary accretion. In its current position, these verses serve no obvious function, and it is difficult to imagine the intent of an author who inserted them here. On the other hand, they serve perfectly well as a coda for the whole narrative, bringing the hearer/reader up to date on the current status of the characters (A. Berlin, *Poetics and Interpretation*), pp. 107-10.

In Act One, the first episode (2 Kgs 4.8-17) orients us to the characters, identifies a need (at least from the point of view of Gehazi and Elisha) and promises the birth of a son. Elisha travels through Shunem with his נער Gehazi, who functions in the various roles pointed out in the general discussion above as he accompanies his master on a journey. A wealthy woman (אשה גדולה, v. 8) prevails on him to accept favors, first of meals, then of lodging. In other words, she takes the initiative to become a patron of this holy man. Eventually, Elisha seeks to return the favor, and become patron rather than client by finding a need that he can supply. Elisha (v. 11) is lying (שכב) in the chamber that the woman had prepared for him, and directs his נער Gehazi to summon her. She stands before him (עמד לפניו, v. 12),[17] but Elisha does not address her directly. Instead, he tells Gehazi what to say to her, using his נער as a go-between or intermediary, perhaps even interpreter.[18] Her response, 'I live among my own people' (v. 13),[19] not only indicates that she feels no need of Elisha's assistance, but also helps to complete the contrast with the נערה קטנה[20] of 5.2, who lives among her captors.

Not satisfied, Elisha asks Gehazi for a suggestion, relying on him for knowledge of her situation, which perhaps he has through interaction with the local servants. Gehazi is once more ordered to summon the woman, and this time she stands specifically 'at the door' (v. 15). At this point, Elisha provides for her a favor that she has not sought from him, and which she in fact tries to discourage him from giving (v. 16).[21]

Episode Two (4.18-25a) creates complications by the loss of the promised son. After the birth of her son (בן, v. 17), the child (הילד, v. 18) is with his father at the harvest, and he becomes suddenly ill. A נער (evidently performing agricultural work, but perhaps as a personal attendant or companion on a journey[22]) carries him home, where he dies

17. Standing before and sitting or reclining are another set of contrasts in this narrative, and seem to reveal dependency or status.

18. We assume that all these characters shared a common language, but this is not inevitably the case.

19. All English translations come from the NRSV, except when indicated.

20. An insignificant serving girl is the perfect opposite of the grand dame in terms of status and opportunities, although the ironic reversal in the narrative makes the former dependent, while the latter possesses wisdom.

21. The granting of a child removes her from the unusual (for a woman) role of religious patron and restores her to the more 'normal' ideal of Israelite womanhood, that is, mother of a son.

22. See below, p. 63.

in his mother's arms (v. 20). She sets out with a נער and a donkey to see the 'man of God'.[23]

Upon seeing her, Elisha dispatches Gehazi, the נער, to inquire about her well-being (serving as a go-between), but she refuses to be diverted from seeking Elisha himself. Gehazi attempts to bar her access (functioning as doorkeeper), but she succeeds in addressing her accusations to Elisha.

Episode Three (vv. 25b-31) relates the unsuccessful restoration or healing attempt of Gehazi. Gehazi is sent ahead with the prophet's staff and directions for its use: he is to lay it on the face of the נער.[24] Gehazi returns to Elisha to report that he has been unable to restore the child. Episode Four (vv. 32-37) depicts how Elisha, with prayer and ritualistic actions, accomplishes the resuscitation himself and returns the 'son' (בנך, v. 36) to the Shunammite woman.[25]

Act Two is the story of Naaman, commander of the Aramean army, whose need for restoration is part of our first introduction to him as a great man (איש גדול, 'great man', v. 1).[26] The first episode of this act (5.1-7), in reverse order to the first act above, chronicles the inability to heal. The great man, who has power and success, needs the advice of a captive Israelite serving girl to begin his quest for healing. This man, who would ordinarily be a patron himself in most circumstances, goes to his king, who agrees to function as a broker to facilitate Naaman's plea for help to the king of Israel, offering a selection of gifts to seal the transaction (vv. 5-6). The king, acknowledging that he is not God (v. 7) and has no power to bring about wholeness, suspects that this interchange is some sort of trap. The second episode of this act (vv. 8-10), which brings a promise of healing, begins by reminding us that Elisha, by contrast to the king, is a 'man of God' and can provide instructions for a healing ritual.

---

23. According to the text, she saddles the donkey, but the נער handles it (v. 24). The נערים are frequently associated with donkeys in various narratives.

24. During the entire period when the child is endangered, he will be referred to not as 'child' or 'son', but as נער, a phenomenon that will be discussed more fully in Chapter 6.

25. The seven sneezes of the נער parallel the seven times Naaman immersed himself in the Jordan.

26. This phrase forms a brilliant series of contrasts: the Shunammite woman (אשה גדלה), the Israelite captive maiden (נערה קטנה), Naaman (איש גדול) and the flesh of a נער קטן. Of course all of these characters, who suffer a lack of one kind or another, are contrasted to the איש אלהים קדוש, who is able to restore.

In Episode Three (vv. 11-14), we encounter a refusal to be healed. The great man's pride causes him to refuse healing at first (compare the great woman's initial refusal to identify her lack), but ultimately, upon the urging of his servants (עבדיו),[27] he performs the sevenfold washing in the Jordan that restores the condition of his skin to that of a נער קטן. In this episode, as in Act One, Episode Three, Elisha works through an intermediary, this time an unnamed messenger (v. 10), who we have no reason to believe is Gehazi, and this time he is successful, in v. 14, which constitutes a brief fourth episode.

Act Three might be subtitled 'Reward and Punishment'. The episodes are: (1) Refusal of deserved reward (5.15-19a); (2) Procuring undeserved reward (19b-24); (3) Health taken away (25-37); and (4) the corresponding Health restored. In the first episode, the intent of the entire narrative is revealed: Naaman acknowledges that there is no God anywhere but in Israel. Using the language of a grateful client,[28] he offers gifts. In the second, Gehazi fabricates a story about visitors from the hill country of Ephraim, two נערים of the בני־נביאים, and this unsuccessful healer procures the reward for the successful healing.[29]

The third episode of Act Three sees Gehazi's health taken away. The flesh of the נער Gehazi becomes white as snow, as Naaman's affliction is transferred to him.[30] Gehazi, who like all נערים should have been a source of information to his master, does not provide the truth when asked where he has been (v. 25). Episode Four is present in the narrative only as an ellipsis. The careful symmetry of the story up to this point requires a matching scene in which Gehazi's health is restored. Its absence from the account makes a powerful statement.

The final sequence of the narrative, 8.1-6, is an abbreviated account that functions as a coda for the entire story, updating us on all the characters, breaking off the narrative and bringing us to the present.[31] The assistance that the Shunammite woman did not need from Elisha in the

27. Once again, the information or exhortation necessary for successful restoration is mediated to the powerful through low-status persons, just as when the original advice was given through the Israelite captive.

28. In just four verses (15-18), he self-refers as עבדך five times.

29. Which is carried by two נערים (v. 23), probably of Naaman rather than Gehazi, although the antecedent of the pronominal suffix is ambiguous.

30. Theories of contagion from the handling of contaminated gifts, while intriguing, are not necessary to understand this event.

31. Berlin, *Poetics and Interpretation*, pp. 107-10.

first act, she now needs because of the famine. The word to the king that was offered in 4.13 is provided by Gehazi, and results in the restoration to her of her land, which had been lost through a seven-year sojourn in the land of the Philistines.[32] Gehazi, the נער of the man of God, is able finally to accomplish a restoration, this time relying on the power of Elisha's past deeds. No mention is made of leprosy, and indeed all finally appear to be whole.

The character portrayals in the story of Gehazi are especially interesting and varied. The child born to the Shunammite is a mere agent, with no development at all.[33] Similarly, the Shunammite's נער, as well as other groups of נערים and עבדים, are simply props for the story. Another group of characters are 'flat' or 'types', displaying only a 'stereotyped range of traits'. These include the נערה (who is described as קטנה and Israelite, and functions like the typical נער in knowing the inside information about a healer-prophet), and the husband of the Shunammite (who is described as זקן, and who appears briefly with his harvesters and with his son). The major characters in this story—the Shunammite, Naaman, Elisha and Gehazi—all receive much richer portrayals. They are full-fledged, rounded characters, although in the case of Gehazi perhaps less fully than a cursory examination would seem to suggest.

The Shunammite woman is described as 'wealthy' (or 'grand' or 'important'), a description that is reinforced by the presence of livestock and נערים at her disposal, not to mention the means to provide room and board for an itinerant prophet. She takes initiative, acts, speaks, and is at times the focalizer for the narrative. We know her actions from her direct discourse with her husband, and we know something of her inner life from her discussion with her נער: her sense of urgency is clearly conveyed by her command to him not to slow the pace of the trip on her behalf.

Naaman is described rather more extensively than biblical characters usually are: he is a great man, in favor with his master, a victorious commander, a mighty warrior, and leprous. From his reaction to Elisha's suggestion to wash in the Jordan, we learn that he is proud and perhaps a little disdainful (although not too proud to follow the advice of a serving girl or ultimately to yield to the urgings of his servants). From his

32. The loss through seven years' absence is the mirror image of the restorations through seven (sneezes, immersions) of the prior scenes.

33. See the discussion on the three character subgroups suggested by Berlin in Chapter 2 above.

offer to Elisha of gifts after his cleansing we learn that he is grateful and also pious and dutiful. His inner life is revealed (v. 15) when he says, 'Now I *know* that there is no God in all the earth except in Israel', and he is the focal point of the narrative through a substantial section of it.

Elisha, also, provides the point of view for a large section of the narrative, and is given speech, action and description as 'a holy man of God' (v. 9). We learn of his itinerancy in the woman's discussion with her husband about providing a stopover place for him. What we know of his inner life, his thoughts and plans, comes through his conversations with Gehazi, his נער. Indeed, serving to bring the interiority of other characters to expression is a frequent role of the נערים in biblical narrative.

Gehazi speaks, is addressed and takes action, but with the exception of the scene of his transgression, all these are done in the service of developing other characters, not his own. His conversations with Elisha tell us what Elisha is thinking. His actions are those that Elisha orders. His attempt to prevent the Shunammite woman from falling at Elisha's feet tells us that her emotion has caused her to lose her composure. When Elisha sees her coming and dispatches Gehazi to make inquiries, it serves to carry the focalization back and forth between the two locations, giving us a sense of time and distance. Similarly, when he is sent ahead of Elisha and the Shunammite to attempt a healing, he carries the story's point of view back and forth between the two scenes. Elisha's power to heal is highlighted by contrast with Gehazi's inability to heal. All of these things, which would ordinarily serve to sketch out a character for the reader, serve instead to give depth to the other characters and to the action of the narrative.

Only in the scene of his greed do any of these devices serve to give color to the character of Gehazi. We learn what he thought, what he wanted, and what he did to get it. For a moment, the point of view seems to be with him. Yet even here we find that his focalization serves to highlight the distance between Naaman and Elisha, as the former travels homeward after being healed. The initiative that Gehazi demonstrates serves as a contrast to Elisha's refusal to accept payment and in the end puts more flesh on Elisha's character than on Gehazi's. Finally, in the 'coda', Gehazi functions once again as a type, providing, in the expected way, the inside information that the king needs about the great deeds of Elisha.

In summary, although Gehazi seems to be a major player, by virtue of being the apparent subject of an extended narrative, we find instead that, in addition to being a servant in the world of the narrative, he is a tool in the hands of the narrator. Clearly, his status is as a subordinate, a dependent.

Ziba

A second case of a נער who is named and who is also a participant in an extended story-line is that of Ziba, a retainer in the house of Saul, in 2 Samuel. This narrative, like the story of Gehazi, is broken up by the intercalation of other material, whether by the original author or by a redactor weaving his sources. With only a few exceptions,[34] scholars do not treat this narrative and the social realities it depicts as a unity, but concentrate on the larger stories of David's fortunes and the political realities that those tales depict. The 'Succession Document' in 2 Samuel 9–20 and 1 Kings 1–2, as identified by Rost,[35] encompasses the three scenes that make up this narrative. Rost already argues against Caspari and Gressmann, who would delineate an independent Absalom cycle within 2 Samuel, making the first of these three pericopes, in which Ziba figures, originate from a separate source from the other two.[36] Of the proposition of an Amnon-Tamar novella and an Absalom novella, he says:

> It must be admitted that both of these *novellen* should be credited with a certain amount of independence in so far as in each of them a different character is, or seems to be, the centre of interest. Against this we should note that no peculiarities of language or style can be discerned and that in terms of content the threads are interwoven. So the most likely solution is that we should recognize just one author, in which case the

---

34. J.P. Fokkelman, 'King David (2 Sam. 9–20 and 1 Kgs 1–2)', in *idem, Narrative Art and Poetry in the Books of Samuel: A Full Interpretation Based on Stylistic and Structural Analyses* (Assen: Van Gorcum, 1981), pp. 23-40; S. Lasine, 'Judicial Narratives and the Ethics of Reading: The Reader as Judge of the Dispute between Mephibosheth and Ziba', *HS* 30 (1989), pp. 49-69.

35. L. Rost, *The Succession to the Throne of David* (Historic Texts and Interpreters in Biblical Scholarship, 1; Sheffield: Almond Press, 1982), pp. 65-114.

36. D.W. Caspari, 'The Literary Type and Historical Value of 2 Samuel 15–20', in D.M. Gunn (ed.), *Narrative and Novella in Samuel: Studies by Hugo Gressmann and Other Scholars, 1906–1923* (trans. D.E. Orton; JSOTSup, 116; Sheffield: Almond Press, 1991), pp. 59-88; H. Gressmann, 'The Oldest History Writing in Israel', in Gunn (ed.), *Narrative and Novella in Samuel*, pp. 9-58 (31).

somewhat unlikely possibility exists that we should attribute the present form of the whole text to a final redaction by this same writer... But just one look at the uniform style or the structure of the succession story proves that there is a unifying plan underlying the whole text which does not owe its origins to the industrious hands of some editor.[37]

In his traditio-historical treatment, Carlson's division of 2 Samuel into 'David under Blessing' (2–7) and 'David under Curse' (9–24) likewise maintains all the parts of this story of Ziba in one unit.[38] McCarter, more recently, has suggested the Story of Absalom's revolt (2 Sam. 13–20), as one of the materials that 'probably derive from the time of David', at least in its original form.[39] Neither Noth[40] nor Cross[41] counts these verses as the work of the Deuteronomists, but rather as part of their sources. Veijola assigns certain of these verses to DtrG (9.1, *7, *10, 11b, 13aβ; 19.22-23, 29),[42] and along with Dietrich assigns the rest to a late prophetic source.[43] McCarter argues against both Dietrich and Veijola, suggesting a Northern, pre-Deuteronomistic provenance for these, as well as certain other prophetic materials.[44]

The interpreters mentioned above were not focusing primarily on the story of Ziba the נער in their division into sources, and the splitting into two different strata of the parts of that narrative was an unimportant and unnoticed by-product of the process of applying their criteria to 2 Samuel. Fokkelman, however, argues for the integrity of a story that he refers to as 'The triangle: David–Ziba–Mephibosheth', with his more

37. Rost, *Succession*, p. 67.

38. R.A. Carlson, *David, the Chosen King: A Traditio-Historical Approach to the Second Book of Samuel* (trans. E.J. Sharpe and S. Rudman; Uppsala: Almqvist & Wiksell, 1964), pp. 24, 30.

39. P.K. McCarter, Jr, *II Samuel: A New Translation with Introduction, Notes and Commentary* (AB, 9; Garden City, NY: Doubleday, 1984), p. 9.

40. M. Noth, *The Deuteronomistic History* (JSOTSup, 15; Sheffield: JSOT Press, 1981), p. 56.

41. F.M. Cross, *Canaanite Myth and Hebrew Epic* (Cambridge, MA: Harvard University Press, 1973), pp. 285-89.

42. T. Veijola, *Die ewige Dynastie: David und die Entstehung seiner Dynastie nach der deuteronomistischen Darstellung* (Annales Academiae Scientiarum Fenicae B, 193; Helsinki: Suomalainen Tiedeakatemia, 1975), quoted in McCarter, *II Samuel*, p. 7.

43. W. Dietrich, *Prophetie und Geschichte: Eine redaktionsgeschichtliche Untersuchung zum Deuteronomistischen Geschichtswerk* (FRLANT; Göttingen: Vandenhoeck & Ruprecht, 1972), pp. 134-39.

44. McCarter, *II Samuel*, p. 8.

deliberate focus on the narratives of the book. 'The analysis in Chapter II below not only demonstrates that II Sam. 9 belongs with 16.1-4 and 19.25-31 on the basis of the material, but on the basis of style, structure, and theme as well.'[45]

In its present form, the interpolation of the stories of David–Bath-sheba–Uriah, the Ammonite wars, the Tamar–Amnon–Absalom tragedy and the details of Absalom's revolt serve to delay the progress of the story of Ziba, heightening tension while at the same time supplying additional information that explains the motivations and situations of various characters in the little drama. We shall see that Ziba shares with Gehazi of 2 Kings not just the fact of being named, but also the fact of being depicted as guilty of self-interest, opportunism and duplicity. (In this they share with other *unnamed* נערים a tendency to behave badly unless rigorously trained and supervised.)[46]

Ziba's story begins with David wondering whether Saul has any surviving descendants to whom he might be gracious as a gesture in memory of David's friend, Saul's son Jonathan (9.1). Since this question bears no relationship to the listing of David's administrative personnel with which ch. 8 closes, some scholars have tried a rearrangement that links the first verses of ch. 9 with 2 Samuel 21, in which David executes the last of the Saulides, allegedly to avenge the Gibeonites.[47] This emendation is not necessary for the sense of the text. Furthermore, given the position of servants (עבדים as well as נערים) as members of the household in the ancient Near East, even at times as heirs,[48] it seems likely that the narrator is suggesting that Ziba was brought forward, not initially as an informant on the possibility of a blood descendant of Saul, but rather as the only surviving member of the household himself. Indeed, the rhetorical question about a survivor לבית שאול (v. 1) is answered immediately by the narrator's answer: לבית שאול (v. 2), there was a servant (עבד) by the name of Ziba. To David's question, 'Are you

45. Fokkelman, 'King David', p. 18.

46. E.g. Ruth 2.9, 22; Prov. 20.11; 22.6; 2 Kgs 2.23.

47. For example T. Veijola, *David: Gesammelte Studien zu den David über-lieferungen des Alten Testaments* (Schriften der Finnischen Exegetischen Gesell-schaft, 52; Helsinki: Finnische Exegetische Gesellschaft; Göttingen: Vandenhoeck & Ruprecht, 1990), pp. 68-69; H.P. Smith, *A Critical and Exegetical Commentary on the Books of Samuel* (ICC; New York: Charles Scribner's Sons, 1899), p. 310.

48. As, for instance, when Abraham (Gen. 15.2, 3) laments that Eliezer of Dam-ascus, a slave (עבד) born in his house, will be his heir.

Ziba?' comes the ingratiating reply, 'עבדך, your servant'.[49] This detail is important for understanding this narrative, since I believe that intentional obfuscation based on ambiguity about who is Ziba's master (that is, of whom he is servant) lies at the heart of the plot of this tale.

David presses Ziba: Is there no one *else* left לבית שאול (v. 3), and Ziba replies that there is still Jonathan's crippled son. Ziba has heard only that חסד אלהים, the grace of God, was to be dispensed; he was not present when David relayed his wish to grant grace 'for the sake of Jonathan'. Thus, although Ziba may have wished to diminish Mephibosheth,[50] by calling attention to his crippled condition, and to distance him from 'the house of Saul', he unwittingly portrayed him as exactly the person David is seeking.

Ziba's answer to David's next question alerts the careful reader to the possibility that the faithful retainer may be more self-serving than traditional reading of this text has cast him. Mephibosheth has not been under the care and service of Ziba of the House of Saul in the interval since the deaths of his blood relatives. Rather he has been in the protection of Machir son of Ammiel (v. 5). When summoned, Mephibosheth too places himself in clientship to the king with the phrase עבדך (v. 6). David's offer of patronage includes not just the return of his grandfather's lands (had they been in the hands of Ziba perhaps?), but a place

---

49. Throughout the Hebrew scriptures, this word, עבדך, is used to indicate subservience, yet more, to indicate a desire to be the client in a patron–client relationship. In using this form, the speaker indicates a wish *not to be treated as an equal*, but rather as an inferior. By doing so, he implicitly places himself under the protection of the other person by acknowledging his superiority. In an agonistic society, such a display of modesty and humility precludes a contest for dominance by declaring the outcome in advance. The rules of patronage in such societies make it a dishonorable thing to do battle in any form with one's clients, since their honor is embedded in the honor of the patron. Thus the address 'your servant' in the scriptures is placed on the lips of many who are patently *not* functioning in serving capacities. Its use allows the speaker to opt out of a battle, physical, verbal or otherwise, which he would surely lose. This behavior is found also in the animal kingdom: among canines, a male dog frequently rolls onto his back (a very vulnerable position) and urinates on himself (as a puppy does) in a gesture designed to reassure a more dominant dog that he is no threat and will not mount a challenge for the position of 'leader of the pack' (v. 2).

50. I will, with MT, use the name Mephibosheth throughout, rather than following Chronicles or LXX in calling him Meribbaal, notwithstanding the possible editorial polemic included in the name.

at David's table (v. 7), and Mephibosheth responds with appropriate gratitude (v. 8).

David's next responses, while some textual uncertainties exist in these verses (vv. 9-13), accomplish a number of reversals. Ziba, who had been previously identified as a servant (עבד) to the house of Saul, is now נער of Saul[51] for the first time. Whether this reflects a degree of being cast off or uprooted is not immediately obvious, but careful examination of the rest of ch. 9 hints that it may indeed do just that. Suddenly, everything that belongs to Saul and to *all his house*, that is, including what belonged directly or indirectly to Ziba, is turned over to Mephibosheth, who is identified as 'the son of your master' (v. 9). This terminology takes on added significance in light of the fact (whatever may be the rearrangements needed to fit the parts of v. 11 in their proper place in the narrative)[52] that Mephibosheth is said to eat at the king's table as 'one of the sons of the kings'. Thus Mephibosheth is, at one and the same time, the son of Ziba's late master, Saul, and in effect the adopted son of David, who for all intents and purposes is Ziba's present master. Ziba has repeatedly acknowledged this by calling himself עבדך.

The demotion is completed (v. 10) when the 'servant' is directed to 'serve': David directs Ziba to work the land for Mephibosheth. Furthermore, Ziba's 15 sons and 20 servants, those who might have fancied themselves in line to inherit oversight of Saul's estate, are to join him in that labor. This is the only biblical נער who has built his own 'house' with sons and servants, an unusual situation facilitated, no doubt, by Saul's death and Mephibosheth's absence, which allowed Ziba temporarily to head the household. Working the land must have been considerably more rigorous work than functioning as retainer or steward to a king, and the observant reader will notice that this is a duty that takes Ziba out of the city (where he seems to have been when the king was wondering about Saul's survivors) into the countryside (where apparently Mephibosheth was living prior to being invited to court life in Jerusalem). In contrast to Ziba's large household, Mephibosheth has

---

51. Syriac manuscripts lack this phrase.

52. The emendations most commonly employed here are to repoint the verb to 3ms perf with the Greek or to emend to imperfect, which has textual support from two manuscripts and the Vulgate. MT's 'my table' must then also be emended to 'his table', i.e. the table of David, the king. See A.A. Anderson, *2 Samuel* (WBC, 11; Dallas: Word Books, 1989), p. 140; McCarter, *II Samuel*, p. 259; Smith, *Samuel*, p. 312.

only one son, and a small (קטן, perhaps 'insignificant'?) one at that, but everyone dwelling in the household of Ziba was serving Mephibosheth by working the lands of his ancestral estate, while he, crippled in both feet, was dwelling in Jerusalem.

The next chapters interrupt the story of Ziba and Mephibosheth, but whether as secondary material or a device of the author is not important. Our next encounter with Ziba is in ch. 16, while David is retreating from Jerusalem as a result of Absalom's insurrection. The narrator calls our attention to him (הנה) and to the donkeys[53] loaded with bread and fruit and wine (v. 1). With these provisions, Ziba is 'going' to meet 'him' (לקראתו). Has Ziba, loyal follower of David, brought supplies to David, or has he gone over to Absalom, who was just entering Jerusalem in the last verse of ch. 15? Bringing agricultural products *into* the city makes more sense than bringing them out of the city, especially since we saw above that Ziba was likely in a rural location (surely Saul's estate was in the vicinity of Gibeah), tilling the soil. At any rate, he carries a considerable supply of food and drink.

Ziba's reply to David's question is ambiguous (v. 2) and noticeably lacking in humble and ingratiating formalities. 'The asses are for the household of the king to ride' (does this mean David or Absalom or whoever comes out on top?), the foodstuffs are for his troops[54] (again, whichever king we may be talking about) and the wine for those who 'grow faint in the wilderness'. For none of these responses is the referent established, and our understanding of Ziba's words will depend on our notion of his character. (Indeed, if the report of an attempted coup by Mephibosheth were substantiated, even he and his followers could be the referents.)

In v. 3, David only appears to ask about Mephibosheth when he asks, 'Where is the son of your master?' When he last appeared (9.11), Ziba's final words were clear: 'According to all that *my master the king* has commanded his servant, thus your servant will do.' Consequently, while we hear the question as, 'Where is the son of your [former] master Saul?', namely Mephibosheth, it can quite as easily mean, 'Where is Absalom, the son of your [present] master?', namely David.[55] The reply

53. Once again, a נער is associated with the handling or leading of donkeys.

54. On נערים as troops or 'gang members', see the section on military contexts, Chapter 4, pp. 70, 72, 83-87.

55. For that matter, it could mean, 'Where is Micah, son of Mephibosheth?' except that the narrator is careful to avoid describing Ziba as עבד מפיבשת, although

Ziba gives works either way, since both Absalom and Mephibosheth
were last seen in Jerusalem and either could be waiting for the handing
over of their father's kingdom. Such an expectation is, of course, pre-
posterous in the case of Mephibosheth, crippled and without any support base that we know of,[56] but Absalom, by contrast, has declared his
intent to take over the kingdom. Thus the often-cited difficulties in
ascertaining Ziba's true motives and character[57] are simply an outcome
of our inability to ascertain exactly what he is saying in these responses.
Although the ambiguity may confuse us, it provides David with an
opportunity to hear the words he wants to hear. He transfers the estate
to Ziba, to which Ziba replies with formalized gratitude and self-
abasement.

When the story continues in 2 Samuel 19, a different assemblage of
characters have gone to the Jordan to meet the now-victorious King
David. The people of Judah come to the Jordan to bring home their
monarch. Shimei, who cursed him in ch. 16, is present, accompanied by
a delegation of Benjaminites, as is Ziba, who met him either by accident or design in that chapter. At this point, the narrator identifies Ziba
as נער of the house of Saul, a suggestive progression from נער of Saul
in ch. 9 and נער of Mephibosheth in ch. 16. Now his full retinue accompanies him: 15 sons and 20 servants. The account leaves the impression
of everyone tripping over each other in their haste to show their loyalty
to the victor, Shimei 'hurrying' (מהר, v. 16), Ziba and his contingent
'rushing' (צלח, v. 18), anxious to do his bidding.

In contrast to the scurrying of the guilty, the innocent proceed with
more dignity and deliberation. Just as Judah came (בא, v. 16) to meet
David, so too Mephibosheth comes (v. 26) to meet him. That he is not
the guilty party in the accusation and counter-accusation of treason is
subtly suggested by the narrator in v. 25. We learn that Mephibosheth
had exhibited the unkempt appearance of one who grieves during the
entire time that David's kingship was in doubt. That this was not a mere
ploy, adopted for show, is clear from the information the narrator gives
us: he had neglected his grooming from the time David departed *until*

he does refer to him as the נער of Mephibosheth.

56. The fact that Mephibosheth has a small son, however, may have been provided by the narrator (9.12) to give a tiny glimmer of possibility to the notion of
establishing a Saulide dynasty.

57. Fokkelman has compiled an intriguing list of positions on the character
issue (Fokkelman, 'King David', p. 33).

the day that he came in peace, namely that very day. Thus presumably it was not an unkempt son of Jonathan who came to greet David, making a show of his acts of mourning, but one groomed according to normal standards. Furthermore, the very choice of details, which are an unusual set of descriptions, makes 'faking it' for show improbable: untrimmed beard, unpared toenails, dirty clothes are much more difficult to produce on short notice than are the sackcloth and ashes, which seem, in biblical narrative, to be donned at times for appearances' sake.[58] No, Mephibosheth's grief was genuine during the period when the kingship was in doubt, although even King David would understand that grief to be more for the loss of his secure and comfortable place at the king's table than from any deep devotion to the king.

The logic behind David's decision to split the property between Ziba and Mephibosheth has been ascribed to a number of causes: his not knowing who the real villain was, his lack of wisdom, his naivety.[59] We have just seen him forgive a confessed scoundrel, Shimei, and provide assurances for his safety (vv. 18-23); extending mercy in a less clear-cut case may have simply been part of the goodwill of the day. Indeed, retaining the services of an extensive servant household may have just been good management. Whether he failed, in this instance, to exhibit 'the wisdom of Solomon' is a question I will leave to other speculators, since it does not relate to my principal task.

The portrayal of the נער Ziba in this staccato narrative is one of the most elaborate pictures of נערים in the Hebrew scriptures. Ziba, indeed, is one of the co-stars of this drama. He speaks, he acts, he is given a name. Yet when we consider some of the other criteria of a full-fledged characterization,[60] we find that he is more a 'type' than a rounded character. Although he is named at the opening of each scene in which he appears, he is always placed into relationship, and a serving relationship at that, to some other person or collective of persons: עבד of Saul, נער of Saul, נער of Mephibosheth, נער of the house of Saul.

Biblical characters are frequently not explicitly described except by their words and deeds,[61] but Ziba not only lacks description, but also

58. For instance, 1 Kgs 20.31; 21.27; 2 Kgs 6.30; 2 Sam. 3.31.
59. H.W. Hertzberg, *I and II Samuel* (OTL; London: SCM Press, 1964), p. 367; Smith, *Samuel*, p. 365; Anderson, *2 Samuel*, p. 238; but see especially Lasine, 'Judicial Narratives'.
60. Berlin, *Poetics and Interpretation*, pp. 23-42.
61. Berlin, *Poetics and Interpretation*, p. 38.

focalization. His words and deeds are always described from the view-point of another character. In scene 1 (2 Sam. 9.1-8), Ziba is the foil for David's musings about a chance to show respect for his deceased friend Jonathan by an extension of grace to his survivors, if any can be found. Scene 2 (vv. 9–13) uses Ziba to expand on that idea, by showing that Ziba will be an agent (as the administrator) of the good that David will do toward Mephibosheth. In scene 3 (16.1-4), we find that Ziba has taken some initiative, but since we are not privy to his inner life, we experience his actions only through their impact on David. By scene 4 (19.16-30), Ziba is not an actor but an extra, part of the crowd scene at the crossing of the river. We are told that David gave half of the estate of Saul to him, but we never see him again.

Narratively, Ziba serves as a 'type' against which the character of Mephibosheth can be contrasted, and both serve the portrayal of the character of David. In terms of a social study, he performs a range of functions that we have already seen to be very typical of the נערים. He serves as an informant, although in this case he can rely on first-hand knowledge of the situation of the household of Saul rather than on local gossip. He is given the tasks of tilling and harvesting (or, more likely, supervising), which may not have been the expected role of a נער since these tasks are enumerated, not assumed. Among servant נערים, Ziba alone has offspring and servants himself. His spouse is not mentioned. Ziba's obsequiousness shows the dependency of his position in society, at least with reference to the king. His servitude has not made him dull-witted, as his responses to David demonstrate when they meet during David's flight from Jerusalem. In short, although he is unusual in being given a name, nothing about the portrayal of Ziba alters our understanding of the נער as servant. We know nothing about his family or ancestry, his home town or ethnicity, nor about how he came to be in the service of Saul.

Agricultural Workers

General Considerations
Journeys. One of the commonest roles in which to find a נער is as a companion on a journey.[62] In addition to the story of Abraham and

---

62. We also find נערות accompanying their mistresses on journeys, but they seem to be permanent moves rather than excursions. When Abigail goes to become David's wife, her five 'maids' are with her (1 Sam. 25.42). Rebecca also travels

Isaac mentioned above, we find Balaam getting up, saddling his donkey and setting out with the officials of Moab (Num. 22.21). As he rode his donkey, his two נערים were with him (עמו), although they play no other explicit part in the tale.[63] When Saul sets out to search for his father's lost asses, Kish instructs him to take (לקח) one of the נערים with him (1 Sam. 9.3). In 1 Samuel 25, Abigail loads provisions onto donkeys (v. 18), then sends her נערים ahead of her on her journey to appease David. The Levite who becomes the object of the attentions of the mob in Gibeah (Judg. 19) is accompanied by his servant and a couple of donkeys (v. 3) when he sets out for Bethlehem to retrieve his concubine. In 2 Samuel 13, we find Absalom away from Jerusalem at Baal-hazor, where his sheep are being sheared, and he addresses the נערים who are there with him (v. 28). When Elijah goes to the top of Carmel to end the drought, his נער is with him (1 Kgs 18.43), as he is when Elijah flees to Beer-Sheba, although he is left behind (נוח) when Elijah ventures a day's journey into the wilderness. In each of these situations, the נער is present with the main character on a journey, where his role as traveling companion varies, although general duties as a personal attendant seem likely, especially since each of these 'masters' is an individual of some stature. Even more striking is the presence, in each of these cases, of animals, whether for transporting goods or persons or for sacrifice. The job of the נער quite likely involved the handling of these animals, a job that could be arduous, dirty, and might involve ritual contamination.

Livestock. The נערים could be involved with livestock in other ways as well. Abraham's נער (Gen. 18.7) prepared (עשׂה) the calf, a task that may have involved slaughtering as well as dressing and cooking the meat. During the time when Joseph served his half-brothers (sons of Bilhah and Zilpah, Gen. 37.2) as a נער, he shepherded their flocks. In 1 Samuel 25, Nabal's shepherds are called נערים (vv. 8, 14), and their tasks apparently also included the slaughter of meat to feed the shearers (v. 11).[64] In the prose prologue to the book of Job, the first three waves of destruction involve נערים along with oxen and donkeys (Job 1.14, 15), נער along with sheep (v. 16), and נערים along with camels (v. 17).

with her 'maids' when she goes to become Isaac's wife (Gen. 24.61).

63. The נערים may have an implicit role in the sacrifice of a ram and bull that Balak and Balaam offer in Num. 23.2.

64. Similarly, the dressed sheep that Abigail loaded on donkeys in v. 18 were presumably slaughtered and dressed by the נערים of v. 19.

Obviously, these were servants charged with tending or handling these livestock.

In the story of Absalom's revenge against Amnon for the rape of his sister Tamar (2 Sam. 13.23-29), Absalom is in the countryside with shearers (גוזזים, v. 24) who are harvesting the wool from his flock. His נערים are instructed to watch for the moment when Amnon's guard is down from drinking so that they may kill him. The נער (vv. 28, 29) may be the same individuals who are identified as shearers. Perhaps the association of נערים with livestock and slaughter means that they were considered appropriate persons to handle dead animals, with the concomitant ritual uncleanness. Similar reasoning could also explain the other times when a נער was requested to kill a human being as well (see, e.g., Judg. 8.20; 9.54).

Kish's Servants

A נער whose function seems to have been agricultural[65] is the one who accompanies Saul, searching for donkeys, when he first encounters Samuel and is secretly anointed for kingship (1 Sam. 9.1–10.1). The narrator introduces both Kish and Saul by genealogy and by description: Kish is a man of substance (גבור חיל, v. 1) and his son Saul is a fine young man (בחור וטוב, v. 2). The 'fellow' Saul takes along is only *one* of the נערים in their employ. The function of this נער is nowhere made explicit, but we can assume that he will be a personal attendant to Saul and that he may handle the donkeys once they are recaptured.

After considerable wandering, the two come to the land of Zuph, where Saul speaks to the נער about the possibility of turning back and learns that a seer is in the neighborhood. Although Saul is uncertain about a gift for the seer, he learns that the 'fellow' has in his possession a quarter-shekel of silver, and the two proceeded into town where the seer was. Throughout this dialogue (vv. 5-10), the נער serves as a narrative tool to give us access to the interior thoughts of Saul. We learn what Saul is thinking, wondering, worrying about, by his discourse with the נער. Furthermore, this whole episode turns on the piece of information that the נער has about the local seer. On their way into town, Saul and the נער encounter some of the local נערות who have come out to

---

65. Contra Macdonald, who suggests that this נער is a 'military escort' (Macdonald, 'Status and Role of the Na'ar', p. 159.) In his zeal to demonstrate that the נערים were 'crack troops' or an 'élite corps', Macdonald makes several similar strained identifications.

draw water. They provide the more immediate details about Samuel's whereabouts, as is typical for נערים and נערות in these narratives.

The vignette provides only two more brief glances at the נער: at the shrine, he is ushered, along with Saul, into the dining chamber, but once there he neither speaks nor acts. Then, after spending the night in town, they arise and depart, this time accompanied by the prophet. At the edge of town, Samuel sends the נער on ahead, thus giving emphasis to the fact that Samuel and Saul were well and truly alone at the time of Saul's anointing. The נער is not seen or heard from again. Sociologically, he functions as a servant, probably with, among other things, agricultural tasks. Narratologically, he has served to demonstrate the status of two of the story's characters and as a tool to reveal the musings of one of them.

Boaz's Servants, Male and Female
Most of the situations in which נערים are involved in agricultural contexts mentioned above involved livestock. In the story of Elisha and the Shunammite, the נער was in the field with her husband along with the reapers (הקצרים, 2 Kgs 4.18), and no mention is made of animals. Likewise, Ziba fills this sort of horticultural role when he is directed by David to 'work the land' for Mephibosheth.

The second chapter of Ruth, likewise, involves no mention of animals; the נערים (and נערות) are occupied with the grain harvest, reaping (הקוצרים, v. 7). Boaz, like Kish, is described as a man of substance (גבור חיל, v. 1). The נערים are agents in this story, not full-fledged characters: they serve only to demonstrate Boaz's graciousness. Nevertheless, they provide a few clues to the role of נערים. Boaz asks the נער who served as foreman[66] over the other נערים who were reaping to identify Ruth for him (vv. 5-6), with the clear expectation that her identity will be known among the workers. After the נערים have served this narrative function, we hear about the workers only indirectly, through Boaz or the narrator: their words and actions are never again recounted directly. The נערים draw water (v. 9), with which Ruth is invited to refresh herself, and they are instructed to leave some grain that will be easy for her to gather (v. 15). Most intriguing of all, though, is his

66. Finding a נער in a supervisory capacity is no more an indication that these are 'high-born' young men than the presence of a Hebrew foreman among the slaves in Egypt indicates that the Hebrews who built the storehouses were of noble birth (Exod. 5), contra Macdonald ('Status and Role of the Na'ar', p. 155.)

instruction to them not to bother her, suggesting that נערים might need to be reminded not to accost an unaccompanied woman whom they find in a field. Notwithstanding his warning to them, Boaz suggests that Ruth stay close by his female workers (נערות, v. 8), but curiously, Ruth reports to Naomi that he urged her to stick with his male workers (נערים, v. 21). Naomi, who apparently understood the risks better than Ruth did, corrects her, suggesting that she remain with the נערים (v. 22), which she did (v. 23).

Cultic Contexts

In several instances, the נערים have cultic or at least quasi-cultic functions. Certainly, all of the cases mentioned above that involve the slaughter of livestock are candidates for consideration in this regard, because of the close association in ancient Israel between slaughter and sacrifice. More explicitly, the נערים of the people of Israel, whom Moses sends (שלח) to the altar at the foot of the mountain, offer up (עלה) and sacrifice (זבח) animals on behalf of the people, under Moses' direction (Exod. 24.5). Kish's נער unwittingly plays a role in the anointing of Saul (1 Sam. 9), while Elisha dispatches a נער actually to perform the anointing of Jehu (2 Kgs 9). In both of these cases, the anointing was a divinely directed rite mediated by the prophet. Not only do prophets like Elijah and Elisha have נערים in their service, but so did priests, as in the report of the meat-stealing servants of the priest in 1 Sam. 2.13-17. The only time when Joshua is called a נער is in Exod. 33.11, where it is reported that he remained in the tent of meeting outside the camp night and day, even when Moses returned to the camp.

Young Levite: Priestly Functions
One story within which the function of the נער is clearly cultic is the tale of the young Levite in Judges 17 and 18. We learn that he comes from Bethlehem in Judah, and that he is something of a vagabond, traveling to the hill country of Ephraim, looking for a position of some sort. Micah takes him into his household (v. 12), as one of his sons (v. 11). The נער then is installed in Micah's personal shrine as a priest, whose duties appear to be oracular, since the narrator reports the presence of ephod and teraphim, but no mention is made of sacrifices. The voice of the נער (v. 3) is recognized by the spying Danites, who investigate his situation and avail themselves of his divination services. When the full

force of Danites returns (v. 15), they proceed to the shrine and carry off the cultic gear, over the initial protests of the נער serving as priest. Eventually he joins them on their northward migration, and apparently becomes the founder of a dynasty of priests for the tribe of Dan.

This narrative uses the נער as an agent, not a full-fledged character so much as a necessary personage at the shrine, first in Ephraim, then in Dan. We learn very little about him, except that he is rootless, evidently without prospects at home with his family of origin, and opportunistic, taking advantage of the best option for employment offered to him. The Danite spies count on him (Judg. 18.3) as a source of information about the local situation, just as we have encountered in so many other narratives. Of his actual cultic duties, these chapters tell us very little, apart from what we can infer from the presence of an idol, along with the ephod and teraphim. His position in the household of Micah was one of dependency, while after the trip to Laish he ceases to be referred to as a נער and may have become more independent. Given the likelihood that 18.30 is secondary, it can contribute little to our understanding of his role.

Conclusions

From the many examples we have examined of נערים who operate as servants in either the domestic or agricultural sphere, we see certain commonalities. They are depicted as dependent and subservient, and can be categorized as clients. Their genealogies are not elaborated, and even their fathers are seldom mentioned. Indeed, for the most part, they themselves are not named. Within the narrative, their serving roles are far less important than their roles as dialogue partners for the other characters, in order to render in discourse those pieces of information that might otherwise be conveyed by the narrator. This is in keeping with the preference of biblical narrative for telling a tale through direct discourse as much as is possible. Both within the social world of the narrative and within the structure of the narrative itself, the נערים are secondary personages and serve the needs of others.

Chapter 4

FIGHTING MEN AND BATTLEFIELD ASSISTANTS

General Considerations

In the last chapter, we examined the role and function of those נערים whose service was in the domestic or agricultural sphere. Although a few of those individuals may have had some potential for involvement in military situations, their primary duties were in the households or fields of their masters, doing domestic or farm work, running errands, and generally serving as personal attendants. The present chapter is concerned with נערים whose function, or at least the realm in which they are depicted functioning, is explicitly military. This does not preclude their serving in the more mundane aspects of life. The נער who carried equipment into battle may well have been the one who prepared food for the forces during bivouac. He may also have had domestic or agricultural responsibilities back home when his master was not called away by battles great or small. Since the scriptures do not follow any individual נער through an appreciable expanse of time, we have no way of knowing whether such switching between roles occurred. Such flexible functioning seems likely, however, and the texts give us no hard evidence of specialization by particular נערים.

The texts in which נערים function in explicitly military situations are found principally in the Former Prophets. With the exception of one citation in the Pentateuch, one in Joshua and several in a section of Nehemiah, they fall exclusively in the narratives of Judges through Kings, with the books of Samuel possessing the largest concentrations. This is in contrast with the rather more ubiquitous distribution of נערים as servants, but is perhaps not surprising given the quantity of material in Samuel that is given over to accounts of battles. The comparative absence of נערים from the 'battle-laden' chapters of Joshua may be owing to the fact that Joshua depicts wars of conquest in which people on the move are taking possession of the land, as compared to the territory wars of a more settled people.[1]

Our lone Pentateuchal example comes from Abram's rescue of Lot, after he had been taken hostage when the coalition of kings led by Chedorlaomer plundered Sodom and Gomorrah. Genesis 14.14 tells us that Abram took 318 'trained men, born in his house' (אֶת־חֲנִיכָיו יְלִידֵי ביתו) to effect the release of all the goods and citizens of Sodom as well as Lot, his nephew. His forces included 'his servants' (עבדיו, v. 15) and his allies, Aner, Eshcol and Mamre (vv. 13, 24), who were presumably other propertied residents. The king of Sodom asked Abram for the return of his citizenry, but offered to allow him to retain the 'liberated' goods. Abram replied that he was bound by oath to El Elyon (v. 23) to refuse his offer, but his allies, being under no such constraint, were to be given their shares. Abram would take 'nothing but what the נערים have eaten' (v. 24). In this case, נערים might refer to the trained men of v. 14, although the trained men were more likely his actual fighting force of עבדים. By analogy with stories which appear in 1 and 2 Samuel, the נערים are likely to be the porters and equipment handlers who accompanied and attended his fighting men, although the boundaries between the two groups may have been fluid. Food may have been provided for the regular troops, but these subsidiaries may have been expected to 'live off the land' or perhaps to take food from the plundered supplies that they were charged with transporting. In any case, these נערים were dependents of Abraham, engaged in a military operation.

The book of Joshua recounts the tale of Rahab the prostitute and the Israelite spies. In Josh. 2.1, the spies are referred to as 'men' (אנשים, also 6.22), thus presumably adults, and the king of Jericho identifies their ethnicity as 'Israelite' (בני ישראל, 2.3). Only in v. 23, when they are dispatched to bring out Rahab and her family in preparation for the destruction of the city are they called נערים. As in the case of domestic servants called נערים, these men act in response to the sending of someone more powerful than they. And as we shall see in numerous other cases, they seem uniquely able to traverse boundaries, in this case enemy lines, just as in Chapter 3, in the section on domestic servants, we saw how frequently the נער or נערה was the one who crossed the threshold of the home, functioning both inside and outside the private

---

1.   No evaluation, either for or against, should be assumed from this remark about the historicity of these accounts, only about their subject matter.

space of the family. The נערים whom Joshua sent were expected to have access to information on local conditions, in their case being explicitly called spies (מרגלים, Josh. 2.1), from their contact with the 'under-classes' among the local populace, similar to the 'inside information' provided by servants, as mentioned above.[2]

Thinning the Ranks

An intriguing example of this ability to cross enemy lines is found in Judges 7 in the story of Gideon and the battle with the Midianites. Fortified with the signs provided by the fleece and the dew (Judg. 6), Gideon is prepared to go into battle, but in order to demonstrate whose power will win the battle, Yahweh thins the ranks, first dismissing those who are fearful, then those who used their hands to get a drink.[3] As a final reassurance of Yahweh's role in this battle, Yahweh sends Gideon into the outer fringes of the enemy camp. The narrator records Yahweh's directive to Gideon to go with his נער Purah (v. 10) and relates that Gideon went with his נער Purah. After that, the נער is not mentioned again. At the outpost of the camp, Gideon hears one man tell another of his disastrous dream, which the Midianite hearer interprets as a sign that God has delivered their army into the hand of Gideon. Gideon, in turn, passes on his renewed courage to his troops, and indeed is able to recruit other Ephraimite hill country residents to join the battle. We are not told of any attempt by Gideon either to hide himself or to disguise himself on his reconnaissance mission. This, combined with the disappearance of Purah from the narrative, suggests that a נער was an anonymous figure unnoticed in the camp and that, accom-

---

2.   Apparently, עבדים (servants, followers, perhaps clients) could also some-times be counted on to report what they had seen and heard, as suggested by 1 Sam. 22.7-8, in which Saul berates 'his servants who stood around him' for not having reported to him on the conspiracy between David and his son Jonathan. The silence is broken (v. 9) when Doeg the Edomite reports what he knows, but by contrast with נערים in various narratives, who are simply assumed to possess critical infor-mation, Doeg's knowledge has been specifically set up by the narrator, who has carefully explained in advance (1 Sam. 21.7) that he was present when David came to Ahimelech at Nob for supplies.

3.   Boling suggests, 'The story thus gives even greater credit to Yahweh, who chose not only a smaller force but also those less suitable to a military enterprise'. His basis for this is the suggestion that those who lie down and lap up water are less alert to possible attack from behind. (R.G. Boling, *Judges: Introduction, Transla-tion and Commentary* [AB, 6A; Garden City, NY: Doubleday, 1975], pp. 145-46.)

panied by Purah, Gideon was able to slip into the camp without attracting attention. After having served as 'cover' for Gideon, Purah is of no
further use to the narrator of the tale.

A story that resembles Judges 7 in its victory by means of a diminished fighting force (which is thus greater glory for Yahweh) appears in
1 Kings 20, when King Ben-hadad of Aram and a mighty force of allies
besieges Samaria (v. 1). King Ahab of Israel initially agrees to Ben-
Hadad's demand for silver and gold, wives and children (v. 4), but the
Aramean king asserts his right to take whatever suits him (v. 6). On the
advice of the elders and people, Ahab finally resists (v. 9), resulting in a
vow of total destruction by Ben-hadad (v. 10).

Into this scene of complete and utter hopelessness comes an unnamed
prophet (v. 13), who relays Yahweh's promise of victory (v. 13). Ahab,
thinking logically, is skeptical, since he knows that his forces are no
match for the allies of Ben-hadad. The prophet's response is to suggest
that he think *theologically*, and he reassures Ahab that the victory
promised by Yahweh can be won with only the נערים of the provincial
governors as a fighting force.[4] Ultimately the day is carried, not by
mighty warriors and experienced men of valor, but by servants, whose
role in warfare usually involved carrying the equipment and perhaps
attending to other baggage, including transporting the spoils of war.
Referred to consistently in relationship to the district governors whom
they serve, these נערים are mustered (v. 15) and led out in the battle
(vv. 17, 19), which results in a victory for Israel and great loss of life
for Aram (v. 21). With the help of Yahweh, the lowly נערים[5] are able to

4.   This suggestion, indeed, is similar to the boast by the Jebusites that 'even
the blind and the lame' would be able to prevent David from entering Jerusalem
(2 Sam. 5.6).

5.   Montgomery wants to see נערים here as 'a technical military term, like the
correspondent Arab. *ġulam*, employed in the Arabic chronicles of the Crusades for
the young knights; *cf.* the parallel in Sanskrit *marya*' (Montgomery, *Kings*, p. 323).

Similarly, Gray, who sees them 'as a mobile force of professional soldiers, who
were employed in skirmishing in the encounter of Joab and Abner at Gibeon…
Here they are obviously a military group, lesser feudal retainers of district commanders, under whom Omri had probably organized the realm for military purposes… In the present passage the young soldiers were probably less ostentatiously
equipped than their seniors and so escaped detection as soldiers (v. 18), but were
nevertheless a picked body of striking troops' (J. Gray, *I & II Kings*, pp. 376-77.

This hypothetical specialized military designation is purely fanciful, as is demonstrated by the present discussion of the use of נער in military contexts, where the

snatch victory for Israel from the jaws of what seemed absolutely certain defeat.[6] Our נערים, though they may have been an inexperienced
group of attendants, were certainly assisted in their victory by the arm
of Yahweh and by the foolishness of the leadership of the Aramean
allies, who seem to have been rather tipsy at the time of the battle.

Crossing Boundaries: Informants and Messengers
Although the story does not give sufficient information to ascertain
exactly what he was up to, the נער from Succoth, captured by Gideon
when he was returning from battle with Zebah and Zalmunna, was outside the city at the 'ascent of Heres' when he was intercepted. Once
again, the נער provides information about the local scene (Judg. 8.14),
this time a listing of Succoth's elders and officials, whose refusal of
supplies to Gideon's army will be punished.

When David and Abishai had crept into Saul's camp undetected and
stolen Saul's spear and water jug (1 Sam. 26.6-12), David calls across
the wadi to taunt Abner with his inability to maintain the inviolability
of the camp (vv. 13-16).[7] David mocks the king with elaborate rhetoric
of clientship (vv. 17-20), and Saul is reduced to entreaty (v. 21) and
gives David his blessing (v. 25). In the midst of this conversation,
David suggests that Saul send one of the נערים of Saul's retinue (v. 22)
to cross the lines and fetch the spear that David now holds as proof of
the success of his escapade of bravado. Not only crossing 'thresholds'
but also functioning as a 'gofer' or 'go-between' are the province of
נערים in military as in civilian life.

An intriguing example of both a נער and a נערה crossing boundaries
and serving as informants appears in the midst of the story of Absa-

most widespread common denominator of the various circumstances in which the
word is used is that the task that these men shared most frequently was the carrying
of armor or baggage, scarcely the hallmark of an élite corps! To draw parallels with
an etymologically unrelated Arabic word from the time of the Crusades is simply
anachronistic and illogical, while conferring some sort of unusual prowess to this
group of fighters deprives the narrative of its *intention*, namely to demonstrate that
it is the power of Yahweh that is decisive and not Israel's military strength.

6. See Chapter 8 for a similar evaluation of the *N'rn* at the battle of Kadesh.
7. Issues of honor and shame are raised by the ability of a man to guard that
which is entrusted into his safekeeping, whether the life of the king, as here, or sexual access to women, as in the case of the Levite's concubine, as well as other
נערות. (See Chapter 6, as well as K.A. Stone, 'Gender and Homosexuality', pp. 87-
107; *idem, Sex, Honor, and Power*, pp. 90, 121.)

lom's revolt in 2 Sam. 17. David has fled and Absalom is ensconced in Jerusalem, listening to the advice of the turncoat Ahitophel and that of the double agent Hushai, an apparent turncoat who was secretly still loyal to David. Hushai passed information about Absalom's plan of attack to Zadok and Abiathar, priests who had returned with the ark to Jerusalem (v. 15). Their sons, Jonathan and Ahimaaz, were waiting at En-rogel for the intelligence report that was generally conveyed from their fathers via a נערה (v. 17), but they were spotted by a נער (v. 18), who reported what he had seen to Absalom, forcing the two priests' sons to hide in a well in Bahurim. They survived with the assistance of the quick-thinking wife of the householder, who covered the well and spread grain over it (v. 19) and who lied to Absalom's servants when they came searching (v. 20). Clearly the city's outskirts are the province of נערים, נערות and fugitives.

In 1 Sam. 30, in the wake of the destruction of Ziklag and the capture of its women (including David's wives Ahinoam and Abigail, v. 5), David receives Yahweh's command to pursue the Amalekites, from whom he is assured he will be successful in rescuing the women (v. 8). He pursued as far as the Wadi Besor, where 200 of his men, too exhausted to go on, are left behind to guard the baggage,[8] while the remaining 400 proceeded with the hunt (v. 10). They intercepted an Egyptian נער, servant (עבד)[9] to an Amalekite, who had been abandoned by his master because of illness (v. 13). In exchange for food and for assurances that he would not be killed or returned to his master, the נער shows them how to find the raiding party responsible for the destruction at Ziklag (v. 15). This story is a poignant example of the expendability of the נערים and the fear they presumably had of their masters, who effectively held the power of life and death over them. The shallowness of the loyalty that this sort of treatment inspired is illustrated not only by the example of this Egyptian who led David to the Amalekite

---

8.   David's army, prior to his kingship, appears to have been a rather egalitarian organization. His men seem all to have been נערים rather than men who had one or more נערים serving *them*. In this instance, the task of remaining behind to guard the livestock and gathered plunder is given to the most fatigued of the fighters.

9.   This is one of the clearest examples of the difference between status and function. The fellow's *status* (נער) is with respect to his former situation: cast off or cast out of Egypt, no longer growing up in his father's household. His present (at least until yesterday) *function* (עבד) is to serve an Amalekite raider, totally dependent upon his master for food and shelter.

encampment, but by the behavior of the other נערים who were serving the Amalekites in their camp. When David attacked the camp, far from participating in its defense, 400 נערים fled on camels (1 Sam. 30.17), and whether they were camels belonging to their masters or part of the spoil from Ziklag is unclear.[10] These נערים seem to have been serving the Amalekites as porters to carry off the spoil they took in their raids.[11]

Several other miscellaneous duties of a military or quasi-military nature fall to the נערים. When the Philistines had imprisoned Samson, they brought him in to make sport of him at the sacrifice to their god Dagon. His request to touch the pillars that supported the structure was made to the נער who restrained him (הנער המחזיק בידו, Judg. 16.2), who apparently was either a prison guard or a servant of the guards.[12] Similarly, after Absalom had assassinated his brother Amnon at the sheep-shearing festivities, the safety of the rest of David's sons is reported by the נער keeping watch (הנער הצפה, 2 Sam. 13.34), a task that may have included guarding the king's person in addition to watching, and which could be considered a military position.

Guarding of another sort is in view when the tale of Sheba's rebellion is recounted in 2 Sam. 20. After Joab's cold-blooded murder of Amasa, a man from the נערים of Joab stations himself beside the body, covering it and urging those who stopped to stare at the body to rejoin the battle (20.11). This corpse-guarding would seem a grisly example of the task of the נערים who was left behind to tend the animals or watch the baggage or war materiel or plunder.

Given the involuntary nature of corvée labor, the designation of Jeroboam, נער of Solomon, as head over the forced labor pool for the house of Joseph, can also be understood as a military function, although the narrative provides few details.

When Sennacherib of Assyria had captured Lachish and Hezekiah of Jerusalem had paid tribute, Sennacherib sent emissaries (את־תרתן ואת־רב־סרים ואת־רב־שקה) from Lachish with a large army (2 Kgs 18.7). Their arrogant speeches at the wall of Jerusalem in the hearing of the

---

10. This scene is reminiscent of the portrayal of *na'arim* described by Mayer-Opificius in the depictions of the Battle of Kadesh, to be discussed in Chapter 8.

11. Cf. the *n-'-rú-na* of the Merneptah Inscription, discussed in Chapter 8.

12. Macdonald's suggestion that Samson, as a high-status prisoner, was permitted his own personal attendant seems strained, in part because of its assumption that the Philistines would honor the social class of a captive in their treatment of him (Macdonald, 'Status and Role of the Na'ar', p. 159).

people demoralized everyone, not least of all Hezekiah, who sent for the prophet Isaiah, who in turn reassured the king through his messengers, referring to the representatives of Sennacherib, clearly military functionaries, as נערים—perhaps 'flunkies'—of the king of Assyria (נערי מלך־אשיר, 2 Kgs 19.6; also Isaiah 37.6). In all probability, these functionaries would not consider themselves (or be considered within their own society) as נערים, but Isaiah dismisses them as minor players, choosing a word that perhaps reflected their present function, carrying messages back and forth between camps.

In Nehemiah, the נערים appear to have military roles that overlap with those we have observed in the Pentateuch and Former Prophets. When the work of rebuilding the wall was resumed (Neh. 4.10 [Eng. 4.16]), half of the נערים worked on the actual construction, while the other half held the armaments, here enumerated by type rather than lumped together as 'armor' (כלים). They worked round the clock, building during the day and standing guard at night (v. 16 [22]). The נערים served as guards again, after the rebuilding was accomplished, when Nehemiah had them keep the gates closed to prevent the transaction of commerce on the sabbath (Neh. 13.19). The נערים are listed, along with Nehemiah and his 'brothers', as lending money and grain to try to prevent their fellow Jews from sliding into poverty and slavery (Neh. 5.10), while others are taking advantage of the plight of their fellow Jews and making money from their misfortunes. This text makes it obvious that some נערים were involved in certain financial transactions, as was Kish's נער, who provided Saul with the silver coin for a gift for the prophet when they visited Samuel at Ramah (1 Sam. 9).[13]

Armor-Bearers

An extensive list of נערים are involved with the bearing of 'armor',[14] and indeed, those discussed above in various military situations may

---

13. A number of seals have been found which indicate that נערים sometimes served as stewards, in which case they would undoubtedly be involved in commerce, albeit on behalf of their masters rather than on their own accounts. See Chapter 8.

14. The Hebrew word that is translated 'armor' in these instances is כלים, which is used in a number of other situations to indicate the sexual organs of David's men (1 Sam. 21.5), the vessels of the temple (1 Kgs 7.45; 2 Kgs 12.14), men's garments (Deut. 22.5, which are not to be worn by women), general baggage (1 Sam. 17.22),

have been 'equipment bearers' or 'military porters' (נשׂא כלים), even if
not designated as such by the texts. On the other hand, in some
instances, a man is called נשׂא כלים but is not specifically designated as
נער. Given the probable strenuousness of this work, they too are likely
to have been military servants of the same sort. Thus the 'armor-bearer'
who was at Saul's side when he was struck by Philistine archers
(1 Sam. 31; 1 Chron. 10) was probably a נער, as also was Naharai of
Beeroth, armor-bearer of Joab, who is listed among the 'Thirty' in the
roster of David's warriors (2 Sam. 23.37; 1 Chron. 11.39). The נערים of
Neh 4.16 carry 'armor' along with a whole list of defensive equipment,
as well as serving as construction workers on the rebuilding of the wall
of Jerusalem. Presumably, in a period when a citizen militia, rather than
a professional standing army, served to protect the interests of a particular group, those citizens who had נערים serving them in peacetime
simply took this attendant along to perform some of the heavy work
when they were mustered for warfare.

Orders to Kill: Assassinations and Assisted Suicides
One of the most striking things about the נערים who serve as armor-
bearer is how frequently they are asked to kill. The parade example, of
course, comes from the story of Abimelech in Judg. 9.50-57. After the
destruction of Shechem, Abimelech's forces besieged Thebez. The
people of the city shut themselves up on the roof of a tower, and when
Abimelech approached the tower to set it afire, a 'certain woman'
heaved a millstone over the side, crushing his skull. At Abimelech's
request, the נער who carried his armor put an end to him in order to

even cooking pots (Lev. 6.21). Given the likely cumbersomeness of Iron Age
weapons of war, a porter would have been helpful for transporting any of these
implements, and thus a translation of 'equipment' may be more accurate than the
usual 'armor'. Additionally, such a translation is less likely to predispose readers to
imagine a medieval battlefield complete with 'knights in shining armor' adhering to
a code of chivalry, such as Macdonald seems to have in view. (Macdonald, 'Status
and Role of the Naʿar', pp. 158-59.)
    The cumbersome equipment of ancient warfare, as well as the servants enlisted
to carry it, can frequently be seen in reliefs depicting ancient battles. Orthostats
from the Nimrud palace of Ashurnasirpal II, for instance, show warriors in battle
and behind each of them is at least one beardless porter holding arrows or shields.
Many of these porters are marked as servants by their ear-piercings (Y. Yadin, *The
Art of Warfare in Biblical Lands in the Light of Archaeological Study*, II [New
York: McGraw–Hill, 1963], pp. 388-89.

spare him the ignominy of having been killed by a woman.

Another well-known example of the use of the נער in assisted suicide comes in the scenes depicting the death of King Saul. In 1 Samuel 31, the narrator tells us that after the deaths of his sons Jonathan, Abinadab and Malchishua, and once Saul realized that his wounds were fatal, he asked his armor-bearer, not explicitly referred to as נער, to complete the process, lest the Philistines have the opportunity to torment him. The armor-bearer refuses in fear,[15] so Saul takes his own life, whereupon his assistant joins him in suicide.

By contrast with this account that the narrator gives of the last moments of Saul's life, another tale is told by the man who arrived in Ziklag from Saul's camp, bearing the marks of grief, in 2 Samuel 1. To David's inquiry about the outcome of the battle between Israel and Philistia, he relays the occurrence of widespread desertion and the deaths of Saul and Jonathan. When David asked the נער (v. 5) how he could be certain of their deaths, he reported finding a moribund Saul with mounted enemy closing in. Saul's first question was about the homeland of the man, and hearing that he was an Amalekite, Saul asked him to end his life.[16] The נער reports to David, perhaps expecting to be commended for his good deed, that he complied with the request and has brought the tokens of Saul's office to David. Far from being pleased, David then commands one of his נערים to execute the Amalekite, which he does forthwith.

A similar, though more stealthy, assassination is carried out by the נערים of Absalom. Some two years after Ammon's rape of Tamar, when Absalom had gathered all of David's sons to celebrate the shearing of his sheep, he instructed his נערים to watch for the moment when Ammon was intoxicated and then at Absalom's signal they were to strike

15. This fear is without doubt because of the fact that Saul is the Lord's anointed, not because of the נער's 'youthfulness' or reluctance to take the life of someone with higher status than himself because of some 'knightly code of honor', as suggested by Macdonald. Certainly David was considered a hero for his unwillingness to harm Saul (as in 1 Sam. 24.6; 26.9), and his restraint was depicted as strength, not weakness (R.W. Klein, *1 Samuel* [WBC, 10; Waco, TX: Word Books, 1983], p. 288; Macdonald, 'Status and Role of the Na'ar', pp. 158-59.)

16. To ask about the ethnic identity of a potential 'angel of death' may seem odd, but perhaps Saul wanted to be certain he was not a Philistine, or perhaps he knew that only a foreigner would feel free to kill Israel's anointed king, even at his own request, although David clearly feels that even an Amalekite should not have done so.

Ammon and kill him. Apparently, this was an order that a נער was in some fear of carrying out, since Absalom enjoins them to be courageous and assures them that the deed will be his responsibility, since he has ordered it (2 Sam. 13.28). The text then reports simply that the נערים did as they had been directed (v. 29), which resulted in the flight of the remainder of Absalom's brothers.

Another incident in which an order to execute an enemy is given occurs in the aftermath of the death of Saul and his three sons, when the Israelites, along with a remaining son of Saul, called variously Ish-bosheth or Ishbaal by MT and LXX respectively, lost heart (2 Sam. 4.1). The two raiding band captains of Ishbosheth, Baanah and Rechab, sons of Rimmon of Beeroth, came to Ishbosheth during a midday siesta. Pretending to deliver wheat, they struck him in the stomach as he lay in his bed, decapitated him, and then fled. Thereupon they proudly carried the head to David, assuming that the enmity between himself and Ish-bosheth would cause him to welcome the assassination. Quite the contrary, David made reference to the way he had greeted the news of Saul's death, and calling in the נערים, commanded them to execute the brothers (v. 12) and remove their hands and feet for good measure.

A final example of נערים who kill on the *implied* orders of their master occurs in 2 Sam. 18.15 in the battle between forces loyal to David, led by Joab, Abishai and Gittai, and Israelite forces who had rallied behind Absalom. David had repeatedly asked his generals to 'deal gently' with Absalom, but they had discouraged him from coming into the battle along with them. Absalom's gorgeous hair had gotten him hung up in a tree when the mule on which he rode had ducked under a low branch, and an observer reported this state of affairs to Joab. To Joab's suggestion that he would have rewarded him for putting an end to Absalom right then and there, the man responded that he would not dream of acting contrary to King David's wish for clemency in dealing with Absalom. Joab, in impatience and disgust, takes three spears and drives them into Absalom's heart, whereupon ten נערים, Joab's armor-bearers, finish him off. The narrator does not record an order from their master, but clearly they were carrying out his wishes.

A נער who refuses an order to kill is featured in the story in Judges 8 of Jether.[17] In one of the stories of Gideon, in a passage that shows

17. Indeed, his unwillingness to carry out his father's directive, whether because of fear or moral scruple or whatever, may be the reason that he is termed a נער, since disobedience or insubordination might well result in removing one from the

some signs of interpolation,[18] Gideon questions the captured Midianite kings, Zeba and Zalmunna, about the men that they have killed at Tabor (v. 18). On hearing of their resemblance to himself, he realizes that the kings have killed his brothers, and he directs Jether, his first-born (בכורו, who appears here for the first time), to kill them (v. 20). Jether refuses, being 'afraid because he is a נער'. Soggin suggests that his hesitancy is because 'the boy seems very young, frightened and inexperienced', which may account for the repetition of the term נער.[19] This text will be considered again with the group of individuals who are נערים because they are at risk for one reason or another, but it is another example of a נער being asked to kill on behalf of his master, even though the reason for calling Jether a נער remains less clear cut than with many others.

Jonathan and his Armor-Bearer Do Battle with the Philistines
The only narrative in which an armor-bearing נער plays an extended role is the story of Jonathan and his נער single-handedly attacking the camp of the Philistines at a time when the war seemed to have ground to a stalemate (1 Sam. 14). This individual is twice identified as the נער bearing his 'armor' (נשא כליו, vv. 1, 6); in subsequent verses, he is called simply the 'armor-bearer' (vv. 7, 12-14, 17), or probably more accurately, 'weapon-bearer'.[20]

The narrator presents us with an Abstract in the form of Jonathan's suggestion to the נער who carried his weaponry: 'Come, let us go over to the Philistine garrison on the other side' (v. 1), and then proceeds to provide an Orientation that sets the scene and explicates the situation.[21] The Abstract is repeated in v. 6, after we have been informed that Saul knew nothing of this. The position of Saul and his 600-strong army, and of the priest Ahijah and the ephod as well, is specified, as well as the fact that the people were not aware of this sortie, and the ruggedness of

control and protection of one's father. See Chapter 5 for more on Jether.
    18. The reference to a battle that the Midianite kings had fought at Tabor, and to Gideon's brothers, comes without prior narrative preparation, for instance.
    19. J.A. Soggin, *Judges: A Commentary* (OTL; Philadelphia: Westminster Press, 1981), p. 155. Certainly this seems a more straightforward explanation than Macdonald's suggestion that Jether feared to kill a man who outranked him (see above).
    20. See Klein, *1 Samuel*, pp. 129-34.
    21. The terms 'Abstract' and 'Orientation' are from Berlin's appropriation of William Labov's 'sequence of well-formed narrative', as discussed in Chapter 1 above (Berlin, *Poetics and Interpretation*, p. 102.)

the pass that the two men traversed is described. Only in these two rep-
etitions of the story's Abstract is the term נער used, as the narrator
clarifies the status of the characters in the opening description of the
story.

In the two episodes of 'dialogue' (in reality, monologue) with his נער,
the first quite brief (v. 1), the second slightly more detailed (v. 6), direct
discourse gives us access to Jonathan's thoughts. The weapon-bearer,
far from having thoughts of his own on the subject, simply serves to
endorse Jonathan's plan. 'Do all that is in your mind. I am with you; as
your mind is, so is mine' (v. 7). Indeed, from the point of view of the
narrative, the two possess only one mind between them. Only one of
them thinks, then both act as one. This appears to be yet another
example of נערים crossing battle lines, and once again the two might
have crossed undetected had it not been for the decision to deliberately
reveal themselves to the Philistines (v. 8). The reaction of the Philistines, whether they will warn the two men off or invite them to come
ahead for a confrontation, is set up as a test of Yahweh's approval of
the scheme. The Philistines, who identify the men as 'Hebrews' (v. 11),
are ready for some action and suggest that the two men come up to 'see
something'. Perhaps they were under the impression that they were
dealing with two נערים out looking for a meal.[22] Scrambling up the
rocks, the two produced panic amongst the Philistines, with Jonathan
knocking them down and the weapon-bearer finishing them off,[23] not
apparently under direct orders to kill, but clearly following his master's
wishes. The ensuing panic is total, involving the camp, the field, the
whole army, even the garrison and the raiders (המצב והמשחית, v. 15).
Saul, realizing finally what Jonathan and the weapon-bearer have been
up to, joins the battle and a great Israelite victory is won. Throughout
the first 15 verses of the chapter, the focal point of the narrative has
been Jonathan; the role of the נער has been in the service of that

22. Indeed, according to v. 21 certain 'Hebrews' who had been in the service of
the Philistines crossed over to the Israelite side when they saw that the momentum
of the battle favored them. The debate about whether this represents a group of the
ḥapiru, as mentioned in the Amarna letters, while interesting, need not detain us
here, but will be revisited briefly in the concluding chapter. But see P.K. McCarter,
Jr, *I Samuel: A New Translation with Introduction, Notes, and Commentary* (AB, 8;
Garden City, NY: Doubleday, 1980), pp. 240-41.

23. In Hertzberg's words, 'the armor-bearer gives them the *coup de grâce*'
(Hertzberg, *I and II Samuel*, p. 113).

focalization. In vv. 16-23, Jonathan and his weapon-bearer are noticed only by virtue of their absence; neither speaks again. Jonathan has served as a *provocateur* to end the stalemate, but the real concern of the extended narrative is the fate of the army of Saul and of the ark (or ephod).

Arrow-Fetcher

In 1 Samuel 20, the story of Jonathan's affection for David and of the risks he took to protect him, a נער figures into the narrative by carrying military hardware, even though he is nowhere referred to as an 'armor-bearer' (נשֹׁא כלים). Within the world of the narrative, his task is to fetch the arrows that Jonathan shoots, ostensibly for practice. David has absented himself from the new moon meal out of fear of Saul (v. 5). Jonathan has agreed to assess his father's mood with respect to David and to send a signal to David that either he may safely rejoin the court or he should flee for his life. The plan is developed privately, out in an open field (v. 11), and David will know whether to approach or escape by whether Jonathan tells the נער to look closer in or further out for the arrows he will shoot (vv. 21-22).

When all have taken their places for the festive meal, Saul notices David's absence and requests an explanation (v. 27). Not easily deceived, Saul becomes enraged, calling his son names and hurling a spear in his direction. The next morning, Jonathan takes a נער קטן,[24] a small or young נער, with him when he goes to the prearranged meeting with David. The boy, oblivious of the message being communicated (v. 39), gathers the arrows and is sent to carry Jonathan's weapons (כליו, v. 40) into town, leaving David and Jonathan truly alone for an emotional farewell (vv. 40-41).

This character, the young נער, has no name, no discourse, no action within the story, except to go where he is taken or sent by his master Jonathan. At no point is the story told from his point of view. He seems to serve merely as a means by which the message between David and Jonathan is communicated, although he is not even dignified with the role of conscious messenger, but rather serves as the insentient tool of his master. For the narrator, however, he serves a somewhat wider function. Just as נערים can serve as 'status indicators' to show the wealth or

---

24. The use of the fixed expression, נער קטן, will be explored in more detail in Chapter 7.

importance of their masters,[25] they also serve the narrator as 'solitude indicators'. When the narrator needs to demonstrate to the reader that a character or characters are completely alone, the dismissal of the נער, as in this story of David and Jonathan and also in the story of the anointing of Saul (1 Sam. 9.27), makes clear that no one, except the parties involved, is aware of what is transpiring.[26] Conversely, the mention of the presence of a נער in an otherwise quite private location is a way for the narrator to signal that he has ways of knowing what goes on behind closed doors. Thus the ancient audience, accustomed as they were to certain classes of persons having constant attendants, was not as immediately skeptical of stories about the most private of encounters as we moderns are.[27] The presence of a נער is a way of introducing 'the fly on the wall' into these ancient narratives. In the case under discussion, perhaps the נער is mentioned specifically as being 'young' (קטן) in order to lessen the reader's expectation that he might catch on to the fact that David was hiding behind a rock and messages were being communicated. In any case, the narrator is quite explicit in this case that the נער knew nothing, only David and Jonathan knew:

והנער לא־ידע מאומה אך יהונתן ודוד ידעו את־הדבר:

David's Band of Rogues

Some clues about the situation and nature of נערים of a certain sort can be deduced from the stories of the band of men who coalesced around David during the time before he became king, which have many points of similarity to various forms of 'social banditry' described by anthro-

---

25. As indicated above, Chapter 4.

26. Speiser makes a similar point in his commentary on 'The Great Temptation' (Gen. 22): 'Abraham says that he intends to go with Isaac onto a mountain to pray... Thus he separates from the servants [נערים], for he can do what he must only when he is completely alone with the child' (E.A. Speiser, *Genesis: Introduction, Translation and Notes* [AB, 1; Garden City, NY: Doubleday, 1964], p. 240.)

27. So, for example, in 2 Sam. 13, in the story of the rape of Tamar by Amnon, our questions about how anyone could know what events had gone on in that room are answered (v. 17) when Amnon calls the נער waiting upon him (משרתו) to send Tamar out of the room. This gesture, which seems to us unspeakably cruel, conveyed to the ancient reader that the deed had been observed. Interestingly enough, the focalization of the story does not remain in the room with Amnon, but follows Tamar through the door to her brother Absalom.

pologists.[28] When David first flees Saul's wrath and goes into hiding, we hear only of him, not of any others with him. Indeed, when David goes to Ahimelech, the first question of the priest at Nob is, 'Why are you alone, and no one with you?' (1 Sam. 21.1). David's reply that he has set a rendezvous with the נערים (v. 2) is the first mention we have of David's followers, and indeed we are not certain whether the priest knows that these are David's band of brigands or whether he assumes that David is still traveling with a division of Saul's regulars (1 Sam. 18.13). David's reply to the inquiry about the state of sexual purity of his נערים (1 Sam. 21.4) seems deliberately vague: 'Indeed women have been kept from us as always when I go on an expedition; the vessels of the young men [כלי־הנערים] are holy even when it is a common journey; how much more today will their vessels by holy?' (v. 5).

The classic description of the men around David during this time is stated in 1 Sam. 22.2: 'Everyone who was in distress, and everyone who was in debt, and everyone who was discontented gathered to him; and he became captain over them. Those who were with him numbered about four hundred.'[29] Clearly his is a band of fugitives and malcontents, not the societal ideal of obedient sons living in their fathers' houses, waiting to inherit the patrimony. That these were not youngsters is reflected in the fact that, in addition to the references to them as נערים, the most frequent reference is to David and the *men* that were with him (דוד ואנשים אשר אתו, e.g. 1 Sam. 22.6) or David and *his men* (דוד ואנשו) in, among other places, 1 Sam. 23.5, where their activities

28. E.J. Hobsbawm, 'Social Banditry', in H.A. Handsberger (ed.), *Rural Protest* (New York: Barnes & Noble, 1973), pp. 154-56. For a fuller treatment of the phenomenon, see E. J. Hobsbawm, *Bandits* (New York: Pantheon, rev. edn, 1981).

29. כל־איש מצוק וכל־איש אשר־לו נשא וכל־איש מר־נפש ויהי עליהם לשר.

McCarter describes them as 'disfranchised, disenchanted and embittered' (P.K. McCarter, Jr, '1 Samuel: Notes', W.A. Meeks (ed.), *The HarperCollins Study Bible: New Revised Standard Version* [New York: HarperCollins, 1993]). The perils of leading a band of misfits and malcontents is made clear, however, in 1 Sam. 30.22, when the text reports that some of the 400 who had pressed the raid against Ziklag ('corrupt and worthless fellows', כל־איש־רע ובליעל) were disinclined to share the booty with the 200 who had remained behind with the baggage at Wadi Besor. In response, David declares an egalitarian principle of sharing the spoil (v. 24), which the narrator asserts continues in practice to the present (v. 25). This egalitarianism is further suggested by the fact that, in these stories, David's 'men' or נערים are never said to be 'serving' or 'waiting on' him. He seems to have been a נער among נערים, leader and captain perhaps, but first among equals.

included engaging the Philistines and taking plunder. Their numbers apparently grew, being noted as 400 in 1 Sam. 22.2, then 600 in 1 Sam. 23.13, where it is observed that 'they wandered wherever they could go' (ויתהלכו באשר יתהלכו).[30] In contrast to the 400–600 'men' who traveled with David, Saul goes in search of them with 3000[31] 'select fighters' (שלשת אלפים לפים איש בחור), although David and his men manage to elude Saul.[32] Their center of operations seems to have been the rougher parts of the countryside (e.g. 1 Sam. 22.1; 24.1).

Settling themselves and their families in a Philistine-held village, David and his band of six hundred lived by marauding (1 Sam. 27.2-8), killing residents of towns and carrying off plunder. David himself is under apparent clientship to the king of Achish, who is kept ignorant about which towns have been the targets of David's raids. The trust of Achish is so thoroughgoing that he appoints David as his lifelong 'bodyguard' (שמר לראשי, 28.2).

One of the activities that David's men carried on in order to support themselves appears to have been a 'protection racket'. In 1 Samuel 25, the נערים of David have been 'accompanying' the נערים of Nabal, a wealthy livestock raiser, as they keep his flocks in the hills. During this time, Nabal's shepherds have not suffered losses, evidently either from predators or from bands of raiders similar to David's.[33] When the time for shearing came,[34] David sent ten נערים to Nabal at Carmel (v. 5) with greetings of 'peace' to remind him of the benefits that David's men

---

30. This phrase is reminiscent of the נער from Bethlehem, identified as a Levite, who was likewise itinerant, if not rootless (Judg. 17.8, 9):

וילך האיש מהעיר מבית לחם יהודה לגור באשר ימצא

The verb in 1 Sam. 23.13, the hithpael case of הלך, is used of David's men also in 1 Sam. 25.15, 27 and 30.31. Perhaps the modern notion of fellows 'hanging out with' or 'running with' David is not too far off the mark.

31. Or possibly three 'divisions of', see: R.G. Boling, 'Judges: Notes', in Meeks (ed.), *The HarperCollins Study Bible*, p. 369. Cf. also 'three thousand chosen men' in 1 Sam. 26.2.

32. Other references to David's 'men': 1 Sam. 27.2, 3, 8, 9; 28.1; 30.1, 3, 4, 6, 9, 10, 24, 26; 2 Sam. 2.2. Saul's troops are referred to as 'chosen men', as in 1 Sam. 24.1; 26.2.

33. Raids on livestock were evidently part of the stock in trade of such bands. 1 Sam. 23.5 reports that David brought away the *livestock* (את־מקניהם) of the Philistines in the rescue of the city of Keilah.

34. Shearing time was a time of celebration and feasting, as in the story of Amnon's murder by Absalom, 2 Sam. 13.

have provided to his shepherds (v. 7) and to request a portion of the festive foods (v. 8).

Nabal's reaction upon hearing the request that David's נערים delivered (v. 9) gives a good summary of how someone of Nabal's social location (i.e. landed gentry) regarded someone of David's social location (i.e. captain of bandits): 'Who is David? Who is the son of Jesse? There are many servants today who are breaking away from their masters' (v. 10). Indeed, during the time when David was serving as נער in Saul's court, we are told that he 'fled and escaped' (ברח וימלט, 1 Sam. 19.18). Our vantage point suggests that David was justifiably fleeing for his life, but from the point of view of the 'master class', David was no doubt just another runaway. From Nabal's viewpoint, men like David should have been under the control and supervision of someone like himself, kept in a subservient rather than a leadership role. His answer amounted to a declaration of war, and David armed his troops for battle in the familiar ratio of 400 fighters to 200 'baggage handlers' (ומאתים ישבו על־הכלים, v. 13).[35] All-out war is averted when one of Nabal's נערים alerts his mistress (v. 14), and she gathers an offering to placate David's affronted pride (v. 18), which she transports to David's encampment with the help of her נערים (v. 19). Pleading ignorance of the request of the נערים sent as messengers by David (v. 25), she offers the gifts for David's נערים and ingratiates herself with the most self-abasing rhetoric (vv. 28-31).[36] The offer is accepted and warfare averted; the only casualty is Nabal himself, who basically 'drops dead'

---

35. Cf. the numbers from the Battle of Ziklag, 1 Sam. 30.10, 21, 24. Among David's troops, the division into a corps of fighting men and a corps of porters seems to have been ad hoc, as opposed to a class distinction, as it seems to have been in some other cases. The role of the נער in carrying off booty is perhaps illustrated in the story of the pursuit of Abner by fleet-footed Asahel in 2 Sam. 2. Abner attempts to shake him off by urging that he turn in one direction or another and 'seize one of the נערים and take his spoil' (v. 21). This certainly suggests that there were any number of נערים at hand carrying plunder.

36. Given the effect of gift-giving as a challenge requiring a response in an agonistic society (Malina, *The New Testament World*, rev. edn, p. 34), proffering these foodstuffs as an offering for David's נערים may be a way of suggesting that these gifts are far too humble to require a response from a person of such a stature as David. Alternatively, this may be an example of the נערים being provided for by 'offerings' from the local populace (see Gen. 14.24), whereas army regulars may have been provided for by transported supplies.

at the thought of the honor that David has received at his expense
(vv. 36-38).

Sociologically, the נערים are dependents, either of Nabal or of David,
and they do their masters' bidding. At one level of the story, they are
the provocation for the crisis, since the acceptance of protection by
Nabal's נערים sets the stage for the confrontation. Within the narrative,
they serve merely as messengers and go-betweens, with no words other
than the words of their masters.

A narrative that has fueled a great deal of speculation is the story of
the contest of the נערים in 2 Samuel 2. David has been proclaimed king
over Judah at Hebron (v. 4), but Saul's son Ishbaal is still nominally
ruler of the northern tribes. At Gibeon, Ishbaal's army commander,
Abner, encounters David's commander, Joab, and suggests that the
נערים perform a contest (וישחקו) for them (v. 14). A dozen men represent each side (v. 15), and David's 'servants' prevail (v. 17). Whether
this was a contest of 'picked champions' or of 'expendables' of the
order of a gladiatorial amusement is a matter of dispute, but it seems
not to have been a token battle that was to decide the outcome by
proxy.[37] The narrative reports that David lost 19 men (in addition to
Asahel, who died pursuing Abner, v. 23), while inflicting casualties of
360 on their enemies (v. 31). Parallels with other ancient contests of
champions are tenuous at best, and these נערים should probably be
regarded as warriors' attendants, armor-bearers and baggage handlers,
whose lives were held in such low regard that their masters were willing to use them for sport.

In 2 Sam. 4.12, David orders his נערים to execute the assassins of
Ishbosheth, as discussed above. This is the last appearance of David's
נערים in the scriptural narrative. In 2 Samuel 5, with David's anointing
as king over all Israel, his men, whether called explicitly נערים or not,
disappear from view, and his retinue takes on the hallmarks of more
usual court life.[38] Only in 2 Sam. 16.2, [39] in the words of Ziba, do we

---

37. A. Rofé, 'The Battle of David and Goliath: Folklore, Theology, Eschatology', in J. Neusner *et al.* (eds.), *Judaic Perspectives on Ancient Israel* (Philadelphia: Fortress Press, 1987), pp. 117-51.

38. 1 Chron. 12.29 (Eng., v. 28), in a listing of the troops who participated in his
ascension at Hebron, mentions one Zadok, a נער warrior or perhaps a נעו *of* a warrior (נער גבור חיל), by name.

39. See p. 59 above.

hear of David's נערים again, and Ziba's duplicitousness gives us doubt as to exactly whose servants are intended by his statement.

David

The stories of David's earliest history are a good illustration of the ways in which individuals, usually young people, came to be נערים (or נערות) serving masters in agricultural, domestic or military contexts. 1 Samuel contains two quite different accounts of how David came to be serving in Saul's court.[40] For our purposes, the relative ages of these two accounts, their authorship, or their historicity (or lack thereof) need not concern us.[41] All of these stories depict roughly the same sort of social world, and in two of them David is referred to explicitly as a נער.

In the narrative of Samuel's trip to Bethlehem to anoint one of the sons of Jesse (1 Sam. 16.1-13), the prophet sets out on his portentous journey, taking with him a heifer as part of the cover story of performing a sacrifice, which ruse he will use to avoid incurring Saul's murderous wrath (v. 2). Yahweh has indicated to Samuel that at the sacrifice he will indicate his selection of the one from among Jesse's sons to become the next 'Lord's anointed' (v. 3). Seven sons appear before Samuel, and seven sons are not selected (v. 10). Then Samuel asks, in v. 11, התמו הנערים, which is often translated, 'Are all your sons here?' Given the situation that is about to be described for David, and in light of what we know about נערים, Samuel's inquiry is whether there are any other sons who are *away from home*, out of the nest, not at the moment under the father's direct control, fledglings perhaps. Samuel is saying, in effect, 'I have seen all the sons who live under your roof. Are there others who live away? Do there still remain נערים that I need to see?' Jesse answers that there is indeed one son, the youngest (הקטן) working outside of the household, watching the flocks. David is brought

40. In 1 Sam. 16.14-23, David comes to Saul's attention as a musician. 1 Sam. 17 contains the composite account of David's defeat of Goliath, by which he became known to Saul.

41. For good reviews of the problems associated with these narratives, see J.C. Trebolle, 'The Story of David and Goliath (1 Sam. 17–18): Textual Variants and Literary Composition', *BIOSCS* 23 (Fall 1990), pp. 16-30; A. van der Kooij, 'The Story of David and Goliath: The Early History of Its Text', *ETL* 68.1 (1992), pp. 118-31.

home, Yahweh confirms his selection (v. 12), and he is duly anointed in the presence of his brothers (v. 13).

In a subsequent narrative describing David's arrival at court (1 Sam. 16.14-23), David is not specifically called a נער, but the events leading to his serving Saul are probably typical of the ways that individuals left the homes of their fathers and became servants or attendants in another household (or military camp). Saul is afflicted with some sort of melancholy or dementia (v. 14), and some of his servants suggest that a skilled musician be sought to soothe his troubled mind (v. 16). One of his נערים[42] is aware of a son of Jesse the Bethlehemite who, among his many virtues,[43] is a capable musician (v. 18). Saul requests Jesse to send his son (v. 20), and Jesse complies, sending also a donkey loaded with bread, wine and meat (v. 20). David 'entered Saul's service' and 'became his armor-bearer' (v. 21), a typical description of the situation of a נער. David is so successful in his role that Saul wishes to extend the term of service, asking Jesse to allow David to remain as his attendant (v. 22).

The second account of the engagement of David at Saul's court is in the context of the battle with the Philistines in 1 Samuel 17. The first 11 verses of the chapter set the scene, describing the taunts of Goliath the Philistine and his proposal for a battle of champions. Verses 12-31, which are missing from LXX, describe David as one of *eight* sons of Jesse, who here is called זקן. The oldest three of Jesse's sons are part of Saul's army, while David, the youngest, alternates between keeping his father's livestock and carrying provisions to his brothers in the field. Although nothing in these verses is inconsistent with our expectations of the situation of a נער, nowhere in them is David referred to as such.

Beginning with v. 32, the text is once again found in LXX, and the story continues with David adressing the king with the formal language of clientship,[44] identifying himself to Saul as עבדך, your servant. Saul tries to dissuade David, reminding him that he is merely a נער, whereas Goliath has been a warrior (איש מלחמה) since the days when *he* served

---

42. A נער 'in the know' about local situations, see Chapter 3 above.

43. Among the phrases that the נער uses to describe David is איש תאר, which suggests that in the mind of the composer of this narrative (or at least in the mind of the final redactor) David was no longer a child.

44. See Chapter 3, p. 57.

as a נער (v. 33).[45] David's description of the risks he has incurred in the past while tending livestock (vv. 34-37) is a reasonable, though heavily theological, portrayal of the life of a נער serving in an agricultural context. Having put aside the weaponry of a professional soldier and armed himself with the weapons of a shepherd, David sets out to do battle with the Philistine (vv. 38-41). Although the warrior holds him in contempt because he is a נער (v. 42), David prevails, not only downing the Philistine, but decapitating him with his own sword (v. 51). Saul, observing this heroic effort, inquires as to the parentage of this נער (v. 55).[46] Abner does not know whose son David is, and is directed to find out (v. 56). Abner brings David before Saul, and the king asks him directly, 'Whose son are you, נער?' (v. 58).

Other information about the status of a נער can be gleaned from subsequent narratives from the time David served in Saul's court. In 1 Sam. 18.1, when Saul becomes jealous and angry, he hurls his spear at David, suggesting that the master may well have held the power of life and death over the נער who served him. That the נער was a person of low status is confirmed not only by the low regard with which the נער David was held by both Saul and the Philistine when he announced his readiness to fight the more experienced warrior,[47] but also by the self-deprecating response of David to the proposal that he might become the son-in-law of the king (1 Sam. 18.18). In response to the growing enmity that he felt for David, Saul removed him from his court service and placed him at the head of a division of the army, where David was very successful (18.13). In 18.27 David became in fact the king's son-in-law, not by marriage to Merab as had been originally promised, but by marriage to Michal. With these two increments in his status, David is never again referred to as נער. No longer is he the displaced son of his father's household, living away from his father's patronage and protection. Henceforth he is the head of his own household, and indeed we find in 1 Sam. 19.11 that Saul sends messengers to David's house,

45. In fact מנעריו, which is frequently translated 'from his youth', although 'since his *na'arship*' is a possibility that will be discussed in Chapter 7.

46. Verses 17.55–18.5 are, like 17.12-31, missing from LXX.

47. If the נערים were a crack fighting corps, as suggested by Montgomery, Gray and others, David the נער would seem the *most* likely of candidates for a contest of champions and the dismissive remarks of Saul and Goliath would seem out of place.

בית דוד. Soon David will be the patron of other displaced persons, as we have seen in the section above on David's men.[48]

Conclusions

As with נערים serving in the domestic or agricultural sphere, the military נער is a dependent, subservient to his master or commander, performing what was probably hard physical labor. He is away from his father's household, serving in a military camp, without the care and protection that a father might ordinarily be expected to provide. The circumstance that led to this status could have been capture, as we might suspect in the case of some of the נערים whose foreign origin is identified. Others may have been sold into service in the payment of a debt, or they may simply have been, as perhaps in the case of David, one of the later-born sons in a family with many surviving sons. As such, their prospects in their father's households would likely be limited, and becoming clients in the service of another household, even in the court of the king, may have offered opportunity, or at least survival.

---

48. Significantly, after David's anointing at Hebron (2 Sam. 5), the men of his retinue are never again referred to as נערים.

Chapter 5

DANGEROUS SITUATIONS

At-Risk Individuals

All of the נערים discussed in Chapters 3 and 4 are servants, probably technically free men, not slaves in many cases, although economic necessity often makes the distinction irrelevant. The translations invariably use the word 'servant' in these cases quite appropriately, since that describes their *function* accurately. Their social location, on the other hand, may be what is at issue in the use of the Hebrew term. Certainly Joseph and David are no ordinary servants. The fact that they too are called נערים should alert us to look at what other characteristics these individuals all share. One such characteristic is the fact of dependence on a patron, whether an employer, a master or a charismatic leader, who is not an actual biological father. Each person called a נער is away from home in someone else's household or camp.

Far more interesting, however, are those individuals who become נערים not by being servants, but by being at risk in some way, deprived by circumstances of the oversight and protection of their natural patrons, which is to say their fathers.[1] As shall be demonstrated below, the need

---

1. Only by a curious combination of the *serving* functions of the נערים that were discussed in Chapters 3 and 4 and the alleged *high birth* or *nobility* of the נערים discussed in the present chapter is Macdonald able to say, 'I had little hesitation in defining him [the נער] as "squire" ' (Macdonald, 'The Status and Role of the Naʿar', p. 169). The characters that qualify as 'at risk' here are manifestly *not* servants in any form (with the exception of Samuel's attendance on the priest Eli). Furthermore, the evidence provided for the 'nobleness' of birth seems merely to be the fact of being *named* by the narrator. In considering the question 'to what families or social class *nᵉʿārîm*...belong', Macdonald includes the servants of 'wealthy Boaz' and the attendant who accompanies Saul to a feast (p. 148). Clearly, however, the narrator has given us some evidence of the status of the *master* in these cases, not of the *servant*. Worse yet, here too Macdonald is less than accurate in his

for a patron can come about because of the death or absence of the
father, through estrangement, as a result of grave illness from which the
father is unable to protect the נער, or by being removed from the father's
household by dedication to God. Indeed, in a number of instances, the
נער has no other patron on whom to rely except God.

General Considerations

Certain young men are reported to be נערים at the time of their growing
up, leaving home and striking out on their own. Indeed, being a נער
seems to be a liminal state, at the threshold between two realities. After
Esau and Jacob have grown up (יגדלו, Gen. 25.27), they are referred to
as נערים, but each is a full-grown man, living on his own, pursuing his
own occupation: Esau as a hunter, Jacob 'living in tents'. They are
neither 'boys' nor servants, but they are clearly living away from their
father's home. A similar transitional experience is surely in view with
the blessing of Ephraim and Manasseh by Jacob in Gen. 48.16. After
'adopting' the sons of Joseph (to insure their inheritance alongside their
father's brothers, 48.5), Jacob intones a poetic blessing over all three of
them. As they are about to lose their grandfather to death, Jacob refers
to them as נערים. In his blessing, Jacob commends them to another's
care, indeed to the care of Yahweh who has been *Jacob's* protector.

A most striking example of an individual who is referred to as נער by
the narrator at a vulnerable moment is Moses. In Exod. 2.6, when the
baby boy has been set adrift in his little basket in the river, Moses is
called a נער. He is but a few months old (and indeed is also called ילד);
surely his age is not what he shares with Esau and Jacob, Ephraim and
Manasseh. But he is about to enter a wider world, without protection.

Death of the Father

Those whose fathers were deceased were obviously lacking this patronage. When Eli heard the news about the Philistine rout of the Israelites
and their capture of the ark, as well as the deaths of his own two sons,
he apparently succumbed to a heart attack. Shortly afterward, his daugh-

citing of the biblical narratives. He says, 'Abraham's son by Hagar is so called [i.e.
נער] (Gen. 21.12, 17, 18, 20; and 22.12)' (p. 148). In actuality, the Gen. 22.12 reference is to Abraham's son *Isaac*, whose mother was *Sarah*. His statement, 'Joseph
son of Jacob is a *na'ar* (Gen. 37.2)' (p. 148), is footnoted by the comment, 'So also
described by Judah in speaking to Jacob (Gen. 43.8); cf. Gen. 44.22, 31-34' (p. 148
n. 2). Those verses, of course, mention *Benjamin* in the role of נער, not Joseph!

ter-in-law, widow of Phinehas, died giving birth to a son (בֵּן, v. 20), but we are told that she named the נַעַר Ichabod, for she realized the peril into which the infant would be born, without family support (1 Sam. 4.21).

Another 'fatherless child' is Jeroboam, son of the widow Zeruah, who is also called נַעַר (1 Kgs 11.28) during his period as a servant (עֶבֶד, v. 26) of Solomon. DeVries points out that 'although Jeroboam has a patronym [son of Nebat, v. 26], we would know that his father was dead not only from the fact that his mother is identified as a widow but also from the unusual fact that she is named [Zeruah]'.[2] Jeroboam is certainly past childhood, even adolesence, and is referred to as אִישׁ and גִּבּוֹר חַיִל, but little can be elaborated about his social location beyond his vulnerability, a vulnerability that is a consequence of the fact that his father is deceased. Gray is quite correct in noting that Jeroboam's father's death has enormous implications for the young man's future, but he has probably overreached the evidence in his analysis: 'Jeroboam, though a young man in the service of Solomon, had succeeded to the property of his father, who had died early, since his mother is designated as a widow.'[3] The simple designation 'widow' is insufficient evidence to suggest that Jeroboam has inherited property; indeed his service as a נַעַר suggests quite the opposite.[4]

2.   S.J. DeVries, *1 Kings* (WBC, 12; Waco, TX: Word Books, 1985), p. 150.
3.   J. Gray, *I & II Kings*, p. 273.
4.   Paula Hiebert points out that, in the Middle Assyrian laws, a woman is *almattu* (and therefore destitute) if both her husband and her father-in-law are deceased and she thus lacks a male guardian. Rook suggests a semantic shift in the meaning of Hebrew אַלְמָנָה over time, since Jeroboam, a grown son, could presumably have functioned as a male guardian for his mother. The issue, I think, is not simply the presence of an adult male protector, but also a 'household' headed by that adult male in which protection can be provided. In the case of a grown son who has become the new head of a household once headed by his father (*her* household of residence), both protector and protection are available. Jeroboam, however, was a נַעַר and thus had no immediate prospect of becoming a head of household. He served the 'house' of Solomon, which was likely not a household to which his mother could become attached (P.S. Hiebert, '"Whence Shall Help Come to Me?": The Biblical Widow', in P.L. Day [ed.], *Gender and Difference in Ancient Israel* [Philadelphia: Fortress Press, 1989], pp. 125-41 [128-29]; J. Rook, 'When Is a Widow Not a Widow? Guardianship Provides an Answer,' *BTB* 28 [1998], pp. 4-6 [5]).

Solomon himself is called נער by David his father in a speech made
in anticipation of his own death (1 Chron. 22.5). David takes pains to
make provisions in advance for the building of the temple, since his son
is, in his view, נער and רך, or 'soft, tender'.[5] His speech is repeated,
verbatim, in 1 Chron. 29.1, but this time the transfer to the protection
and patronage of Yahweh is made more explicit. The verses just prior
to 29.1 provide the context for the statement that Solomon is נער:

> David said further to his son Solomon, 'Be strong and of good courage,
> and act. Do not be afraid or dismayed; for the LORD God, my God, is
> with you. He will not fail you or forsake you, until all the work for the
> service of the house of the LORD is finished' (1 Chron. 28.20).

Solomon's son Rehoboam is characterized in the same words (נער and
רך, 2 Chron. 13.7), in the description of the rebellion and secession that
Jeroboam had accomplished upon Solomon's death. The narrator's
description of this critical time of transition, and of the importance of
guidance and protection to a man who has just lost the oversight and
influence of a father, is very revealing:

> Then King Rehoboam took counsel with the older men [זקנים] who had
> attended his father Solomon while he was still alive, saying, 'How do
> you advise me to answer this people?' They answered him, 'If you will
> be kind to this people and please them, and speak good words to them,
> then they will be your servants forever.' But he rejected the advice that
> the older men gave him, and consulted the young men who had grown
> up with him [ילדים אשר גדלו אתו] and now attended him (2 Chron. 10.6-
> 8).[6]

His peers tell him the things he wishes to hear, and in his arrogance he
rejects the mentoring of men who could have helped him hold his kingdom together.

Josiah, who was thrust onto the throne in the wake of a palace coup
against his father Amon (2 Chron. 33.24, 25), is another young king who
is in need of good advice. When the historian refers to Josiah as נער
(34.3), he is probably highlighting his vulnerability and lack of such

---

5.   BDB suggests that the word implies 'undeveloped character'. Since supervision, guidance and character development were among the responsibilities of a
father or, I suggest, the master of a נער, David's impending death will indeed render
Solomon vulnerable (and make any further development of his character unlikely).

6.   For inscriptional evidence related to this phenomenon, see N. Fox, 'Royal
Officials and Court Families: A New Look at the (yĕlādîm) in 1 Kings 12', *BA* 59.4
(December 1996), pp. 225-32.

mentoring, since most נערים are well into adulthood and are not, as Josiah is, mere boys of eight.

Hadad of Edom, fleeing to Egypt after the extirpation of every Edomite male (including most certainly Hadad's father, since they were of the royal family), is called נער קטן (1 Kgs 11.17), a fixed expression that appears a number of times and which will be explored in Chapter 7. His youthfulness may be alluded to by the use of the adjective, but surely the noun reflects his vulnerable state as a fatherless refugee, dependent on the patronage of Pharaoh (v. 18).

Estrangement or Absence
Even short of death or orphanhood, the same sort of transfer of patronage[7] appears in stories of alienation or of endangerment. At precisely the moment in the narrative in which the father is no longer willing or no longer able to protect his son, the terminology changes and the son becomes a נער.

Ishmael. During the early years of his life, Ishmael is described as Abraham's 'son' (Gen. 16.15; 17.23, 25, 26; 21.11). As his disenfranchisement approaches, he begins to be known as Hagar's son (21.9, 10) or the son of a slave woman (21.13). In Gen. 21.12, God recognizes the change in Ishmael's status by referring to him as נער for the first time. In v. 17, God hears the voice of the נער, and Ishmael continues to be referred to in that way in vv. 18-20. The patronage of Abraham, his father, has been lost. From this point on, God will provide protection and advancement of the interests of Ishmael.

The story of Ismael is generally agreed to be composite; the age of Ishmael at the time he was placed on his mother's shoulder and carried off, helpless, into the wilderness would have been roughly 17,[8] if a

7.   According to Halvor Moxnes, patronage is the relationship between patrons and clients, such as fathers and sons, lords and vassals, landlords and tenants. 'Patron–client relations are social relationships between individuals based on a strong element of inequality and difference in power. The basic structure of the relationship is an exchange of different and very unequal resources. A patron has social, economic, and political resources that are needed by a client. In return, a client can give expressions of loyalty and honor that are useful for the patron' (Moxnes, 'Patron–Client Relations', p. 242).

8.   According to Gen. 16.16, Ishmael was born when Abraham was 86. Gen. 17.24, 25 reports the circumcision of Abraham and Ishmael when they were 99 and 13 respectively. The birth of Isaac occurred when Abraham was 100 (Gen. 21.5;

single narrative were here represented. At that age, he should have been providing for his outcast mother, rather than the other way around. Beyond that agreement, however, little else is unanimous. Although they differ as to the exact assignment of the first seven verses of ch. 21, both Speiser and Skinner agree that vv. 8-21 should be assigned to the Elohistic source.[9] Westermann points to differences between this and Gen. 20.1-18, another supposed Elohistic text, and suggests, 'A narrative from the patriarchal period was available to the interpolator'.[10] This agrees with our findings so far that the use of the word נער occurs in narratives from old sources, although the concept of a 'patriarchal period' should be replaced, perhaps, by 'premonarchic period'.

Ishmael, in this narrative, is not a full-fledged character. He does not act, speak, see or focalize. Indeed, in this account he is not even named; we infer his name from the earlier accounts of his birth and circumcision. Strictly speaking, the possibility exists that this tale refers to yet another son of Abraham by Hagar, an unlikely possibility, but one that would resolve the chronological difficulties inherent in this pericope. What the son of Hagar lacks in character development he makes up by the power of the attention focused on him. Although he does not see or speak, he is the object of all sight and speech in this story. Significantly, he is named נער by God and the messenger of God. Hamilton has come close to a description of the social location of a נער in his exegesis of this narrative:

> It is interesting that every time God refers to Ishmael, he calls him a *lad* (*na'ar*; cf. vv. 12, 17 [2 times], 18, 20). But when Abraham or Hagar refer to him they call him a *child* (*yeled;* cf. vv. 14, 15, 16). The latter word denotes a biological relationship. The use of the former by God minimizes Ishmael's relationship to Abraham as son. Thus Ishmael is a

Ishmael by inference was 14), and the banishment of mother and child happened only after the *weaning* of Isaac, surely at least two years later, perhaps three. The phrase ואת־נער seems awkwardly inserted in v. 14, but whether it is so placed as an attempted gloss (so C. Westermann, *Genesis 12–36: A Commentary* [trans. J.J. Scullion; Minneapolis: Augsburg, 1985), p. 341] or is a deliberate strategy of the narrator to provide emphasis (so L.L. Lyke, 'Where Does "the Boy" Belong? Compositional Strategy in Genesis 21.14', *CBQ* 56.4 [1994], pp. 637-48 [647]), the anachronism remains between this tale and the earlier stories of Ishmael.

    9.   E.A. Speiser, *Genesis*, p. 151; J. Skinner, *A Critical and Exegetical Commentary on Genesis* (ICC; New York: Charles Scribner's Sons, rev. edn, 1910), p. 320.

    10.   Westermann, *Genesis 12–36*, p. 338.

yeled to Abraham and Hagar, but he is a *na'ar* to God. It is almost as if God is siding with Sarah in calling Ishmael Abraham's *na'ar* rather than his *yeled*.[11]

Neither the mother nor the son are given voice to protest the severance of the bond of protection between father and son; the divine voices are left to name the reality for what it is. Trible makes a similar observation quite concisely: 'To minimize Abraham's relationhip to Ishmael, God calls him "the lad" rather than "your son".'[12]

Isaac. A most dramatic example of this phenomenon of severance of paternal protection comes in the story of the 'binding of Isaac'. After Abraham has taken him away from home and has decided on a course of obedience to God's demands that will culminate in his son's death, God's angel refers to Isaac as נער (Gen. 22.12). The author of this narrative undoubtedly means to indicate more than youthfulness by this term, since he also uses it to indicate the servants whom Abraham has taken along on this painful mission, who were presumably more than mere boys (Gen. 22.3, 5, 19). Moreover, Isaac is manifestly not, in this narrative, a servant of any sort.

Skinner, who refers to this story as the 'literary masterpiece of the Elohistic collection', typifies the assignment of this narrative to the 'E' source.[13] Von Rad calls it 'the most perfectly formed and polished of all the patriarchal stories', but suggests that its lack of tight connection to the prior narratives implies 'that it existed a long time independently before it found its place in the Elohist's great narrative'.[14] More recently, Westermann argues against evidence of an Elohist source here, but suggests that 'Gen. 22 is to be traced back to an older narrative'.[15]

---

11. V.P. Hamilton, *The Book of Genesis: Chapters 18–50* (NICOT; Grand Rapids: Eerdmans, 1995), p. 81.

12. P. Trible, 'The Other Woman: A Literary and Theological Study of the Hagar Narratives', in J. Butler, E. Conrad and B. Ollenburger (eds.), *Understanding the Word: Essays in Honor of Bernhard W. Anderson* (JSOTSup, 37; Sheffield: JSOT Press, 1985), pp. 221-46 (232).

13. Skinner, *Genesis*, p. 328. Also Speiser, *Genesis*, p. 166, and Hamilton, *Genesis 18–50*, p. 99.

14. G. von Rad, *Genesis: A Commentary* (trans. J.H. Marks; OTL; Philadelphia: Westminster Press, 1972), p. 238.

15. Westermann, *Genesis 12–36*, p. 354, also pp. 401-402.

The narrative prepares us for the horror of the stark moment when the father's decision will cast the young man out of the warm glow of the protection of his father into the cold darkness of the possibility of death by a heaping up of phrases that sketch the tight bonds of love between Abraham and Isaac: 'Take your son, your only son Isaac, whom you love...' (22.2). He takes along two of his נערים and *his son* Isaac (v. 3) and sets off. The נערים, who are servants, provide nothing in the way of dialogue or action to advance the plot, but they do, just as we have seen in other cases, serve as a narratorial device for indicating solitude: once Abraham sees the location, he asks them to remain with the donkey, while he and Isaac proceed ahead (v. 5). The decision to carry out this terrible sacrifice seems irrevocable, and the term נער, used in reference to his beloved son, is uttered by Abraham: 'The נער and I will go over there and worship, and then we will come back to you.' (22.5)

Up to this point, the spotlight has been on Abraham. Isaac has merely been a prop, the object of his father's preparations and actions. By calling his son a נער (an ominous term) and with the laying of the wood on the back of his son, Abraham transfers the focalization of the story to Isaac (vv. 5, 6). Isaac finds his voice (v. 7), and we readers find ourselves inside his heart, feeling his uneasiness, his helplessness.

Just as abruptly, the focus returns to Abraham and his preparation of altar and firewood (v. 9). Although his actions are the object of the reader's focus, his interiority is never laid bare in quite the way that Isaac's was.[16] Indeed, as the story reaches its climax, the only part of Abraham that seems to be in view is the outstretched hand, the hand that holds the knife (v. 10). Then suddenly the attention shifts to the heavenly messenger (who joins Abraham in calling Isaac what he has become, a נער) and to the ram that will serve as a substitute sacrifice, instead of his son (v. 13). Leaving aside vv. 15-18,[17] Isaac does not appear again in the narrative, either as character or as object. Indeed the

16. The closest we come to knowing Abraham's feelings is in the way that Isaac is described in v. 2. This is a good example of Berlin's observation that a character's interiority can be shown in the way another character is named. (Berlin, *Poetics and Interpretation*, p. 59.)

17. These verses are generally regarded as secondary to the narrative. See, for example, Skinner, *Genesis*, p. 331; von Rad, *Genesis*, p. 242; Westermann, *Genesis 12–36*, p. 363. However, only the *angel* mentions Isaac (and even here, not by name), saying, 'Because you have done this, and have not withheld your son, your only son, I will indeed bless you' (vv. 16, 17).

biblical texts never again place Abraham and Isaac on the same stage again, except when Isaac and Ishmael, both נערים by virtue of their father's willingness to cast them out in obedience to God's demands, come together to bury their father.

Benjamin. The story of Benjamin is another striking example of a young man who becomes a נער when he is in danger. Genesis 43 and 44 are part of the 'Joseph novella', which extends from Genesis 37 to 50. Westermann presents an excellent survey of the gradual scholarly departure from attempting to extend the J and E sources[18] into the Joseph story and instead to see it as a unified story (with perhaps interruptions at Genesis 38 and 48–49) related to the earlier patriarchal traditions, but with a very different shape and style.[19] He refers to it as

> an artistic narrative, the fruit, not of oral tradition, but of the literary plan of an artist who conceved it in written form. It is a work of art of the highest order, but the writer is not narrating something he himself invented; he is narrating a story of the patriarchs—his own fathers, and the fathers of his listeners.[20]

He points out that, while the Joseph story bears resemblances to the biblical books of Ruth, Esther, Judith and Tobit, only this story is integrated into the larger biblical narrative.

In the whole of this long Joseph story, the word נער is used only of the sons of Rachel.[21] Joseph, when he is away from home tending livestock for his half-brothers (Gen. 37.2) and again when he is in an Egyptian prison (41.12) is called נער. Benjamin, his only full brother, is called the same repeatedly in the two chapters under discussion.

In Genesis 42, the brothers journey to Egypt in search of grain, but 'Jacob did not send Joseph's brother Benjamin with his brothers, for he feared that harm might come to him' (v. 4). Genesis 43 finds them facing severe famine in Canaan again, with the exception of Simeon, who has been detained in Egypt under pretense by Joseph, whom the brothers have not as yet recognized. Jacob wishes to send them to Egypt

18. So, for instance, Speiser assigns both chs. 43 and 44 to the source J (Speiser, *Genesis*, pp. 325, 331).

19. C. Westermann, *Genesis 37–50: A Commentary* (trans. J.J. Scullion, SJ; Minneapolis: Augsburg, 1986), pp. 15-30.

20. Westermann, *Genesis 37–50*, p. 26.

21. And grandsons, if we include the blessing of Ephraim and Manesseh in Gen. 48.16.

once again to seek food, but Judah reminds him that the man (Joseph *incognito*) had warned them that they must bring their other brother (Benjamin) with them if they ever returned (vv. 3, 4). He insists that they will go only if their brother accompanies them. Jacob expresses his dismay that they had even disclosed the existence of another brother (v. 6). Throughout this entire discussion, Benjamin is referred to by his relationship to the others, that is, as 'brother' (vv. 3, 4, 5, 6, 7). Finally, to break the impasse, Judah says, 'Send the נער with me... I myself will be surety for him; you can hold me accountable for him' (vv. 8-9). They have not yet embarked on their journey, but at the moment when Judah has *verbally* wrenched Benjamin from his father's protection, he is labeled נער. Jacob finally acquiesces (v. 13), and suggests that the brothers take a present of 'choice fruits of the land' (v. 11), another example of the frequency with which נערים are associated with journeys, donkeys and agricultural products.

Once they arrive in Egypt, the group (referred to repeatedly as 'men', 43.16, 17, 18, 24) tries to make amends for their prior visit, when the money with which they had purchased foodstuffs mysteriously reappeared in their baggage (they were unaware that this had happened through Joseph's machinations). When Joseph returns home, he is touched by the sight of his younger brother, and during this peaceful moment in the narrative the narrator once again uses the relational term with respect to Benjamin (vv. 29, 30). Arrangements are made for the brothers to be treated to a banquet, and they sit down to enjoy it, 'the firstborn according to his birthright [הבכר כבכרתו]²² and the youngest according to his youth [והצעיר כצערתו]',²³ and they are once again referred to as 'men' (v. 33). Then, Joseph arranges for his silver cup to be planted in Benjamin's bag (44.2). In the morning the men are sent on their way, but the steward catches up with them, and a search (v. 12) 'beginning with the eldest [גדל] and ending with the youngest [קטן]' reveals the missing cup. Significantly, this narrator chooses words such as קטן and צעיר to convey 'youngness',²⁴ saving the word נער, which is

22. Cf. Gen. 25.31, 32, 34; Deut. 21.17; 1 Chron. 5.1, 2; Gen. 27.36.
23. Cf. Josh. 6.26; 1 Kgs 16.34; also Jer. 48.4.
24. See, e.g., Gen. 42.13, 15, 20, 32, 34; 43.29; 44.12, 23. Indeed, at no place in the biblical text is the word נער part of a comparative or superlative expression indicating 'younger' or 'youngest'. That concept is most frequently conveyed by קטן, as in Gen. 9.24; Judg. 9.5; 1 Sam. 16.11; 17.14; 1 Chron. 24.31; 2 Chron. 21.17; 22.1.

so frequently translated 'young', to describe Benjamin, vulnerable and away from his father's protection.

The brothers are so certain that the cup will not be found among their things that they suggest the steward make a search, and if it should be found, they will all become slaves (44.9). He counters that only the one in whose possession the cup is found should be enslaved (v. 10). When the cup is found in Benjamin's bag (v. 13), they return to the city, where Joseph insists that the brothers should return home, but that Benjamin will remain behind as his slave. Judah steps forward to plead the case, explaining about his father's elderliness and his great affection for Benjamin, and the great grief that will come to their father if they go home without their youngest brother. Judah reminds Joseph that when he had requested that they bring Benjamin to Egypt, they had explained, 'The נער cannot leave his father, for if he should leave his father, his father would die' (v. 22). Once again, the word נער is invoked precisely when the conversation turns to leaving the house of the father, and thus being at risk.

Judah goes on to explain what will happen upon their return: '[W]hen I come to your servant my father and the נער is not with us, then, as his life is bound up in the boy's life, when he sees that the נער is not with us, he will die' (vv. 30-31). Benjamin left behind is Benjamin as נער. Judah suggests that, since he agreed to be surety for the נער (v. 32), he should remain as a slave instead of the נער, so that the נער (v. 33) could return. '[H]ow can I go back to my father if the נער is not with me?' (v. 34).

The resolution of the story comes in the first three verses of Genesis 45, in which Joseph identifies himself to his brothers. With the discovery of the presence (and power to protect) of Benjamin's older brother, the narrative never again refers to Benjamin as נער. Once again, he becomes 'brother' (vv. 12, 14), and he is no longer in danger.

Within the narrative, Benjamin is scarcely a fully developed character. He does not speak or act; we have no glimpse of his interior life, of whether he was fearful or courageous, willing or reluctant to undertake this fateful journey. He is merely a prop, a 'bone of contention', that gives tension to the narrative. Regarding our understanding of the word נער as it describes an individual away from the father's house and in some sort of danger, perhaps the most revealing aspect of this story is the question of who uses the word. Throughout this long account, only other characters use the term נער. The narrator and Joseph, both of whom are in on the secret that there is no real danger, never speak it. Understanding the social reality is made easier by understanding the dynamics of the way the narrative is put together.

Absalom. One of the reasons that several commentators have suggested that a נער is a 'noble-born' youth is the fact that, on a number of occasions, one or more of the sons of David are referred to as נערים.[25] Certainly kings' sons would qualify, according to most analyses, as individuals of noble birth, but a careful examination of the texts in which a son of David is so labeled reveals that in each instance the term is used when the young man is in danger of some sort, away from the house of his father.

The first such instance comes in the story of Absalom's revenge against Amnon for the rape of his sister Tamar.[26] Absalom holds a feast in conjunction with the shearing of his flocks, and he invites his father and his retinue to join him (2 Sam. 13.24). When David demurs, Absalom requests the presence at least of his brother Amnon (v. 26), and over David's protestations, he wins approval for the attendance of all of his brothers (v. 27). We can only speculate as to the reasons for David's reluctance, but the ill-will existing between Amnon and Absalom must have been known to their father. After the נערים of Absalom have carried out his plot to assassinate Amnon, his other brothers mounted their mules and fled (v. 29).[27] The news that reached David was that all of his sons had been killed (v. 30), and he exhibited all the signs of grief (v. 31). Jonadab assures David that not 'all the נערים, the king's sons' have been killed, only Amnon.[28] In using this word to refer to David's sons, he recognizes that they had been away from home and in danger.

---

25. Macdonald, 'Status and Role of the Na'ar', pp. 148, 156, 164; Stähli, *Knabe*, pp. 149-57; Stager, 'The Archaeology of the Family', p. 26.

26. The Absalom Cycle also contains mention of נערים of the agricultural and of the military sort, that is, persons who are away from their own father's households, serving either David or Absalom in military or agricultural labor. These are servants with no name and no pedigree; it would be difficult to assert that *they* were of 'noble birth', but in ascertaining the social location to which the term refers, these citations are equally important.

27. Their presence at the sheep-shearing (without attracting particular notice from the participants or from the narrator) suggests that Absalom's נערים are agricultural workers, not military personnel.

28. Commentators are not in agreement about whether the phrase 'the king's sons' is an insertion that should be removed (so Smith) or a corruption of the text

At this point, Absalom fled to Geshur, where he lived for three years as an outcast in the home of Talmai, son of Ammihud, the local king (v. 37). By and by, Joab, using a ruse presented by the woman of Tekoa, is able to persuade David to soften his position. The affront of the murder of his son had dishonored David, and he had responded to this challenge to his honor and authority by leaving Absalom in a state of dishonored exile. David responds to the tale that the woman presents, and to her pointing out to him, in a manner that was obsequious but still risky, that his actions were precisely the same as those of the community who insisted on avenging spilled blood in her parable. He instructs Joab to bring the outcast back to Jerusalem, calling him 'the נער Absalom' (14.21), a phrase that will be used repeatedly by him to describe his son, right up until the moment of Absalom's death, a phrase that acknowledges that this estrangement in the family has left Absalom at risk, away from his father's patronage.[29]

In 2 Samuel 18, we find that the temporary normalization in the father–son relationship has been breached again by Absalom's usurpation attempt. David, having left the city of Jerusalem temporarily under control of his son's insurrectionist forces, announces to his military leaders that he will personally accompany the forces into battle (2 Sam. 18.2).[30] David's commanders will not hear of it, and suggest strategic reasons for him to remain away from the battle (v. 3).[31] Many commentators see here a father's attempt to save his errant son.

> David's intention is to go into battle, but he is made to stay behind at the request of the people. Perhaps his wish conceals the intention of saving Absalom's life, that of the troops, Joab's concern to prevent this... For

that needs to be emended (so McCarter). Neither position is critical to understanding Absalom's position as a נער. A number of biblical narratives have נערים who are sons and נערים who are servants appearing in quite distinct roles in the same stories, with occasional confusion about which is referred to at a particular point in the narrative. See the section on 'Sons and Servants' below (Smith, *Samuel*, p. 333; McCarter, *II Samuel*, p. 331).

29. Contra Smith, who suggests that this word was chosen to emphasize Absalom's youth: 'To his father he was still but a boy' (Smith, *Samuel*, p. 357).

30. In another instance (2 Sam. 11.1, 2), when the narrator seems to indicate that, as king, David *should* have been on the battlefield with his troops, David stayed behind in Jerusalem and had an adulterous affair with Bathsheba.

31. In a similar way, David had tried to use arguments about inconvenience to Absalom as a reason for preventing his other sons from attending the fateful sheep-shearing (2 Sam. 13.25).

Joab knows better than David himself, who is here governed solely by his paternal sensibilities, that a further pardon of Absalom will only lead to a further jeopardizing of the kingdom.[32]

Prevented from accompanying the forces into the field, David rather plaintively entreats his officers, in earshot of all the troops, to 'deal gently for my sake with the נער Absalom' (v. 5). When, in the midst of the fighting, the upstart Absalom's mule runs under a branch and he is immobilized, 'caught by his marvelous hair' (v. 9), [33] a man reports this to Joab, who berates him for not having dispatched Absalom forthwith. The man reminds Joab of David's injunction, using the same phrase, 'the נער Absalom' (v. 12), but Joab, impatient with such sensibilities, carries out the execution himself with the help of other נערים, his armor-bearers (vv. 14, 15). Two runners set out to carry news of victory to David, and each is asked about the welfare of 'the נער Absalom' (vv. 29, 32). Ahimaaz, who had ignored the suggestion that he ought not to be the one to bring this news to the king, seems to realize, when David words his inquiry this way, that he will fare better if he dissembles (v. 29). The Cushite (perhaps himself a נער) fails to hear danger in the king's question and reveals the outcome in echoing David's phrase: 'May the enemies of my lord the king, and all who rise up to do you harm, be like that נער' (v. 32).

Of all the instances where the word נער is used in the Hebrew scriptures, only in this chapter do most commentators see that the use of the word reflects issues concerning the relationship between father and son, but they are not in agreement about what is connoted. Hertzberg says, 'David's clearly given command "Deal gently...with the young man Absalom" shows his confidence of victory and at the same time his readiness to forgive and his weakness as a father, which was already observed in ch. 13'.[34] Conroy suggests that 'the word *n'r* 'young man' explicitly betrays the father's affection for his son in spite of everything.'[35] McCarter asserts 'David's use of *na'ar*, "young (man)", in reference to Abishalom here and in vv. 12, 29, and 32 below is demon-

---

32. Hertzberg, *I and II Samuel*, pp. 358, 359.

33. W. Brueggemann, *First and Second Samuel* (IBC; Atlanta: John Knox Press, 1990), p. 319.

34. Hertzberg, *I and II Samuel*, p. 358.

35. C. Conroy, *Absalom Absalom! Narrative and Language in 2 Sam 13–20* (AnBib, 81; Rome: Pontifical Biblical Institute, 1978), p. 58.

stratively affectionate… As elsewhere, the narrator is intent upon keeping David's love for his son before us'.[36]

Caspari comes close to capturing the authentic essence of the word in
a note on 2 Sam. 18.5: 'נער betrays a loosening of the filial bond yet,
according to K. Budde, leniency for the son.'[37] More recently, Brueggemann has noted some of the complexity that the terminology held,
perhaps especially for its earliest readers. Verse 5 he calls 'an intensely
freighted statement', and points out that

> he does not name Absalom as his son, but only as 'the young man.' It is
> as though David is reticent about identifying the relationship too directly.
> Perhaps there is an intended distance to control the pathos. Second, it is
> to be done 'for my sake', not for the sake of the son. The narrative is cast
> with attention turned completely away from Absalom to David. Even as
> the son of the king, the narrative has no interest in Absalom or sympathy
> for him.[38]

In considering the narrative structure of the Absalom cycle, we see
many points at which Absalom is a fully-fledged character, speaking,
acting, thinking, feeling and focalizing.[39] In the passages in which he is
called נער, however, he is the object of the scheming or concern of others, nothing more. What is at stake in the use of this word is not the
father's affections, but the son's *social location*. Clearly, this estrangement has conferred on Absalom the status of נער: he is a fully adult
male at this point in his life, and he is not the servant of anyone. Yet by

---

36. McCarter, *II Samuel*, p. 405.

37. 'נער verrät Lockerung des Sohnesverhältnisses, doch nach Bd [K. Budde]
für den Sohn mildernde Umstände.' D.W. Caspari, *Die Samuelbücher* (KAT; Leipzig: Deichert, 1926), p. 588 n. 3; Caspari, '2 Samuel 15–20', p. 64.
Conroy disagrees: 'In view of David's reaction (19,1 ff.), it is hard to agree with
Caspari p. 588 n. 3 that the use of *n'r* expresses a loosening of the filial relationship.
The Cushite's use of *n'r* at 18,32b simply re-echoes David's question of v. 32a.'
Caspari, however, advocates the kind of eclectic translation that has for so long
obscured the sociological import of this term: 'In 14.21 the king calls Absalom a
נער because he does not want to accept him into favour, and in 18.5 because he par-
dons him. The tone in which the word is spoken is different in each case' (Conroy,
Absalom Absalom!, pp. 48-49 n. 14; Caspari, 'Literary Type', p. 64).

38. Brueggemann, *First and Second Samuel*, p. 317.

39. E.g., in conversation with and avenging his sister (2 Sam. 13.20-29); in his
efforts to enlist Joab in his reinstatement (14.28-33); in tricking his father and then
usurping his father's position (15.1-12); in plotting to hold onto the kingdom
(16.15–17.14).

his assumption of powers that belonged to his father, the king, he has cast himself outside the household and alienated his proper patron.

Illness or Morbidity

Facing mortal danger or illness, too, takes one outside the protective sphere of the father's house and conveys the status of נער. Thus the term is used for Moses 'in the bulrushes' (Exod. 2.6) and Joseph in an Egyptian prison (Gen. 41.12).[40] When David is away from his father's house at Saul's military encampment, about to face the Philistine Goliath, he is repeatedly called נער (1 Sam. 17.33, 42, 55, 58).

The case of Jether, son of Gideon (Judg. 8.20), is a puzzling example of a נער, but it may be an interesting example of the effect of danger in conferring that status. When asked by his father on the battlefield to slay the Midianite kings Zebah and Zalmunna, Jether, his first-born (בכורו), 'did not draw his sword [ולא־שלף הנער חרבו] because he was afraid since he was still a נער'. The text does not tell us everything which we would like to know about his family circumstances, but we have no evidence that Jether was, at this point, necessarily particularly 'young', which is the usual translation for נער in this verse. His refusal to obey his father's order may have put him at risk of alienation from the father to whom he owed obedience. The fact that 'Gideon had seventy sons, his own offspring' (v. 30), not including less legitimate sons like Abimelech, may have meant that the father's patronage was spread too thin to provide adequate protection. Or the narrator may be seeing ahead to the slaughter of all of Gideon's sons, except for Jotham the youngest, by Abimelech (Judg. 9.5). The possibilities are more complex than in most passages, but here too vulnerability rather than age seems to be operative.

In the story of the rape of Dinah (Gen. 34), the perpetrator Shechem is called נער just once, at v. 19. A number of commentators have suggested that the tale is composite and that Shechem's father Hamor may have been missing from the older of the component versions.[41] Untangling the arguments for the presence of sources is not necessary, however, for understanding Shechem as a נער, since this is another case, similar to that of Jether, in which the father appears to be present, but in

---

40. Joseph is also called עבד here, so that the term נער is clearly not used to indicate his function as a servant.

41. Von Rad, *Genesis*, pp. 320, 330; Skinner, *Genesis*, p. 417.

which the narrator knows that the individual in question will not sur-
vive to the end of the story.

Abijah. In each of these cases, the father is powerless to provide the
protection that could usually be expected from the head of a household.
Even when the father is alive and powerful, he is unable to protect
against fatal illness, a fact of life known only too well in a world in
which fully half of a family's children would die before reaching adulthood.[42]

Abijah, son of Jeroboam, is called נער by his father when he becomes
ill (1 Kgs 14.3) and again at his death (v. 17). The text in which this
event is described has an interesting history. Gray has suggested that
the tale was originally 'associated...with the prophetic circle at Shiloh',
and that '[t]he nucleus of the passage is vv. 1-6, 12, 17'.[43] Long points
out, 'Critics seem to agree that an old tradition has been heavily edited
by the Dtr editor of Kings, especially in vv. 7-11, 14-16'.[44] DeVries
calls vv. 7-11 'Dtr's own oracle against the house of Jeroboam'.[45] It is
precisely the verses that do not come from the hand of Dtr, the verses of
the old prophetic tale, in which Abijah is called by the term נער. The
connotation of the term is most concrete and specific in the earliest biblical materials.

Shunammite's Son. Another story of a child who comes to be נער when
illness and death place him beyond the protection of his father is told in
2 Kings 4. Many details of this narrative are covered in Chapter 3,
where Gehazi, the נער of Elisha is discussed.

The Shunammite woman has initiated a relationship with Elisha, providing him with meals and lodging (2 Kgs 4.8-10). In return for this
material support, the prophet felt a need to demonstrate reciprocity, not
gratitude. To do otherwise would have placed him in a position of
clientship, with the woman as his patron.[46] Expressed in modern terms,
Elisha did not want to be 'beholden'.

42. C.L. Meyers, *Discovering Eve: Ancient Israelite Women in Context* (New
York: Oxford University Press, 1988), pp. 112-13.
43. Gray, *I & II Kings*, p. 304.
44. B.O. Long, *1 Kings with an Introduction to Historical Literature* (FOTL;
Grand Rapids: Eerdmans, 1984), p. 154.
45. DeVries, *1 Kings*, p. 178.
46. For a discussion of gift-giving as a 'challenge' requiring a 'response' to
avoid loss of honor, see B.J. Malina, *The New Testament World: Insights from*

Elisha has Gehazi summon her, and through Gehazi, he inquires about areas of life in which she might need his intervention in order for her to obtain patronage from people of great rank and power, such as the king or the army commander (vv. 11-13). In other words, he offers to serve as a 'broker'.[47] She rejects his offer, indicating that her situation is secure.

Elisha, however, will not be deterred, so he asks Gehazi what could be done for the woman. The נער responds by pointing out her childless state and her husband's age (v. 14), two factors that could leave her a widow (אלמנה) without a male advocate at her husband's death. Once more, Elisha has Gehazi summon her (v. 15) and, addressing her directly this time, he promises her a son, over her protests (v. 16). She acknowledges her indebtedness by referring to herself as שפחתך, 'your servant' (v. 16), which is the feminine equivalent of the use of עבדך to indicate indebtedness, humility or client status (see Chapter 3).

Elisha's intervention is successful, and the woman bears a son (בן, v. 17). Sometime later, while in the field with his father and the reapers, he is stricken with some sort of affliction that affects his head (v. 19). His father has the נער carry him home to his mother, on whose lap the child (ילד, v. 20) dies. After laying him on Elisha's bed, she requests the use of one of the נערים and a donkey from her husband, indicating only that she plans to go quickly to the 'man of God' and return (v. 22). His inquiry about what religious observance was prompting her journey is met with evasion: שלם, 'It is all right' (v. 23). Seeing her from a distance, Elisha sends Gehazi to inquire about her, her husband, her child (v. 26), but she brushes him off with the same evasion, שלם, and goes directly to Elisha.

Gehazi tries to restrain her, but Elisha realizes that the patronage that he has brokered has had tragic results and Yahweh (called by name here for the first of three times) has not announced it to him (v. 27). To this point, the boy has been called 'son' and 'child' (three times each), but with this temporary eclipsing of Elisha's confidence in Yahweh's faithfulness (or perhaps in his own ability to deliver the patronage of Yahweh), Elisha for the first time calls him נער. The boy will continue to be

---

Cultural Anthropology (Louisville, KY: Westminster/John Knox Press, rev. edn, 1993), p. 101.

47. The broker 'functions as a mediator who gives a client access to the resources of a more powerful patron' (Moxnes, 'Patron–Client Relations', p. 248).

called by that term through the entire period when his recovery is in doubt. Elisha sends Gehazi ahead with his staff and instructions to place it on the face of the נער (v. 29), at which juncture the narrative joins the prophet in referring to the woman as the mother of the נער. Swearing by Yahweh, she declares her intention to accompany Gehazi (v. 30), who goes to her home and lays Elisha's staff on the face of the נער, then returns to report that the נער has not awakened (v. 31). The narrator, as well as Elisha and his servant, designate the child as נער; the parents, as has been the case in other stories that we have examined, do not.

Elisha arrives in person and finds the נער dead, lying on the bed (v. 32). Entering the room with the body and closing the door, Elisha prays to Yahweh (whose name is invoked here for the third and last time), and, as he lays upon the child (ילד), the flesh of the child begins to warm (v. 34). With the change in nomenclature, there begins to be hope, but the resolution is deferred. The crisis is not quite past: the narrator tells us that the נער sneezed seven times and the נער opened his eyes (v. 35). The woman is summoned and instructed to take not her נער but her son (בן), so she takes her son and goes. Prior to his illness, the boy was always 'son' or 'child', but as long as he is at risk, he is called נער, not once but seven times. Once healed, he is once again 'son', never again נער. Unless we wish to assign these semantic shifts to mere coincidence, the narrator must have intended to indicate a change in status by the use of one word in preference to another.

Bathsheba's Child. Just as with the son of the Shunammite woman, mortal illness seems to be the reason that David uses the term in praying for his son by Bathsheba when he becomes ill (2 Sam. 12.16). When the child was born (11.27), he was called בן, as he is again when Nathan predicts that he will die (12.14). As he falls ill (v. 15) and again after his death (v. 18), the boy is called ילד. Only when David understands that the boy's life is beyond his power to protect, when he pleads for Yahweh to assume the patron's role and save the boy, only then is he called נער. McCarter has captured the dynamic of the moment in explaining the odd form that David's 'grief' took during this tragedy:

> From the servants' viewpoint David seems to be mourning at the wrong time. From his viewpoint, however, David is not mourning at all. By his fasting and self-humiliation he is imploring Yahweh to spare the child. ('David entreated God on behalf of the boy,' v. 16.) Whereas it would be

illogical to stop mourning when someone dies, it is logical to stop
imploring God when one's petition has failed.[48]

This boy will not find another patron who can protect when his father is
powerless to do so.

   Although all three of the narratives of sons who become נערים when
they are stricken with illness involve the mediation of a prophet and
prayers to Yahweh, only the son of the Shunammite is restored to
health. The sons of Jeroboam and of David are not so fortunate.

Dedication

In addition to the work of field and home and military encampment,
another sort of service seems to result in the status of נער: the act of
dedication, by one's parents, to the deity.

Samson. In the story of the birth and dedication of Samson, an old narrative from the book of Judges, Samson is called 'son' (בן, Judg. 13.3,
5, 7, 24) or 'boy' (ילד, 13.8, 24), but in his being set apart as a Nazirite,
he becomes נער (Judg. 13.5, 7, 12, 25).[49] Clearly, the act of dedication
interrupts the usual relationship between father and son and substitutes
a different sort of patron to provide guidance and protection. Whereas,
in the case of Samuel, the dedication is carried out by ordinary human
means, that is, the two parents simply packed up the boy and took him
to the priest in the sanctuary, in Samson's case the dedication is the
result of not one but two theophanies. Indeed the angel is the first to call
the boy נער, immediately after specifying the practices that will set him
apart and mark him as someone other than an ordinary son of his
father's household (Judg. 13.5). When Manoah's wife recounts this
visitation to her husband, she retains the same order of discourse: first,
the conditions that will set Samson apart, then calling him 'a נער who
will be a Nazirite to God from birth to the day of his death' (v. 7).
Manoah requests a return visit from the angel (v. 8) in order to confirm
the conditions concerning the נער. When the theophany is granted,
those conditions for the נער are the only inquiry that Manoah presents
to the messenger (v. 12). The simple narrative of Samson is interrupted
by a lengthy interchange between the father and the angel about the
appropriateness of a sacrificial meal in honor of the visitor (vv. 15-

   48. McCarter, *II Samuel*, p. 301.
   49. Boling places this narrative with the oldest material in the book of Judges
(Boling, *Judges*, pp. 30, 224).

23).[50] Finally, the birth and naming are reported, and we are told that 'the נער grew and the Lord blessed him' (v. 24). Samson the נער will indeed find himself without the protection of any patron except God, and even that patronage will fail him when his hair, symbol of his being set apart, has been cut.

Samuel. Samuel's mother had 'no children' (ילדים, 1 Sam. 1.1), although her faithful husband Elkanah reassured Hannah that he was of more value than 'ten sons' (בנים, 1 Sam. 1.8). When, with Yahweh's intervention, Hannah conceived, she bore a 'son' (1.20) and nursed her 'son' (1.23). However, at the moment of his dedication (1 Sam. 1.22), and from the time he is handed over for service to the priest (1 Sam. 1.24, 25, 27; 2.11, 18, 21, 26; 3.1, 8) he is called נער.

All commentators agree that the integrity of the text has been disturbed in the first chapters of Samuel. Klein has suggested, 'At the end of v. 24 MT is incomprehensible'.[51] This incomprehensibility has not dissuaded a number of scholars from proposing novel solutions to the problems in these verses.[52] McCarter suggests a reason for the disturbance of the text at this particular point: 'The unintelligible expression *whn'r n'r* is the remnant of a long haplography due to *homoioteleuton*, suggesting that the Hebrew tradition behind MT at this point was substantially the same as that behind LXX.'[53] Fortunately, understanding the social location of the נער Samuel in this narrative is not dependent on a final resolution to these issues.

Of more significance, when comparing young Samuel's story to the accounts of other נערים, is the relative age of the sources of the narrative. Klein suggests that '[t]he Song of Hannah probably once had a separate existence', and that 'Deuteronomistic notices appear in 2.27-36 and 3.11-14'.[54] These are precisely the portions of this story in which the word נער does not appear, and it is consistent with our earlier

---

50. Gray posits an 'Aetiological Myth of the Rock-altar of Zorah' in vv. 13-24. (J. Gray, *Joshua, Judges, Ruth* [NCB; Grand Rapids: Eerdmans, 1986], p. 219).

51. Klein, *1 Samuel*, p. 3 (note on v. 24).

52. R. Althann, 'Northwest Semitic Notes on Some Texts in 1 Samuel', *JNSL* 12 (1984), pp. 27-34; S. Frolov and V. Orel, 'Was the Lad a Lad? On the Interpretation of I Sam 1.24', *BN* 81 (1996), pp. 5-7; R. Ratner, '"Three Bulls or One?": A Reappraisal of 1 Samuel 1.24', *Bib* 68.1 (1987), pp. 98-102.

53. McCarter, *I Samuel*, p. 57.

54. Klein, *1 Samuel*, p. xxx.

observations that it is a word from old prose narratives, never found in the bona fide work of Dtr and rarely used in poetry.

Once Samuel has been weaned and handed over as promised to remain with the priest at Shiloh, he appears to serve as a domestic helper in much the same way as other נערים whom we have encountered. As the narrator describes the boy's ongoing 'growth', he repeatedly uses the familiar term משרת to indicate his service to Eli the priest. The remarkable thing about Samuel is not the nature of his servanthood, but the circumstances by which he was taken from the house of his father and handed over to serve in the house of Yahweh, בית יהוה (1.24).

Sons and Servants

In several narratives of the Hebrew Bible, נערים who are servants exist alongside נערים who are clearly *not* servants, but rather are sons, individuals who receive their status as נער from being at risk. In a number of these instances, the narrator appears to be using the ambiguity of the term deliberately, highlighting the common social location that the sons of the main characters momentarily share (as a result of narrative circumstance) with unnamed domestic or military personnel. English translations that have rendered the term 'servant' on the one hand and 'son' on the other have short-circuited this aspect of the narrator's art. This brief section will focus on several of these instances, in an attempt to recover some of the forcefulness that this play on words gives to the stories in which it appears.

Job 1: Job's Sons and Servants

The word נער occurs in Job only seven times: three times in the poetical dialogues (Job 24.5; 29.5, 8) and four times in the prose prologue (Job 1.15, 16, 17, 19). Additionally, the feminine plural נערות (with second masculine singular suffix) appears once (Job 40.29). The first chapter of Job sets the stage for reading the friends' speeches that follow, and it colors our understanding of the term נער when it appears in those later dialogues as well. Accordingly, it is within the prose passages that we will attempt to establish a context for translating this word.

Scholars have offered widely divergent theories about the provenance of the story that provides the framework for the poetic dialogues of Job. Pope, for instance, see it as a traditional tale that the writer of the poetry of Job has used for his own purposes:

Most critics, however, regard the Prologue-Epilogue as part of an ancient folk tale which the author of the Dialogue used as the framework and point of departure for his poetic treatment of the problem of suffering. Whether this ancient folk tale was in written form or transmitted orally, it had probably attained a relatively fixed form and content which the author of the Dialogue could not modify in any radical fashion. It has epic style and the charm and flavor of an oft told tale.[55]

Habel, on the other hand, suggests that the parallelism and 'episode repetition' of the prologue suggest that the author who crafted the long poetic speeches also used intentional narrative techniques to set up the plot.[56] Clearly, a final consensus has not been reached on the age of the narrative material in Job.

A variety of schemes have been offered for outlining the contents of the prologue to Job. Clines suggests that the structure consists of five scenes that alternate between an earthly and a heavenly location, followed by a sixth that accomplishes the transition from the prologue to the dialogues. Thus,

1. Job's piety (1.1-5).
2. First dialogue of Yahweh and the Satan (1.6-12).
3. Disasters announced to Job (1.13-22).
4. Second dialogue of Yahweh and the Satan (2.1-7a).
5. Personal afflictions of Job (2.7b-10).
6. Arrival of Job's friends (2.11-13).[57]

In support of this structure he points out the parallels between scenes 2 and 4 and the recurring phrase 'there came a day when...' The literary artistry is shown by the fact that the author has given the plot a double complication (1.6-21; 2.1-10).[58]

The 'plot analysis' sketched by Habel does not break the narrative into radically different segments, but it serves to highlight slightly different features. Only the first episode is outlined below.[59]

55. M.H. Pope, *Job* (AB, 15; Garden City, NY: Doubleday, 1965), pp. xxii-xxiii.
56. N.C. Habel, *The Book of Job: A Commentary* (OTL; Philadelphia: Westminster Press, 1985), p. 81.
57. D.J.A. Clines, *Job 1–20* (WBC, 17; Dallas: Word Books, 1989), p. 6.
58. Habel, *Job*, p. 7.
59. Episode 2, in this analysis is 2.1-10b; Episode 3 is 2.11–3.1ff. (Habel, *Job*, pp. 79-80). Berlin's categories of Abstract, Orientation, Complicating Actions, Evaluation and Resolution can equally effectively be applied. Her Coda would correspond to Clines's, Scene 6 or Habel's Episode Three (Berlin, *Poetics and Interpretation*, pp. 102-103.)

Pretemporal Background (1.1-5) Introducing Job, his character and his world

Episode 1: Yahweh versus the Satan

Setting (1.6-7)	The council of heaven; Yahweh and the Satan.
Catalyst (1.8)	Yahweh boasts about the blameless character of Job.
Conflict	
Challenge (1.9-11)	The Satan challenges Yahweh's boast and predicts a conflict between Job and God if Job is afflicted.
Challenge accepted (1.12)	Yahweh accepts the challenge and gives the Satan power to afflict Job.
Execution (1.13-19)	Job is afflicted according to the decision in heaven.
Apparent resolution (1.20-21)	Job passes the test and Yahweh is vindicated.
Closure (1.22)	Narrator's verdict: Job does not express contempt for God.

In the prologue of Job, the word נערים is found only in the section that Habel has labeled the Execution, which corresponds to Clines's third scene, which is enclosed by the two 'scenes in the heavenly court'. This section (Job 1.13-22) is a free-standing vignette that could function as a compelling story not only without the speeches of the friends, but even without the remainder of the prose portions of the book.

It is the first day of the cycle of feasting of Job's sons and daughters, and they are holding their accustomed festivities at the home of the oldest son. The complicating actions appear in four waves, vv. 13-19, in the form of the successive catastrophes that gradually erode Job's blessedness and prosperity. Habel has pointed out 'the forcefulness of episode repetition in the fourfold reference to the "boys/servants" being killed (1.15, 16, 17, 19)'.[60] The power of this account comes from the relentless waves of tragedy that wash over Job, one right after the other, giving him no time to react, and it is the fate of the various groups of נערים that gives the unit its structure. One by one, the hallmarks of Job's success and prosperity are erased, but not until v. 20 do we finally see Job take on the signs of grief. The narrative has set out to answer the question of Satan: what would Job do if he *did not* have all the things with which God had blessed him? The first answer comes in v. 21, when Job makes his statement and blesses the name of the Lord.

60. Habel, *Job*, p. 82.

The word נער in the prose prologue of Job appears only in the complicating actions within this sub-narrative, where the word provides the connecting link in a beautifully balanced rehearsal of four disasters, each recounted in a series of three steps. At the head of the series of complications, the stage is set (v. 13) and we are subsequently reminded of this domestic scene, in which Job's sons and daughters are eating and drinking in their eldest brother's home, by an almost verbatim reiteration in the second half of v. 18, which heightens the drama by delaying the inevitable completion. Four messengers arrive (vv. 14, 16, 17, 18), each one still speaking when the next one arrives. Clearly, this is a rapid-fire series of disasters. Following the arrival of each messenger in turn, the substance of the announcement of each stage of destruction is provided (vv. 14b, 16b, 17b, 19). Parallels between these are reinforced by the use, in the first, second and fourth case, by forms of the verb נפל, and a similar balance between forms of לקח, in the first and third cases. The disasters alternate, as has been pointed out by numerous commentators, between raids by humans and 'acts of God', perhaps meteorological phenomena.[61] Finally, in perfectly symmetrical phrases (vv. 15b, 16c, 17c, 19b), we learn of the fate of the נערים, and we hear a refrain, identical to each messenger, that indicates that he alone has survived to tell the tale.[62]

The degree of similarity between each of these segments can be seen when the verses are printed with their parallel portions in juxtaposition.[63]

A (The Scene):

v. 13:
ויהי היום
ובניו ובנתיו אכלים ושתים יין בבית אחיהם הבכור

v. 18b:
בניך ובנתיך אכלים ושתים יין בבית אחיהם הבכור

v. 13:   And there was a day when
his sons and his daughters were eating and drinking wine in the house of their brother, the first-born.

---

61. E.g. J.G. Janzen, *Job* (IBC; Atlanta: John Knox Press, 1985), p. 43; Clines, *Job 1-20*, p. 30.

62. The reader is somehow not bothered by the fact that each messenger claims to be the sole survivor and yet the next messenger (who has obviously also survived) announces additional deaths among the ranks that have apparently been decimated but not eliminated.

63. The translation offered is rather literal in order to highlight the similarities between verses.

v. 18b: your sons and your daughters were eating and drinking wine in the house of their brother, the first-born.

B (Messenger arrives and speaks):

v. 14:   ומלאך בא אל איוב ויאמר
v. 16:   עוד זה מדבר וזה בא ויאמר
v. 17:   עוד זה מדבר וזה בא ויאמר
v. 18:   עוד זה מדבר וזה בא ויאמר

v. 14:   Then a messenger   came to Job and said:
v. 16:   As this one was still speaking, another came   and said:
v. 17:   As this one was still speaking, another came   and said:
v. 18:   As this one was still speaking, another came   and said:

C (Crisis described):

v. 14b: הבקר היו חרשות והאתנות רעות על ידיהם ותפל שבא ותקחם
v. 16b.   אש אלהים נפלה מן השמים ותבער בצאן
v. 17b: כשדים שמו שלשה ראשים ויפשטו על־הגמלים ויקחם
v. 19:   הנה רוח גדלה באה מעבר המדבר ויגע בארבע פנות הבית ויפל

v. 14b: The oxen were plowing and the asses grazing at their side and Sabea fell and took them
v. 16b: The fire of God
         fell from heaven and burned up the flocks
v. 17b: Chaldeans made three columns and attacked the camels
         and took them
v. 19:   See, a great wind came from across the desert
                   and struck the four corners of the house and it
         fell

D (Fate of the נערים and announcement of sole survivorship):

v. 15b: ואת־הנערים הכו לפי־חרב   ואמלטה רק־אני לבדי להגיד לך
v. 16c: ובנערים   תאכלים   ואמלטה רק־אני לבדי להגיד לך
v. 17c: ואת־הנערים הכו לפי־חרב   ואמלטה רק־אני לבדי להגיד לך
v. 19b: על־הנערים וימותו   ואמלטה רק־אני לבדי להגיד לך

v. 15b: And struck the נערים with the mouth of the sword
         and there remains only I alone to report to you.
v. 16c: And on the נערים and consumed them
         and there remains only I alone to report to you.
v. 17c: And struck the נערים with the mouth of the sword
         and there remains only I alone to report to you.
v. 19b: And the נערים and they died
         and there remains only I alone to report to you.

As a result of careful examination of parallel elements in this small narrative we must now question how we are to understand the word נער. Almost all the English translations render the word as servants in the first three instances, but change to indicate Job's children in the final case.[64] In view of the perfect symmetry in all four contexts, the evidence from the narrative does not support this practice. Habel alone maintains a consistent word choice throughout. Of his translation for v. 19, he says, 'The rendering "boys", as in vs. 15, 16, 17, is more forceful and faithful to the MT'.[65] The question remains whether 'boys' is an appropriate designation for servants who have charge of Job's agricultural and trading operation or for his children, who have homes of their own in which to feast. Although one might argue that the word has different meanings, or at least different connotations, in *different* contexts, the author of this short piece has been meticulous in holding the context constant. This observation supports the conclusion that a different understanding of the word in its fourth occurrence from that in the other three occurrences is not warranted. The evidence of this intricate pattern of connections and parallels suggests that every word of this brief story has been chosen carefully and deliberately. The author's intentions are everywhere evident and suggest that his use of בניו ובנתיו in one place and נערים in another is neither by accident nor by caprice.

The simplest and most convincing explanation is that the author means to indicate 'servants' throughout and that the sons and daughters are not, in fact, harmed. The evidence from the rest of the book of Job, in point of fact, supports this possibility. Nowhere, in either the poetic dialogues or in the prose prologue or epilogue, is there unequivocal evidence of the deaths of Job's children. Certainly, the absence of evidence of grief on the part of Job's wife makes us wonder. Nowhere does the book suggest the loss of בנים or of ילדים, only of נערים. Most translations of Job 8.4 assume, and therefore reflect, the deaths of Job's

64. Significantly, most scholars feel a need to justify this practice of rendering the same word into such different English equivalants (Pope, *Job*, p. 14; S.R. Driver and G.B. Gray, *A Critical and Exegetical Commentary on the Book of Job: Together with a New Translation* [ICC; New York: Charles Scribner's Sons, 1921], pp. 17, 18; R. Gordis, *The Book of Job: Commentary New Translation and Special Studies* [New York: Jewish Theological Seminary of America, 1978], pp. 16, 17; E. Dhorme, *A Commentary on the Book of Job* [trans. H. Knight; London: Thomas Nelson, 1967 (1928)], pp. 10, 12).

65. Habel, *Job*, p. 78.

children, but Jastrow sidesteps the difficulty entirely here by suggesting that Job's children were not an original part of this section at all: 'A commentator has added, v. 4 (in prose form). "If thy children had sinned against Him, He would give them up because of their transgression." '[66] An easier case can be made for rendering that verse into English as another 'hypothetical' case: '[*I*]*f* your children have sinned against God, he has delivered (or will deliver) them into the power of their transgression.'[67]

Countering the possibility that Job 8.4 reports the deaths of Job's sons is their presence in Job's speech in 19.17-18. Coogan translates, 'My breath is alien to my wife, and I am repulsive to the sons of my belly,' and points out,'If Job is referring to his own children in this continuation of his response to Bildad, then it appears that they are not dead.'[68] Although he suggests possible ways of dealing with this anomaly, he is finally left with the conclusion that 'at times Job seems to be talking as if his children were still alive'.[69]

As noted above, the word נער appears three other times in Job. Job 24.5 is a much disputed verse whose definitive translation remains elusive, but in any case, the reference is not either to servants or to children of Job, but rather apparently to the offspring of wild asses.[70] In ch. 29, Job is reminiscing about the days when his fortunes were secure; he recalls a time 'when the Almighty was still with me, when my נערים were around me' (v. 5). Obviously, his נערים are no longer around him, but this context does not demand that they be sons rather than servants. In v. 8, Job tells us that, prior to his downfall, when he appeared in public 'the נערים saw me and withdrew, and the זקנים rose up and

66. M. Jastrow, Jr, *The Book of Job: Its Origin, Growth and Interpretation Together with a New Translation Based on a Revised Test* (Philadelphia: J.B. Lippincott, 1920), p. 223 n. 53.

67. Those who assume a different provenance for the dialogues as compared to the prologue will, of course, find no need to reconcile such issues in any case, but will find additional evidence from such supposed contradictions for different sources or authors.

68. M.D. Coogan, 'Job's Children', in T. Abusch, J. Huehnergard and P. Steinkeller (eds.), *Lingering Over Words: Studies in Ancient Near Eastern Literature in Honor of William L. Moran* (Atlanta: Scholars Press, 1990), p. 141.

69. Coogan, 'Job's Children', p. 143.

70. See, e.g., Dhorme, *Job*, pp. 256, 357-58; Gordis, *Job*, p. 253. Even in this rather confused allusion, we see the juxtaposition of 'asses' and נערים, as mentioned in Chapter 4.

stood.' Although NRSV has chosen to translate these as 'young men' and 'aged' (i.e. a merismus of age), I will argue in Chapter 7 that this is a set form that represents (here as well as in other contexts in the Hebrew texts) a merismus indicating the full gamut of *status* rather than age: '[T]he servants withdrew, the elders rose.' In any case, however, this is not an indication of Job's offspring. The lone representative of the feminine form of this word in Job appears in 40.29. This is another verse whose full meaning fails to elicit unanimity, but the most common rendering is 'maidservant' or something similar, but decidedly *not* 'daughters'.[71]

The notion that Job's children were not, in fact, harmed is buttressed by reading the epilogue. In the *opening* scene of Job, we learned that there were *born to him* (ויולדו לו, 1.2) seven sons and three daughters. His livestock included 7000 sheep, 3000 camels, 500 yoke of oxen, 500 donkeys (v. 3). The restoration related by c. 42 consisted of 'twice as much' as before (v. 10), and Job was 'blessed more than at the beginning' (v. 12), which included 14,000 sheep, 6000 camels, 1000 yoke of oxen and 1000 donkeys. 'And Job *had* seven sons and three daughters' (ויהי־לו, 42.13, not *were born to him* as in the first chapter). This choice of words certainly allows the possibility that these were his original children, not new ones, since no birth is mentioned in this chapter. Clearly, the doubling promised in v. 10 or the increase promised in v. 12 are not realized with respect to children, if they were indeed lost to him, although some have viewed it as if this were the case:

> The Epilogue naively assumes that the death of the children can be compensated for by new children and that Job's suffering can be fully recompensed by living twice the normal lifespan. Since Job has been unjustly deprived of his possessions and his offspring, everything is doubled. The number of his daughters, however, remains the same, on the theory that in the case of female offspring enough is sufficient! The doubling of his possessions, his male offspring,[72] and his lifespan is in

71. Gordis, for instance, proposes the following: 'נַעֲרֹתֶךָ here is the Arabic *nughar*un, fem. *nugharat*un, "sparrow, swallow", as noted by D. Winton Thomas (VT, vol. 14 [1964], pp. 114ff) but there is no need to revocalize as נַעֲרֹתֶךָ, since cognates frequently undergo vocalic change' (Gordis, *Job*, p. 319).

72. Gordis here is assuming that שבענה in 42.13 is a dual form and thus represents 14 sons. I will follow Coogan's understanding: 'The form *šib'ānâ* in 42.13 is not, as has occasionally been suggested, a dual (meaning that Job had fourteen more sons), but an archaizing form probably attested in Ugaritic; see Sarna, "Epic Sub-

accordance with the ancient biblical law in Ex. 22.3, 11, which ordains double payment for a theft.[73]

Invoking a dual form here to yield double restitution of the sons and suggesting that this restitution applied only singlefold to the daughters is a strained attempt to make the text fit our presumptions about it; it is not satisfying either logically or grammatically. Still, the thorough-going nature of the calamities leads us to assume the loss of progeny as well as of other blessings.

The careful crafting of the scenario of Job's trials has suggested to some a second possibility: the author has presented us with a deliberate ambiguity. We are not intended to know for certain whether Job's children were lost along with the servants. Habel has proposed that this exploitation of ambiguity is a deliberate authorial device.[74] The author is practising 'reticence'.[75] Clines, too, sees this as the use of the same word to denote two different groups of people, and suggests that the author has given a sort of foreshadowing.

> In this scene, it is the children of Job who are meant; on looking back over the passage, we realize that it is for the sake of this announcement that the term נערים has been used throughout. These are the נערים that really matter, though no doubt their attendant servants also have died.[76]

Perhaps by placing us in a position of limited information, the writer reminds us of the perils that all נערים may face and of the frightening

---

stratum," 17-18, followed by Gordon in *UT* 102-3' (Coogan, 'Job's Children', p. 137 n. 8.)

73. Gordis, *Job*, p. 576.

74. In his note on Job 1.15, he says, 'The translation "boys" (for *neʿārīm*) is retained to preserve the literary effect, though the sense is probably "servants" '. On v. 19: 'Most translations render *neʿārīm* in this verse by an expression which implies a reference to Job's children... But this distorts the literary force of the orginal by making explicit what the narrator leaves the audience to deduce, namely, the death of Job's children... Each disaster account reports the fate of the servant "boys." The last word spoken about them is that they "died." In the last disaster the messenger boy also reports that the servant "boys" were crushed and died, but he omits any reference to Job's family. The most tragic disaster of all, the death of Job's family, is not actually stated. It is left for the audience to deduce' (Habel, *Job*, pp. 78, 92-93).

75. Alter uses this term with respect to characterization, but much of his discussion can apply equally to the actions which advance the plot. (Alter, *The Art of Biblical Narrative*, pp. 114-30).

76. Clines, *Job 1–20*, p. 33.

suddenness with which sons and daughters, living safely nearby as part of an extended family occupying the family compound, can slip into danger beyond a parent's ability to protect them, just as the servants hired or bought by Job live outside the protection of their fathers. This illustration of the porousness of the boundary between offspring who one minute are living in safety under the patronage of their fathers and the next are נערים facing life's exigencies unshielded is consistent with the overall effect of the book of Job as it illustrates the mysterious tenuousness of good fortune.

Eli's Sons and Servants
A similar juxtaposition of son and servant is exploited by the author of the narratives of Samuel's birth, call and displacement of the house of Eli in 1 Sam. 1.1–4.1. The contrast, noted early by Smith[77] and elaborated on by Klein, between the נער Samuel and the נערים Hophni and Phineas (sons of Eli), almost certainly was deliberate on the part of the narrator.

> The word 'boy' or 'attendant' (נער) would seem to be in some tension with the *very* young age presupposed for Samuel[78] in the rest of the story, but the main point of contrast seems to be between the faithful boy Samuel and the evil boys or attendants, namely, the sons of Eli. These sons were in fact 'good-for-nothings'.[79]

Still, this linguistic connection is overlooked by most commentators owing to the inadequacy of the semantic values that have been given to the word נער.

Samuel has been removed from his father's household as a result of the fulfillment of Hannah's vow, becoming a נער in the process. Hophni and Phinehas, while still apparently residing either with or near their father Eli, have removed themselves from their father's control and guidance by their disobedience and wicked ways, and in the process have become נערים (2.17). The use of the same noun in describing all three of them functions to highlight the contrast between the two biological sons of Eli and the 'foster son' Samuel, who is serving a sort of priestly apprenticeship under Eli and has accepted the older man's

77. Smith, *Samuel*, p. 17.
78. Klein here presupposes the commonly accepted understanding of נער as 'youth' or 'young man'.
79. Klein, *1 Samuel*, pp. 24-25.

authority and guidance. Perhaps a third sort of נער is present in this narrative as well, the 'servant of the priest' (2.13, 15), who actually carries out the evil practices of Eli's renegade sons, although some take this to be one or the other of the sons of Eli. Thus the contrast is complex: the good and obedient Samuel, a servant נער, 'ministering to the Lord under Eli' (והנער שמואל משרת את־יהוה לפני עלי), 3.1, a typical description of the position of a servant); Eli's sons, נערים whose 'sin was very great in the sight of the Lord' (v. 17); and 'the priest's servant', נער הכהן (vv. 13, 16), whose obedience to 'sons of Belial' makes him an agent of wickedness, not goodness. For Eli, the apprentice is more faithful than his biological sons.

None of these observations about the opening chapters of the book of Samuel are dependent on any particular view of the development, composition and compiling of these stories. However, an understanding of the stages of development is useful in furthering our knowledge of the place of the word נער within the Hebrew scriptures generally. McCarter sees in these chapters old material that the Dtr editor has only lightly edited, with additions at 2.27-36, 3.11-14 and 4.18b.[80] He also suggests that the 'Song of Hannah', 1 Sam. 2.1-10, as it stands in these chapters, is in a 'secondary context'.[81] Klein, likewise, attributes 2.27-36 and 3.11-14 to the Deuteronomistic historian[82] and recognizes, regarding 2.1-10, 'that this psalm must have had a different setting and function before its ascription to Hannah'.[83] The term נער is used frequently in the portions of 1 Sam. 1.1–4.1 that these commentators consider to be older prose sources, but it is entirely absent from the other portions of these texts. This strengthens our earlier observation that this word is a word of old narrative sources more than of the Deuteronomistic redactor or of poetry, whether archaic or not.

---

80. McCarter, *1 Samuel*, pp. 15-16.

81. McCarter, *1 Samuel*, p. 76.

82. Klein, *1 Samuel*, pp. xxx, 24, 37.

83. Klein, *1 Samuel*, p. 14. More recently, Campbell, while not fully accepting the specifics of any of the theories of Deuteronomistic redaction, nonetheless considers these same elements to have been added by a redactor to older prophetic narrative. See Campbell, *Of Prophets and Kings*, pp. 66-67. Much *earlier*, Smith recognized that the insertion of 2.27-36 is 'of comparatively late date' and refers to the narratives themselves as work of the 'oldest historian' (Smith, *Samuel*, p. 21).

Other Contrasts between Sons and Servants

Although it is not developed nearly as strongly, a contrast between servant נער and a son as נער appears also in Judges 8. In 8.14 Gideon captures a 'נער of the people of Succoth' (or perhaps better 'of the *army* of Succoth'), quite likely a weapons carrier or porter or other military servant. This individual obediently identifies for him the 'officials and elders of Succoth' (v. 14) when questioned by Gideon. Gideon's son Jether, by contrast, refuses the direct order of his father when he is told to kill Zebah and Zalmunna (v. 21). The servant was obedient, the son was not, but both are termed נער by the narrator.

Similarly, in the story of Absalom's revenge against Amnon, Absalom commands his נערים (servants) to watch for the moment when Amnon is tipsy to kill him (2 Sam. 13.28, 29). David, who had resisted allowing his sons to attend the shearing festivities, watches and grieves, fearing all of them have died, but is assured by Shimeah that 'all the נערים the king's sons' have not been killed, only Amnon (13.31). Another נער, serving as watchman, is the first to see that the other sons were returning safely (v. 34). Absalom, as noted earlier, is repeatedly referred to in chs. 14 and 18 as 'the נער Absalom.' Once again, the son is perfidious, while his own and his father's servants exercise their duties faithfully. Obedience issues from the 'fictive' kin, but not from the biological son.

The stories of Elisha in 2 Kgs 2–6 are filled with נערים of various roles and dispositions, although only one is in a relationship of 'sonship', and that is the son of the Shunammite woman. These chapters present a veritable nexus of contrasts (see Chapters 4 and 6 above) along diverse lines. The impertinent נערים who taunt Elisha (2.23) contrast with the innocent son of the Shunnamite, who becomes a נער only when his life is endangered (4.18-37). Gehazi, the greedy נער of Elisha, is contrasted with the faithful נערים of Naaman, who carry the gifts (intended for Elisha) that Gehazi has fraudulently accepted in the name of fictitious נערים of the prophets, supposedly newly-arrived from the hill country (5.19-27). In each of these pairings, the faithlessness of the one who should have been trustworthy is contrasted to the faithfulness of the one who is a mere servant.

From the conspicuous case of the servants/sons of Job to the pairs that receive only the briefest mentions, the use of this same term, נער, seems to be a deliberate narrative device that forces our minds to make the connection between those who are outside their father's households because of unavoidable circumstances and those who have given up that protection because of intentional flaunting of the natural relationship of protection and authority that should have existed between them and their fathers/masters. With a nuanced understanding of the Hebrew word נער we can appreciate the full power and subtlety of the ways the authors of these old narratives have used the word to elicit connections and draw contrasts.

Conclusions

The נערים of this chapter vary in age and circumstances. What they all share, however, is the reality of their vulnerability. Something stands between them and the safety of their father's house: illness, distance, dedication, estrangement or orphanhood. Almost without exception, only God or the narrator (both of whom are in their own way 'omniscient'), use this term of these individuals.[84] At precisely the moment when these characters are 'shaken loose' from the protective arms of their fathers, the narrator terms them נערים. If they are fortunate enough to see that bond restored, from that point on the narrator chooses other words to describe them. Clearly, this condition of risk is what is at issue in the use of this word נער.

---

84. Trible has observed this in the case of Ishmael, albeit without making note of the more general phenomenon: 'When speaking to Hagar about her own child, God never uses the noun *son* or the pronoun *your*. Instead, the deity follows the lead of the narrator by referring to Ishmael as "the lad". Subtly, the motherhood of Hagar is undercut' (Trible, 'Other Woman', p. 236).

Chapter 6

WOMEN: UNPROTECTED AND VULNERABLE

General Considerations

The Hebrew word נערה is invariably translated 'girl, damsel, maid',[1] or perhaps 'young woman' (as, for instance, in the NRSV), thus suggesting a stage of life. In fact 'nubility' or marriageability have been asserted as the nuance of this particular female designation.[2] Close reading of the Hebrew texts in which this term occurs, however, suggest that the word connotes a girl or young woman who is away from home, perhaps in danger or at risk in some way. The uses of the feminine term show many parallels to the ways the masculine term נער is employed. Often, the feminine term seems to have a slight negative or pejorative cast to it, perhaps because to a considerable extent a man's claim to honor was contingent on his ability to keep the women of his household shielded from both danger and scandal. This applied perhaps most strongly to wives, but also to sisters and to daughters.

> Feminine 'shame' as a positive value is characterized by deference and submission to male authority, by docile and timorous behavior, by hiding nakedness, by sexual exclusiveness, and by modesty in attire and deportment. The absence of these qualities renders a woman 'shameless' and dishonors her family—particularly her husband, who cannot 'control' his wife—in the eyes of the community... To protect his honor and social reputation from his wife's shameful behavior, a husband has socially

1. BDB, p. 655 b, c.
2. This is precisely the sort of nuance that Wenham has suggested for בתולה, which is traditionally translated 'virgin'. His case is built by comparison with related words in other Semitic languages as well as an examination of the biblical uses of the word. Thus he argues that the term refers not to the young woman's sexual status (e.g. *virgo intacta*), but rather to the stage of life she has reached (G.J. Wenham, 'Betulah, "A Girl of Marriageable Age" ', *VT* 22 [July 1972], pp. 326-48).

recognized strategies: segregation of his women, insisting that they remain veiled in public, and restricting their social behavior to 'women's spaces'.[3]

Women Servants

A large number of the persons referred to as נערה in the Hebrew Bible are maids or serving girls, frequently under the control and direction of a woman. As we saw in the case of the נערים of Chapter 4, the narrative ordinarily does not describe the tasks with which these women are occupied. Their presence is, as was the case with their masculine counterparts, an indication of the status of their masters or mistresses. Providing food for them seems to be a concern (Prov. 27.27, and perhaps 31.15[4]), perhaps suggesting that when the household suffered times of shortage, the נערים and נערות were the first whose rations were shortened. They are frequently 'sent' (e.g. Prov. 9.3) on errands or journeys and seem to move across boundaries and thresholds, between spaces, frequently with messages and insider information.[5] In the biblical narratives, we seldom find נערות in houses; most frequently they are 'out'. This, of course, is in sharp contrast to the notion that 'women's space' was interior space.

> Female spaces and female things are centered around the family residence and 'face toward the inside', and all things remaining within the home are identified with the female; those taken from the inside to the outside—the male 'space'—are identified with the male.[6]

As part of the artistry of the narrative, the נער serves, by his departure or being left behind, to indicate that the main character is in complete solitude.[7] By contrast, the נערה seems to function to bolster the appearance of propriety in scenes in which a female character is out and about in places where her safety, or at the very least her good name, might be in jeopardy. The narrator indicates that a respectable woman is *not*

---

3.   L.R. Klein, 'Honor and Shame in Esther', in A. Brenner (ed.), *A Feminist Companion to Esther, Judith and Susanna* (Feminist Companion to the Bible, 7; Sheffield: Sheffield Academic Press, 1995), p. 151.

4.   The Hebrew חק is here variously considered either a prescribed portion (i.e. rations) or a prescribed task.

5.   Cf. Chapters 3 and 4.

6.   Klein, 'Honor and Shame in Esther', p. 151.

7.   Cf. Chapter 3.

alone by mentioning the presence of her נערה. Thus, when Pharaoh's daughter walks along the river, her נערות accompany her, serving no other function, apparently, than as chaperones (Exod. 2.5). When Abigail sets out on the journey to become the wife of David, she is accompanied by נערות (1 Sam. 25.42), as is Rebekah when she sets off with Abraham's servant and his men to become Isaac's bride (Gen. 24.61).

The נערות also serve, just as the נערים do, as a device by which the plot of the narrative can be advanced through dialogue rather than narration.[8] We have access to the interior of a character by what is said to the נערה who happens to be standing nearby. In addition, נערות carry information or messages across boundaries between one category of space and another or between groups of people who would not otherwise have information about one another. Thus, the נערות of Queen Esther bring her word of the scene that Uncle Mordecai is creating by taking on the signs of grieving in reaction to the plan to annihilate the Jews (Est. 4.4). They carry the dialogue back and forth between the inside world of Esther and the outside world of her uncle. The Queen's נערות even join her in fasting (Est. 4.16). The captured Israelite girl who served Naaman's wife (2 Kgs 5.2, 4) allows word about Israel's prophet to be inserted into the court of the king of Aram, where ordinarily his existence and powers would not be known. These women have movement and liminality that their more respectable sisters do not.

The servant women in many of these texts are at the disposal of, and in fact are probably the property of, another female.[9] Mace suggests that a 'handmaid' was a customary part of the dowry that a young bride received from her family. 'The freedom with which these wives (Sarah, Rebekah, Leah and Rachel) disposed of their maids shows them to have been in the nature of an individual possession over which their husbands did not share the control.'[10]

---

8. As Alter has observed, 'The biblical preference for direct discourse is so pronounced that thought is almost invariably rendered as actual speech, that is, as quoted monologue... [W]hen an actual process of contemplating specific possibilities, sorting out feelings, weighing alternatives, making resolutions, is a moment in the narrative event, it is reported as direct discourse' (Alter, *Art of Biblical Narrative*, pp. 67-68.)

9. For instance, Rebekah, Abigail, Esther and the daughter of Pharaoh all have women serving them who are called נערות.

10. D.R. Mace, *Hebrew Marriage: A Sociological Study* (New York: Philosophical Library, 1953), p. 176.

The נערה could also be in the service of a man, however, as those in Prov. 27.27, Job 40.29 (English 41.5),[11] and Ruth 2.8, 22, 23; 3.2 seem to be. The type of work performed was generally as household help or personal attendant, although apparently some agricultural work might be performed as well, as in the case of the women working as 'reapers' for Boaz. The texts do not differentiate among the positions of 'hireling' (i.e. a woman working for wages of some sort), 'indentured servant' (i.e. a woman serving a master for a specific term of time), and 'slave' (i.e. a woman in a permanent state of servitude). All three possibilities seem to be covered, at times, by the single term נערה. Indeed, the differences among the three circumstances may have been negligible. All three situations would have involved living in the household of her master or mistress, away from the home of her natural parents.

Only in the case of the servant of Naaman's wife, who had been captured by an Aramean raiding party, does the biblical narrative make explicit how the נערות came to be away from their father's household. In other situations, a father might sell a daughter to meet a debt obligation (or perhaps as collateral),[12] or perhaps a father would send his daughter out to perform paid day labor. In any case, being away from the father's house removed the נערה from the patronage and watchful eye of her father.

Women and Sexual Service

Although debt slaves and captive women might be used as serving girls in field or household, at other times their designation might be explicitly sexual. Even as servant to a woman, a נערה could be made sexually available at the command of her mistress. Furthermore, such a נערה may well have been less than secure against sexual exploitation by men in the household in which she lived, even over the objections of her mistress.

The preferred sequence of events in life for a female child in ancient Israel, during all the stages of its history, was to grow up within the confines of the family to which she was born until the time of her marriage, when she would transfer her residence and her allegiance to the

11. This is the very difficult reference to the leashing of Leviathan. As is frequently the case in poetic citations, little can be ascertained about the social reality underlying the term נערה here.

12. Chirichigno, *Debt-Slavery in Israel*, pp. 63-65, 182-84.

household of her husband. '[H]er father controlled her life until he relinquished her to another man for marriage.'[13] Although at various periods she might have more or less independence with regard to various activities, with regard to her *sexuality*, she was not a free agent. Her *body* was not her own.[14] The result was that, although theoretically she was not chattel and was not 'owned' by father or husband, in reality

> every woman in Israel would normally be under the authority of some man. At first it was her father, but on her marriage she was transferred to the *potestas* of her husband, the head of the new household which she was to help to build up. As long as either was alive, therefore, she had to recognize the authority of her father or her husband.[15]

The restrictions and close supervision of females in such a society seem to us to reduce her to property; in reality their aim is to guard against the misuse of her sexuality, either by her own willful violation of the sexual exclusivity that she owed to the man under whose tutelage she lived or by exposing her to victimization by men who might take advantage of her. Thus,

> the key to the understanding of Hebrew standards lies in the conception of the woman's sexuality as the property of the man under whose *potestas* she was. In the case of her father, this involved the exclusive right of disposal; in the case of her husband, the exclusive right of use.[16]

In either case violation of chastity or sexual exclusivity involved a deep affront to the man who was supposed to control/protect her. 'A wife who was proved guilty of fornication had violated the honor and power of both her father and her husband.'[17]

The נערות of the Bible are each women who are, by reason of circumstance or conduct, functioning outside the control/protection of father or husband. As a result, her chastity may be questionable, or perhaps she may be in a dependent position that renders her ability to maintain her chastity problematic. Unlike the typical woman of the Bible, who was named as someone's wife or someone's daughter, these

13. P. Trible, 'Woman in the Old Testament', *IDBSup* (New York: Abingdon Press, 1976), pp. 963-66 (964).

14. Trible, 'Woman in the Old Testament', p. 964; Perdue *et al.* (eds.), *Families in Ancient Israel*, p. 76.

15. Mace, *Hebrew Marriage*, p. 189.

16. Mace, *Hebrew Marriage*, p. 227.

17. Bird, 'Woman in the Old Testament', p. 964.

females are not designated by the name of their male kin. The vocabulary with which the biblical writer describes them and their activities is illustrative of two realities, both of which must be understood as having negative implications for a woman. First, she is frequently described in terms which put her *exterior*, and thus outside the safety of the home. The נערות are described as 'going out' or 'sent out', they are found on roads, at wells, in the countryside. Second, the stories depict them most frequently as objects of verbs, not as subjects, either grammatically or narratively. They are 'brought' and 'sought', 'found' and 'gathered'. Thus, the social position of a נערה is one of sexual contingency, of ambiguity and vulnerability.

Wives for the Tribe of Benjamin

A shocking example of the sexual vulnerability of young women who are without the protection of their male relatives comes from the story of the plot to obtain wives for the tribe of Benjamin, after the other tribes had sworn not to give their daughters in marriage because of the outrage that had occurred in Gibeah in Judges 19. In the first phase of this horrifying plan, all the men of Jabesh-gilead (a city that had refused the call to muster when the other tribes went out for vengeance against Benjamin), along with all the sexually experienced women, were slain. The remaining 400 young women, deprived now of the protection of fathers and mothers, are referred to as נערה בתולה (Judg. 21.12) and are distributed to the men of Benjamin for sexual purposes, presumably as wives. The second phase of the plan, in which they capture additional wives from among the daughters of Shiloh who are dancing for the annual festival (Judg. 21.19-21), does not use the term נערה to refer to these young women, presumably since their fathers and brothers are still alive and are persuaded to give *ex post facto* consent to the marriages negotiated in this way (v. 22).[18]

Abishag

This beautiful young Shunammite procured for King David in his days of waning potency (1 Kgs 1.2, 3, 4), likewise evidently fatherless and husbandless, was also a נערה. Perhaps she was a captive (or orphan) of war. During Saul's reign, Shunem was the site of a Philistine encampment (1 Sam. 28.4). In any case, she has no husband and appears not to

---

18. We should note that, once again, these women are at risk when they 'go out', in this case as a group for celebration.

be any longer under the care of a father. As is so often the case with
נערות, the text does not name her with reference to the names of the
men of her family (as is usually the case with women), but gives only
her own name and place of origin.[19] Her sexual status remains ambiguous since she was available to the king, but the narrator reports that the
relationship was not consummated, and she continues to be referred to
as נערה.[20]

Because the root *skn/sgn* has a wide range of uses in various ancient
Near Eastern contexts, a few scholars have attempted to find in the term
סכנת, used of Abishag in vv. 2 and 4, a title of some sort of 'high
government official'.[21] I will follow Lipiński, who sees 1 Kgs 1.1-4 as
an example of a usage of the word meaning (in the French) 'intendant',
that is, in English, 'steward' or perhaps 'attendant' or 'governess' or
'nurse'.[22] Whatever a similar term may have designated in Akkadian
documents, the presence of the expressions ועמדה לפני המלך (v. 2) and
ותשרתהו (v. 4) in the two verses in which Abishag is called סכנת clearly
indicate that the semantic domain here is one of servanthood, not of
high royal officialdom. 'Standing before' (i.e. waiting on) and 'ministering' are precisely the terms used to describe the service of other
נערים and נערות, as well as עבדים.[23]

Esther

The manner in which Abishag is procured for King David is echoed by
the manner in which Esther is procured for King Ahasuerus, although

19. Indeed, her name means 'My father is a wanderer' (or perhaps sinner) BDB,
p. 4.

20. In contrast, Esther *ceases* to be called נערה after she 'goes into the king',
apparently because that relationship was consummated and, as a wife, she is once
again appropriately 'attached to' (or 'embedded within') the household.

21. See discussion in M. Heltzer, 'The New-Assyrian Sakintu and the Biblical
Sōkenet (1 Reg 1,4)', in *La femme dans le Proche-Orient antique: XXXIIIe Rencontre assyriologique internationale* (Paris: Recherches sur les Civilisations, 1987),
pp. 87-90; M.J. Mulder, 'Versuch zur Deutung von Sōkenet in 1 Kön 1.2,4', *VT* 22
(1972), pp. 43-54; O. Loretz, 'Ugaritisch Skn-Skt und hebräisch Skn-Sknt', *ZAW*
94 (1982), pp. 126-27.

22. E. Lipiński, 'Skn et Sgn dans le sémitique occidental du nord', *UF* 5 (1973),
pp. 191-207 (196).

23. See, e.g., the uses of the Hebrew words שרת, עמד, לפני in Gen. 39.4; 40.4;
2 Kgs 4.43; 6.15; 2 Sam. 13.17, 18; 1 Kgs 10.5; Est. 2.2; 6.3; 1 Sam. 16.22; 1 Kgs
1.2; 17.1; 18.15; 2 Kgs 3.14; 5.16; Jer. 15.19.

the source of 'dis-ease' for this king is an affront to the royal ego rather than an inability to keep warm.[24] The servants of King Ahasuerus, when the king's pride has been injured by Queen Vashti, seek נערות בתולות for the king's pleasure (Est. 2.2, 3, 4, 7, 8, 9, 12, 13). Perhaps they come from among various captive populations, since Esther's 'Jewish-ness' is pointed out, in which case these women are already sexually vulnerable by virtue of being spoils of war. Whether captive or not, they *became* vulnerable upon being removed from their families at the command of the king. After each 'girl's' night with the king, she was returned to the harem to a status of perpetual sexual ambiguity, not quite a wife, but certainly never again the virgin daughter of her father's household.[25] Parallels between the stories of Esther and Abishag are quite remarkable, as is obvious when verses are juxtaposed:

Est. 2.2	ויאמרו נערי המלך ומשרתיו
1 Kgs 1.2	ויאמרו לו עבדיו
	And the נערים of the king and his ministers said...
	And his servants said to him...
Est 2.2	יבקשו למלך נערות בתולות טובות מראה
1 Kgs 1.2	יבקשו לאדני המלך נערה בתולה
	Let there be sought for the king virgin נערות, good looking...
	Let there be sought for my lord, the king a virgin נערה...
Est 2.7	והנערה יפת־תאר
1 Kgs 1.3	נערה יפה
	And the נערה was lovely to look at...
	a lovely נערה...
Est 2.8	ותלקח אסתר אל־בית המלך

24. The striking similarities between these two stories are given only the briefest of mentions in most of the commentaries and other discussions, e.g., Wenham calls it a 'similar incident'; others note the shared motif. Clines suggests that this part of the Esther tale 'is probably deliberately reminiscent of 1 Kg 1.2-4', although he looks further afield to make a comparison to the basic tale: 'The story of the search for a bride is obviously analogous to that of the *Thousand and One Nights*, where also only one girl (Scheherezade) can charm the king and so become queen' (Wenham, 'Betulah', p. 343; J.D. Levenson, *Esther: A Commentary* [OTL; Louisville, KY: Westminster/John Knox Press, 1997], p. 54; C.A. Moore, *Esther: Introduction, Translation, and Notes* [AB, 7B; Garden City, NY: Doubleday, 1971], p. 26; D.J.A. Clines, *Ezra, Nehemiah, Esther* [NCBC; Grand Rapids: Eerdmans, 1984], pp. 285, 286).

25. Indeed, after their night with the king, neither Esther nor any of the other women is again referred to as a נערה. Esther is ever after referred to as 'queen'; the others simply fade from view.

1 Kgs 1.3   ויבאו אתה למלך
And Esther was taken to the house of the king…
And they brought her to the king…

1 Kgs 1.5   ותשרתהו
And she ministered to him.

These similarities suggest the likelihood that the Esther narrative was an elaboration or expansion of an earlier motif.[26] In reliance on the structure of the Abishag account for his basic story-line, the writer appears to have borrowed considerable language from the older, shorter account. Thus, the use of the term נערה in Esther (as well as נער in other parts of the book), which is obviously a postexilic text may reflect a deliberate archaizing, since the words are used with precisely the same sense that they have when they are found in the much older narratives of Genesis and the Former Prophets.

Significantly, in Est. 2.7 we hear that Esther 'had neither father nor mother', and had been adopted by her cousin Mordecai. As an orphan and 'foster child', Esther is living outside the protection of her natural father. Mordecai, as surrogate father, was not able to provide the same patronage and oversight, perhaps due to his own situation as an exile. Once Esther becomes queen, she is under the king's patronage and is no longer referred to as נערה.

As we have seen in other narratives, Esther as נערה appears as an object in the narrative, one who is sought and gathered and made ready for the king's enjoyment. Only after she ceases to be called נערה does she emerge as a fully-fledged character, with speech and action, thought and feeling and initiative.

Women at Risk

General

In addition to the loss of guidance and protection which a young man experienced when he became a נער, the young woman who was a נערה also became vulnerable sexually, even when she was not explicitly procured for sexual service. The resultant vulnerability to the *possibility* of sexual shame is a prominent characteristic that these women all share.

---

26. If this is an example of the 'type-scene' as discussed by Alter, the ancient hearer would have indeed expected to hear the familiar vocabulary used in the new elaboration of the familiar story (Alter, *The Art of Biblical Narrative*, pp. 47-62).

The proper sphere for a woman was the *interior* space of the home; venturing across the threshold into the *exterior* space confers the status of נערה on a woman in some texts. One of the sites in village life where women mingled freely with those outside the family was the local well. Whether this was so because this was considered a safe space (possibly because adequately 'public') or because it was simply a necessary risk because of the need to draw water is not clear. In either case, it is significant that, in more than one instance, young women at the well are referred to as נערה. Outside the household, women could be vulnerable and fathers would be unable to supervise their activities there. Additionally, one simply could not ascertain the status of a young woman in that situation: she was not easily identifiable as someone's wife, daughter or serving girl.[27]

That the dangers to women at the well were real is suggested by a recent analysis of Ruth 2.7 by Carasik. He has suggested that the fumbling speech of the overseer in response to Boaz's question about the identity of the נערה (Ruth 2.5, 'To whom does this נערה belong?') reflects the overseer's embarrassment because Ruth had been 'sexually harassed' by the reapers of Boaz when she tried to quench her thirst at the water source.[28] The instructions that Boaz then gives her (2.8, 9) suggest that he recognizes the danger and that he has taken some steps to curb the behavior of the נערים, although she is cautioned to avoid eye contact and to stick close to the other female reapers.[29] The same sort of encounter with intimidating behavior at the well is suggested, according to Carasik, by the story of the daughters of the priest of Midian (Exod. 2.16-19). They are protected and assisted there by a complete stranger, Moses.

27. Cf. the Ugaritic poem 'Kirta' (col. III, ll. 9-10), in which the surprise attack on the women occurs at the well (S.B. Parker [ed.], *Ugaritic Narrative Poetry* [Writings from the Ancient World, SBL; Atlanta: Scholars Press, 1997], KRT 1.III.9-10, 16).

28. M. Carasik, 'Ruth 2,7: Why the Overseer Was Embarrassed', *ZAW* 107 (1995), pp. 493-94. Many women of my generation will identify with this episode, spelled out in the manner that Carasik has spelled it out. Not infrequently, young women of high school age had to 'run the gauntlet' of a hallway lined with young men whose remarks or perhaps simply stares persuaded her that she would wait for a drink of water until she got home in the afternoon.

29. In fact, this is another example of the narrative use of נערות to guard against impropriety by providing chaperonage to a woman who would otherwise be alone.

Despite the apparent dangers, women seem to have been the chief drawers of water, and in that position are referred to as נערות. Thus, when Saul and his servant are searching for donkeys and go to consult the seer, 'they met some נערות coming out to draw water' (1 Sam. 9.11). These woman carry the information about the local seer across the social boundary between the village and these two outsiders. Likewise, when Abraham's servant goes to seek a bride for Isaac, he prays that the נערה who says, 'Drink, and I will water your camels' (Gen. 24.14, 16) will be the appropriate bride for his master's son. Apparently, at the well there were no restrictions on conversation with men not of one's own household, including men who were strangers to you. Possibly it was to the local well where Dinah 'went out to visit the women of the region' of Shechem, when she ventured outside the protection of her father's house.[30]

Rebekah
When Abraham's servant arrives seeking a bride for Isaac, Rebekah, too, is a נערה coming to the well for water (Gen. 24.14, 16). After the encounter with the servant, the narrator tells us, the נערה runs to tell the news to her *mother*'s household (Gen. 24.28). The gifts (not bride price) are presented to Rebekah's mother and brother (Gen. 24.53), not to her father as would be the custom, and the arrangements are agreed to. Only the time of departure remains unsettled, and the mother and brother request, 'Let the נערה remain with us a while, at least ten days; after that she may go' (Gen. 24.55). Abraham's servant prefers to set out immediately, and in the end the final decision is made by Rebekah herself: 'We will call the נערה, and ask her' (Gen. 24.57). In the course of the negotiations about departing, her mother and brother Laban give her a great deal more of a voice in decision-making than we would expect.

Rebekah is identified as 'the daughter of Bethuel, Nahor's son, whom Milcah bore to him' (Gen. 24.24, 47), but it is her brother Laban who extends hospitality to the servant. When the servant asks for Rebekah as a wife for his master's son, Laban and Bethuel answer together (v. 50). This is the only appearance of the woman's father in the story, and we

30. Other stories of women, unsupervised by male relatives, at the local well include the story of the encounter between Jacob and Rachel (Gen. 29.1-14, in which Rachel is not called נערה but is tending stock, as נערים so often do), and even the exchange between Jesus and the Samaritan woman (Jn 4.1-38).

sense that something may be unusual about the authority structure in this household. Some have suggested that a later editor has included Laban in v. 50.[31] Perhaps Rebekah's father has died,[32] or been incapacitated, either physically or mentally.

Thus the use of the word נערה for Rebekah reflects a twofold reality: she is out and about, talking to a stranger at the well (a circumstance that has resulted in that designation being used for other women, as we have seen). She may also be fatherless, although not without a male overseer, since she has a brother to speak on her behalf. Surely some of the details of this situation have been lost to us, but, in conjunction with the term נערה, we have in Rebekah a young woman whose status is somewhat ambiguous, and who has more autonomy than we would expect from a young woman under the *potestas patrii*. After her marriage she will not be called by this word, but for the moment Rebekah is a נערה.

Dinah

More willful adventuring seems to have been the case when Dinah explored the world outside the walls of her father's house, with a consequent change in appellation to נערה (Gen. 34.3, 12) once she has been 'humbled'[33] by Hamor.[34] Dinah, daughter of Leah and Jacob, 'went out to visit the women of the region' of Shechem (Gen. 34.1). Perhaps, as with Rebekah and others, this was a trip to the local water source or well, since we do not know of other gathering places for women in ancient times. Her role in the narrative is as object, as 'bone of contention', not as subject. Her ability to initiate action is ended after the first verse in which she took the fateful step of 'going out'. Her help-

31. Skinner, for instance, labels the phrase 'and Bethuel' in v. 50 a 'marginal gloss' or 'textual misadventure'; Speiser suggests that it is 'probably intrusive' and calls it 'a marginal gloss on the part of some ancient scribe who did not realize that the father had no place in this narrative' (Speiser, *Genesis*, pp. 177, 181; Skinner, p. 184).

32. Westermann takes this for a certainty (Westermann, *Genesis 37–50*, pp. 386, 388).

33. Whether rape or consensual extramarital intercourse is indicated is a matter of considerable dispute. In reality, the consent required is her father's, not her own.

34. A good background on the narratological issues in this text can be found in D.N. Fewell and D.M. Gunn, 'Tipping the Balance: Sternberg's Reader and the Rape of Dinah', *JBL* 110.2 (1991), pp. 193-211; M. Sternberg, 'Biblical Poetics and Sexual Politics: From Reading to Counterreading', *JBL* 111.3 (1992), pp. 463-88.

lessness is seen by the rapid-fire series of verbs of which she is the object in v. 2: Shechem saw (ירא), took (לקח), lay with (שׁכב) and 'disgraced' (ענה) her. She does not act; she is acted on, as is underscored by the threefold repetition in this verse of the objective pronoun אתה.

Although Shechem recognized that she was 'Dinah daughter of Jacob', he took the opportunity, when she had left the authority and protection of her father, of 'going out' to rape her.[35] With this act, her status was changed, and the narrative tells us that 'he loved the נערה' and 'spoke tenderly to the נערה' (v. 3). The potential vulnerability has been actualized, and Dinah has moved from 'daughter' to נערה.[36]

Shechem requests of his father Hamor, 'Get me [קח־לי] this girl [את־ הילדה] to be my wife' (v. 4), and his change of terminology reveals two things about his situation. Since he can refer to Dinah as a 'girl', her youth influences our evaluation of this sexual encounter, whether or not force was used.[37] Second, he paints the best possible portrait of Dinah: to his father, he does not describe her as a נערה whose adventures outside the house of her father might have left her chastity, or at least her reputation, damaged. To his father, he describes a 'girl-child' (ילדה) whom he wishes to wed. When making a case to his father about the value of making arrangements for his marriage to Dinah, he presents her as a girl whose purity had presumably been kept properly protected under a father's watchful eye.

During the negotiations with the men of Dinah's family, Hamor likewise uses words that reflect well on Dinah, calling her 'your daughter' (v. 8). Shechem, however, minimizes his own guilt by using less favorable terminology when he adds his eagerness to the discussion. 'Name your price,' he says in effect. 'Only give me this נערה to be my wife' (Gen. 34.12). In addressing her father, he attempts to excuse his behavior by terming her a נערה, calling attention to the failure of

35. Some scholars, including Tikva Frymer-Kensky, suggest that 'forcible rape' was not necessarily the situation here (T. Frymer-Kensky, *In the Wake of the Goddesses: Women, Culture, and the Biblical Transformation of Pagan Myth* [New York: Fawcett Columbine, 1992], p. 274 n. 34) .

36. The reference to Dinah as 'daughter of Leah' in v. 1 establishes her identity within the polygamous family but does not indicate that Jacob had died, as he is present, although not central, in the rest of the narrative.

37. Of the various terms used for individuals of various statuses, situations and ages in the Hebrew texts, ילד and ילדה are the most consistent in indicating a minor, what we would think of as a child, as opposed to a person of dependency or reduced status whose situation might not be solely due to age.

Jacob (as well as Simeon and Levi) to keep his daughter (and their sister) confined to 'women's spaces'.[38] The *honor* of the men of the family, specifically with regard to their ability to control access to the sexuality of their women, has been impugned. The story of the revenge taken by Dinah's brothers suggests how deeply this affront to honor was felt.[39]

Ruth

The same term used for a fatherless young woman (as Rebekah appears to have been) might be used for a widow; both might be called נערה. When the widowed Ruth returns to Bethlehem with her mother-in-law, Boaz inquires, 'To whom does this נערה belong?' (Ruth 2.5, 6). The young woman has come into the community without an apparent patron; her vulnerability to sexual exploitation[40] is clear in Boaz's charge to his reapers not to 'bother' her (Ruth 2.9).

Ruth was the Moabite woman who had married Mahlon, one of the sons of Naomi.[41] Upon her return as a widow to Bethlehem with her mother-in-law, Boaz asks a most revealing question about her, when she appears as a gleaner in one of his fields (a public and vulnerable place for a young woman). Once again we see that the term is used when the attachments of a female are not evident. Whose daughter, whose wife,

---

38. Contra Hamilton, who sees just the opposite effect: 'Note that when Shechem spoke to his father about Dinah he called her a "girl" (*yaldâ*, v. 4) but when he speaks about her to her father and brothers he calls her a *maiden* (*na'arâ*). We understand immediately his purpose in using a word with more dignity attached to it.' The notion that the term נערה is one of 'dignity' is shown to be fanciful by recalling what sorts of women are called by that term, to wit, not wives, mothers and daughters, but servants, widows, orphans and concubines (Hamilton, *Genesis*, p. 361).

39. For discussion of this text from a socio-anthropological viewpoint, see Pitt-Rivers; for aspects of biblical law, see Frymer-Kensky; as a defense of exogamy, see Klein (Pitt-Rivers, *Fate of Shechem*; T. Frymer-Kensky, 'Law and Philosophy: The Case of Sex in the Bible', *Semeia* 45 [1988], pp. 89-102 [95]; R.W. Klein, 'Israel/Today's Believers and the Nations: Three Test Cases', *CurTM* 24.3 [1997], pp. 232-37).

40. And perhaps also the tendency of נערים to be 'troublesome'.

41. For basic background scholarship on the book of Ruth, the reader is referred to E.F. Campbell, *Ruth* (AB, 7; Garden City, NY: Doubleday, 1975); R.L. Hubbard, *The Book of Ruth* (NICOT; Grand Rapids: Eerdmans, 1988); J. Sasson, *Ruth: A New Translation with a Philological Commentary and a Formalist-Folklorist Interpretation* (Baltimore: The Johns Hopkins University Press, 1979).

whose serving girl is the woman? The נער to whom Boaz addresses his question serves merely as a foil for the narrator to provide to Boaz the information that the reader already has about the identity of Ruth. That her presence in this place is a premeditated bid for a patron is reflected by Ruth's announcement of her intentions: I will go to the fields and glean 'behind someone in whose eyes I may find favor' (2.2).[42] That the desired relationship is one of 'fictive kinship' is made obvious by Boaz's addressing Ruth as 'my daughter' (בתי, v. 8).

Throughout the book, Ruth is no mere tool of the narrator. She is a fully-fledged character who speaks and acts, whose interiority we see, who takes initiative. She is not a nameless, faceless, voiceless servant; only her circumstances and Boaz's inquiry make her a נערה. Ruth, who has no father to broker a marriage for her, offers her own sexuality to Boaz at the threshing floor. The patron who should have served in this capacity is missing from her life, so she is called נערה. By accomplishing this marriage, she perpetuates the name of her deceased husband (and of her father-in-law), and in the process provides security for both her mother-in-law and herself.

Once the marriage has been arranged between Ruth and Boaz (but before she has become his wife), the term נערה is used of Ruth just once more, this time by the people gathered as witnesses at the gate: 'Through the children that the Lord will give you by this נערה, may your house be like the house of Perez, whom Tamar bore to Judah' (Ruth 4.12). The people's use of the term is poignant; they acknowledge the possibility that this marriage of somewhat unconventional beginnings may be more productive in building up the house of Boaz than a more traditional one might have been.

The comparison is intriguing, since Tamar, too, was a woman whose sexual status involved some irregularity. Tamar is never called נערה, but like Ruth she takes the initiative to offer, without a male broker, her

---

42. Malina has pointed out the connection between patronage and the Hebrew word חן. 'What clients seek of patrons is favor, and grace is favor. Favor might be defined as receiving something, either that could not otherwise be obtained at all, or on terms more advantageous than could otherwise be obtained. Favoritism is the main quality of patron–client relationships. The frequent phrase in the Hebrew Bible, "to find favor in the eyes (sight) of" means to have a person treat one with all the benefactions of a client...' Hubbard anticipated a portion of this analysis, but without the language of the social sciences, in his discussion of this passage. See Pilch and Malina, *Biblical Social Values*, pp. 83-84; Hubbard, *Ruth*, p. 139.

sexuality. Although the expressed intent of this conception was to save
the name of her late husband from extinction (and provide security for
herself), the result from the long view of the greater scriptural narrative
thread was to perpetuate the name of her unjust father-in-law Judah, as
the genealogy at the end of the book of Ruth makes clear.

Levite's Concubine
The Bible's most compelling illustration of the fate of women who
strayed outside the protected boundaries comes from the story of the
Levite's concubine.[43] Apparently because of some sort of falling out,
the woman leaves the Levite and returns to her father's residence. By
this action, the concubine places her self at risk, 'going out', crossing
the threshold into the world outside her home, which was 'male space'.
In the process, she has entered a state of sexual ambiguity: clearly not
the virgin daughter of her father, but temporarily estranged from her
master/husband. The verb used of the woman is זנה, which suggests har-
lotry or adultery; LXX translates as ὠργίσθη (became angry, spurned),
indicating either an emendation or a *Vorlage* that read זנח. In com-
menting on this verse of the story, Boling suggests 'MT is interpretive.
As Israelite law did not allow for divorce by the wife, she became an
adulteress by walking out on him.'[44] The dishonor that this departure
from her master's household brings upon her family of origin is conveyed by the narrator's repeated reference to 'the father of the נערה'
(Judg. 19.3-6, 8, 9). Once she is restored to the control of her master,
she is once again referred to as פילגשו (his concubine), a status that provides protection for neither her sexuality nor her life.

    Although the climax of this story comes later, when the couple have
stopped for the night at Gibeah, the interesting scenes with respect to
our understanding of the word נערה come during the time when she has
taken temporary refuge in her father's home, for it is only during this
time that the term is used with respect to her. Careful reading of the
text, however, reveals that the word is not in fact ever used of this
woman directly. Instead, during the time when she is in her father's
home, *he* is referred to as אבי הנערה, 'father of the נערה'. Within this
phrase may be hidden the reasons for her status as a concubine and the

43. For general discussion of this story, see, e.g., S. Niditch, 'The "Sodomite"
Theme in Judges 19–20: Family, Community, and Social Disintegration', *CBQ* 44
(1982), pp. 365-78.
    44. Boling, *Judges*, p. 274.

callous disregard with which she is treated by her husband/master. The narrative never tells us why she is called concubine and not wife. No mention is made that the Levite has a primary wife to whom this woman must take second place. However, the phrase אבי הנערה, when it appears in Deuteronomy 22, applies to the father of a woman who has had sexual relations, either as a result of rape or seduction, while still living in the home of her father. As a non-virgin bride, she may have been forever condemned to a secondary status, such as we see in this story. More horrifying still, this designation is used in Deuteronomy for the father of a woman who has been raped and whose rapist is punished by an unrenounceable marriage to her. With echoes of these circumstances ringing in our ears, we cannot help but wonder whether her husband's treatment of her is the result of her being 'used goods', or indeed whether this heartless Levite might even be a rapist.

When she was inside her father's home, she disappeared, becoming a nonentity.[45] Outside, she is an object for rage and lust. In light of the role of נערים and נערות in going out or being sent out to cross boundaries and thresholds, it is significant that it is at the threshold of the house that she is found dead (or dying). Clearly, to be 'out' was a dangerous place. Still, some, like Dinah in Genesis 34, cannot resist the crossing of the threshold, despite the risks. In the process, they become נערות. The possibility is strong that one function of the story of the Levite's concubine among its earliest hearers (and the story of Dinah as well) was as an object lesson for women, to make clear the dangers of taking initiative, of 'going out', of venturing across the threshold of the home in which she was protected by father or husband. This possibility is strengthened when we are attentive to the language used by the narrator in the story of the adventuring concubine, whose father is over and over called 'the father of the נערה'. That phrase is used elsewhere in the Hebrew scriptures in only one place, the collection of laws regarding

---

45. Phyllis Trible has pointed this out: 'The power struggle between the two men highlights the plight of the woman who brought them together but whom they and the storyteller have ignored. Unlike her father, the daughter has no speech; unlike her master, the concubine has no power. A journey "to speak to her heart" has become a visit to engage male hearts, with no speech to her at all. What the master set out to do, he has forsaken to enjoy hospitality and competition with another man. The woman suffers through neglect' (P. Trible, *Texts of Terror: Literary-Feminist Readings of Biblical Narratives* [OBT; Philadelphia: Fortress Press, 1984], p. 69).

the penalties for the misuse, on her own part or on the part of another, of the sexuality of a נערה in Deuteronomy 22. Surely its use in this narrative would sound a note of warning to female listeners.

Legal Material

Among the various law codes and groups of statutes in the Hebrew scriptures, only the Deuteronomic Code deals with the term נערה: the word appears 13 times in Deut. 22.13-29, 3 of which occur in the phrase 'father of the נערה', which was so prominent in the story of the Levite's concubine.[46] These laws (which are part of the Deuteronomic Law Code in Deuteronomy 19–25) are considered by most scholars to have appeared later than the Book of the Covenant in Exod. 20.22–23.33.[47] Steinberg places them in a tenth-century context, and suggests that they helped to consolidate the power of the monarchy, diminishing the importance of the wider kinship network, especially the extended family, by placing limits on the absolute power of the *paterfamilias*.[48] Rofé proposes the eighth century, during the second half of the monarchy.[49] Crüsemann has mounted a very convincing 'plea for a pre-exilic dating' in which he suggests the beginning of the reign of Josiah (639–609 BCE) as the most compelling option to consider.[50] Any of these proposals

46. In Deuteronomy, the Hebrew word is spelled *defectiva* נער (with one exception in v. 19), as it was in Genesis. I will omit discussion of Deut. 22.22 and 22.30, since they neither use the word נערה nor deal with the concepts directly under discussion.

47. For an excellent analysis of these verses, along with a summary of pertinent scholarship to date, see F. Crüsemann, *The Torah: Theology and Social History of Old Testament Law* (trans. A.W. Mahnke; Philadelphia: Fortress Press, 1996), p. 109. See also C. Pressler, *The View of Women Found in the Deuteronomic Family Laws* (BZAW, 216; Berlin: W. de Gruyter, 1993). The reader is referred as well to earlier treatments of these verses found in A. Phillips, 'Another Look at Adultery', *JSOT* 20 (1981), pp. 3-25; von Rad, *Deuteronomy*, pp. 141-43; A.D.H. Mayes, *Deuteronomy: Based on the Revised Standard Version* (NCB; Grand Rapids: Eerdmans, 1981), pp. 309-13; R.J.V. Hiebert, 'Deuteronomy 22.28-29 and Its Premishnaic Interpretations', *CBQ* 56 (1994), pp. 203-20.

48. N. Steinberg, 'The Deuteronomic Law Code and the Politics of State Centralization', in Jobling *et al.* (eds.), *The Bible and the Politics of Exegesis*, pp. 161-70, 336-38 (169). See also Perdue *et al.* (eds.), *Families in Ancient Israel*, p. 60.

49. A. Rofé, 'Family and Sex Laws in Deuteronomy and the Book of Covenant', *Henoch* 9.2 (1987), pp. 131-59 (157).

50. Crüsemann, *Torah*, p. 212.

would accord well with the time frame in which the terms נער and נערה are most frequently found in other biblical sources. Although the laws of Deuteronomy appear to offer some protection to women, in actual practise these statutes are part of an overall loss of power and independence, as the monarchy increasingly centralized decision-making.[51]

This particular section of laws in Deuteronomy deals principally with one issue: the case of a woman who has crossed the threshold of her father's house, who has 'gone out'. The first case is one in which the 'going out' is only suspected (Deut. 22.13-19), and falsely so at that. The husband has accused his wife of not having been a 'virgin' when the marriage began.[52] In other words, the woman is accused of 'going out' from, of 'wandering' from, of 'harloting', her father's house, since presumably the behavior of which she is accused could not have happened when she was supervised within it. Within the description of this case, the woman is not a subject who acts at all. The father of the נערה submits the evidence of the virginity of the נערה (v. 15), the father of the נערה presents his case to the elders (v. 16), the father of the נערה receives the fine from the man who has falsely accused her. Significantly, the father, in speaking of her, refers to her as daughter (בתי, vv. 16, 17), never נערה.

In the case in which the accusation is demonstrated to be true and the signs of virginity of the נערה are not found (v. 20), which is to say that she has indeed crossed thresholds and left a sphere within which she should have remained, then it is to that theshold (פתח, v. 21) that the נערה shall be brought, to be stoned for her act of unfaithfulness (זנה, v. 21).

The remaining cases also reflect the situation of a female, called a נערה because she is away from her father's house, who has sexual intercourse with a man not her husband. In the first situation, she is engaged and the man has *found* her (ומצאה, v. 23) in the city and lain with her.[53] In this instance, because the woman 'did not cry for help'

---

51. Meyers, *Discovering Eve*, pp. 189-96; Steinberg, 'Law Code', p. 168.

52. I will accept here the traditional translation of בתולה as 'virgin'. The debate over this translation, while interesting, is not germane to the issue at hand. For details of that debate, I refer the reader to the articles by Wenham and by Wadsworth (Wenham, 'Betulah'; T. Wadsworth, 'Is There a Hebrew Word for Virgin? Bethulah in the Old Testament', *ResQ* 23.3 [1980], pp. 161-71).

53. Translators make her culpability more explicit than the original author of this legislation by using the less ambiguous 'meet her', which carries the implica-

they are both to be stoned (v. 24), even though the woman has been 'violated' (ענה). In this situation, no mention is made of her father, since she was clearly not under his supervision when the event occurred. The stoning is to take place at the 'threshold' of the city, which is to say at the gate (שער).

In the case of the נערה 'found' in the countryside, the case is strengthened by adding that 'the man seizes her', perhaps suggesting that force is involved (חזק, v. 25). No punishment is to be administered to her, since she is presumed to have called out (v. 26), but was unheard because of the secluded location (v. 27). Whether or not the degree of force involved is greater in this case than in the prior one, a central issue in both cases is that this young woman is at risk and is called נערה. In these two instances, her father is not even mentioned.

The final case involves a virgin who is not engaged, and thus has no obligation to any man except her father. The degree of force is not clear (the Hebrew word here is תפש), the location of the rape/seduction is not specified, only her status as virgin daughter of her father's household not yet promised in marriage to any man is described. Once again, she is a נערה (v. 29), venturing beyond the threshold (or at least acting outside the supervision of her father) and compromising her reputation and marriageability in the process. The man will be penalized by paying 50 shekels to the father of the נערה; she will be penalized by spending a lifetime with the man who has done this.[54] These laws without exception relate to sexual behavior of women who had a responsibility to uphold the honor of a man, that is, father, fiancé or husband. Her own wishes in the episode, her own initiative or carelessness, matter less than does her status as a woman 'attached' to some man, a man to whose honor she could bring shame even if she were the victim of rape.

tion that the woman had a hand in arranging the sexual encounter.

54. Naomi Steinberg has pointed out that, by contrast with the case of Exod. 22.16-17, in which the father could withhold his daughter from this marriage if he wished, in the Deuteronomic Code 'what could have been resolved by the *paterfamilias* in Exodus is in Deuteronomy expressed in categorical terms. Such an arrangement for the administration of legal rights qualifies the power of adult males of the nuclear family and supposedly provides legal protection for women and children. The successful transition to a centralized state comes from both using and subverting existing judicial authority structures, in this case the elders' (Steinberg, 'Law Code', p. 165).

The passage shows clearly that in terms of her sexuality at least, the unmarried girl was under her father's authority, as the married woman was under the authority of her husband... Legally, the woman's status is determined by her relationship (or non-relationship) to a man. As Phyllis Bird has noted, whether a woman's actions toward a man and whether a man's actions toward a woman are offenses or not is determined by whether the woman has obligations to a husband, father, or father in law.[55]

That the Deuteronomic Code escalates these offenses to include the entire community as party to the case does not alter the basic fact that the principal affront is to the man to whom she owed faithfulness.

The Deuteronomic understanding of adultery as an offense against the community, however, does not mean that the Deuteronomic authors did not regard adultery as a violation of the rights of the husband or the father. Rather, it is precisely as a violation of the husband's or father's rights that adultery was perceived as a serious threat to the social order.[56]

Each of these scenarios represents a situation that is not the sexual norm, that is a chaste young virgin whose sexuality is passed on, unblemished, to her bridegroom, who maintains exclusive access to that sexuality. The laws detail the resolution of those situations where the morality of the young woman is in question: how to determine the virginity or non-virginity of the new bride, how to determine the culpability or innocence of the betrothed woman who has had sexual intercourse, and how to deal justly with the chaste daughter who has become 'damaged goods', through no fault of her own, except perhaps her boldness in stepping outside of boundaries to explore, 'to see the women of the land'. Stuhlman, in his study of those offenses for which the Deuteronomic Code prescribes the death penalty, has noted 'the most profound fears and concerns' in the social world of the authors of this law collection:

The greatest threat to the social environment of D is posed neither by foreigners who are 'far away' nor by enemies who are 'close by' but outside the defined boundaries (e.g., Canaanites, Jebusites, Perizzites [7.1]). Rather, the most profound danger to the social order of D is posed

55. Pressler, *View of Women*, p. 43; P. Bird, ' "To Play the Harlot": An Inquiry into an Old Testament Metaphor', in P.L. Day (ed.), *Gender and Difference in Ancient Israel* (Philadelphia: Fortress Press, 1989), p. 77.

56. Pressler, *View of Women*, p. 42.

by wanton individuals/groups who reside within the community boundaries but do not conform to its social and cosmic restraints.[57]

It is precisely at the 'community boundaries' that the term נערה is used.

A Special Case: Amos 2

The third phrase of Amos 2.7, ואיש ואביו ילכו אל־הנערה, is usually
translated by some variation of 'father and son go in to the same girl',
and some sort of violation of incest standards is inferred. However,
only in this verse is הלך used with a sexual connotation. (The verb ordinarily used to suggest sexual congress is בוא.) The phrase also lacks any
designator that would suggest the *same* girl. The Greek translators,
however, already understood it that way (καὶ υἱὸς καὶ πατὴρ αὐτοῦ
εἰσεπορεύοντο πρὸς τὴν αὐτὴν παιδίσκην), although probably without
explicitly sexual content.[58] In reality, it says simply that a 'man and his
father go to the girl'. What this means is the subject of many a commentary and book on Amos, and the breadth of the scope of proposed
solutions to this *crux* is matched only by their creativeness. A sampling
from recent commentators is illustrative.

Wolff's suggestion is typical of a number of scholars, who see this
passage as a sexual injustice, which he places under the rubric of 'Abuse
of Maidens'.

> The נערה is generally a young woman, legally a minor, though her status
> seems less a matter of actual age than of social standing. In our passage
> 'the maiden' is further defined neither as wife nor as sister, nor is there
> anything which indicates that a female servant is meant. The reproach
> addresses the case of a 'man and his father' consorting sexually with 'the
> (same) maiden', since here the expression הלך אל (literally 'to go unto')
> means nothing less than 'to copulate with.' Thus in our text, as often
> elsewhere, נערה simply denotes a marriageable girl. The terminology of
> our passage and the situation it portrays are unattested in the biblical
> legal traditions. To be sure, there are apodictic injunctions against a man
> having intercourse with both a woman and her daughter, or a son with

---

57. L. Stulman, 'Encroachment in Deuteronomy: An Analysis of the Social
World of the D Code', *JBL* 109 (1990), pp. 613-32 [631].

58. The Greek verb εἰσπορεύω does not ordinarily have a sexual connotation,
but means rather 'to enter' or 'to go into' (H.G. Liddell [ed.], *An Intermediate
Greek–English Lexicon Founded Upon the Seventh Edition of Liddell and Scott's
Greek–English Lexicon* [Oxford: Clarendon Press, 1889], p. 234).

the wife of his father, or a father with the wife of his son; but nowhere do we encounter the prohibition of father and son having intercourse with the same young woman. Casuistic law handles a similar case when it provides that a female house slave shall be elevated to the full legal status of a wife if either the householder or his son has intercourse with her (Exod. 21.7-11). Amos, however, is not speaking of a female slave (אָמָה Exod. 21.7), but simply of a young woman, one who is not identified more precisely either as a maidservant or a temple prostitute. If it were the 'exploitation of her defenselessness and servitude' which made the act reprehensible, this dependence and weakness of the woman ought to have been stressed. The only thing that is emphasized as being reprehensible here, however, is the fact that 'a man and his son' consort sexually with 'the (same) maiden.'[59]

It is interesting to note his assertion that the 'dependence and weakness of the woman ought to have been stressed' if this passage intends to indicate some sort of abuse of economic or social power. This stress is, in Wolff's view, absent, although he has not examined the social location (and possible level of dependence and weakness) of an individual indicated by the Hebrew term נערה. On the other hand, he suggests that what is 'emphasized' is the fact that father and son 'consort sexually with "the (same) maiden"', a fact whose emphatic content is surely diminished by the fact that the critical word (same) is not supplied by the biblical writer!

Mays suggests that the transgression in question is not sexual so much as syncretistic, and represents an offense against strict monotheism, although allowing for a possible social and sexual concern:

> The maiden to whom both father and son go could be the cultic prostitute who plays such an important role in the fertility cult of Canaanite religion (Hos. 4.14). The institution of cultic prostitution was strictly forbidden in Israel (Deut. 23.17). But maiden (*na'ᵃrā*) is a neutral word that does not of itself mean sacred prostitute (*qᵉdēšā*). Possibly v. 7b refers to the violation of the rights of a female bond-servant by making her into a concubine for father and son, prohibited in Ex. 21.8. (Cf. also Deut. 22.30.) The emphasis of the line on father *and* son highlights the promiscuity involved. In Israel's legal tradition the juxtaposition of related pairs in sexual relations to a third is the subject of a number of laws (Deut. 27.20; Lev. 18.8, 15, 17; 20.10ff.).[60]

59. H.W. Wolff, *Joel and Amos: A Commentary on the Books of the Prophets Joel and Amos* (Hermeneia; Philadelphia: Fortress Press, 1977), pp. 166-67.

60. J.L. Mays, *Amos: A Commentary* (OTL; Philadelphia: Westminster Press, 1969), p. 46. For a similar treatment, see F.I. Andersen and D.N. Freedman, *Amos:*

Barstad, while noting the general absence of 'religious polemics' in the first few chapters of Amos, believes that these verses are an exception, and stresses, as Mays does, that religious syncretism may be the issue that concerns the prophet. He, however, takes pains to build a case that 'as long as the texts themselves remain silent on this point, the sound scholarly attitude should be to regard cultic prostitution in Israel as non-existent'.[61] He connects this phrase in Amos to a two-generational participation in a *mrzḥ* meal, a banquet of the upper classes of Canaanite society that involved conspicuous consumption and drinking to the point of collapse in a religious setting. The נערה, in this view, would be the 'hostess' of the *mrzḥ* banquet.[62]

This suggestion was already anticipated by Coote,[63] who considered it along with other possible breaches of the social ethic that drives the prophet in the verses surrounding this one, including the possibility that the נערה is a tavern keeper whose giving of credit has brought two generations into indebtedness (or perhaps creditorship):

> I strongly suspect, however, that this line does not refer to intercourse with a peasant slave, but rather to an institution known in considerable detail from Mesopotamian documents: the role of the alewife, or barmaid (the 'girl'), as broker. A man and his father *must* go (the verb may be translated modally) to the alewife to obtain a loan at exorbitant rates or else a man and his father go to the alewife to invest for a usurious return. Either the man and his father are peasants, or they are the ruling elite. The latter alternative *may* fit better with the succeeding line in the oracle. I prefer the former, which by its mention of son and father seems to allude to the breakdown of patrimonial domain.[64]

Coote acknowledges, however, the difficulties with the alewife hypothesis, since the evidence of this institution is lacking in the Syro-Palestinian area, not to mention that all references to it date prior to the middle of the second millennium.[65]

A New Translation with Introduction and Commentary (AB, 24A; New York: Doubleday, 1989), p. 318.

	61.	H.M. Barstad, *The Religious Polemics of Amos: Studies in the Preaching of Amos 2,7b-8;4, 1-13; 5,1-27; 6,4-7; 8,14* (Leiden: E.J. Brill, 1984), p. 31.

	62.	Barstad, *Polemics of Amos*, pp. 34-36.

	63.	R.B. Coote, *Amos among the Prophets: Composition and Theology* (Philadelphia: Fortress Press, 1981), pp. 36-38.

	64.	Coote, *Amos among the Prophets*, p. 35.

	65.	Coote, *Amos among the Prophets*, p. 36.

Paul points out that Amos's concern is with the 'social sphere' and that he evidences little concern about idolatry. The female involved is not referred to as קדשה, nor are shrines mentioned, until the next verse, which Paul cites as evidence *against* understanding this as a cultic transgression. He points out that no biblical law forbids father and son to have sexual relations with the same *unmarried* woman, pointing out that Exod. 21.7-11 are not related to this situation.[66] Still, he says that Amos is expressing disapproval of the 'continuity of the act involved (father setting the example for his son), as well as the lack of shame and promiscuity involved when a father and son both "go to the (same) young woman"'.[67] Although this description is morally satisfying, Paul does not explain how an act that is not prohibited by the law codes can be branded with 'lack of shame and promiscuity'. His view of the נערה as 'just one more member of the defenseless and exploited human beings in northern Israel' confirms our findings, even if the source of exploitation for this particular נערה remains a mystery.[68]

Each of these suggestions is consistent with the picture that we have derived of the social location of the נערה. Whether slave or hired girl, cult prostitute, barmaid or banquet hostess, the young woman mentioned in this problematic verse is *working outside the home*, away from the protection and supervision of her father.[69] If sexuality is involved, it is clearly irregular in some way, not the ideal of marital intimacy within a union arranged and sanctioned by family, but somehow outside the bounds of acceptable sexual activity. This has been reflected in every incident in the biblical texts in which a נערה is involved in sexual activity, whether it is the Levite's concubine, called נערה when she leaves her husband's home, or the נערה of the law codes of Deuteronomy.[70]

66. S.M. Paul, *Amos* (Hermeneia; Philadelphia: Fortress Press, 1991), pp. 76-81.

67. Paul, *Amos*, p. 82.

68. Paul, *Amos*, p. 82-83.

69. Chaney has suggested a solution to understanding this elusive verse in which the נערה ceases to be a woman at all! He suggests, by an extensive comparison with the sociological situation in Neh. 5, that the word here means 'foreclosure', making this a denouncement of societal structures that reduce families to poverty and break the sacred connection between the people and their land. (M.L. Chaney, 'Latifundialization and Prophetic Diction in Eighth Century Israel and Judah', unpublished paper, Colloquium on Reformed Faith and Economics, Ghost Ranch, August 1987).

70. Other נערות (such as Ruth and Esther) cease to be called by that term when their sexual activity is 'regularized' by marriage.

Even if this text from Amos does not address sexual issues directly, it seems clear from the concerns of the prophet in the rest of chapter 2 that the girl is vulnerable in some way (economically). In any case, the full situation behind this verse remains elusive, and our emerging picture of the נערה in ancient Israel is not significantly challenged.

Conclusions

As in the case of the young men of previous chapters, these women who come to be called נערות vary in age and circumstance. Without exception, however, they are beyond the protective reach of their fathers and as a result are vulnerable. In the case of the women, this vulnerability is felt particularly strongly in the area of sexual matters.

Chapter 7

OTHER USES OF נער

Fixed Expressions

The Expression נער–זקן

The Hebrew word נער appears frequently as part of the stereotyped phrase נער–זקן, which establishes antithetic parallelism.[1] No corresponding stereotyped pair based on נערה seems to exist. The phenomenon of stereotyped pairs has been catalogued in both Hebrew and Ugaritic by Dahood, and these uses of the pair נער–זקן function very much in the way he suggested, whether the pair is used together or has been 'broken up'. This particular pair has no parallels in the Ugaritic literature, however, since Ugaritic *dqn* is used exclusively to designate the beard or chin, never a person like the Hebrew elder.[2]

In the Hebrew texts, the phrase functions as a merismus, always indicating the totality of the group by designating the end points of a continuum. Frequently this is made explicit with the use of the prepositions מן and עד. The usual English translations of these passages suggest the full spectrum of age, *from young to old*, and indeed that is probably what is represented in some of the late compositions. Certainly, that was the way these expressions were understood by those who rendered these texts into the Greek of the LXX. More appropriate, in view of our

---

1.   For more on the parallel pairs, see: M. Dahood, *Psalms III: 101–150: Introduction, Translation, and Notes with an Appendix, the Grammar of the Psalter* (AB, 17A; New York: Doubleday, 1970), pp. 445-56; M. O'Connor, *Hebrew Verse Structure* (Winona Lake, IN: Eisenbrauns, 1980), pp. 96-109; W.G.E. Watson, *Classical Hebrew Poetry: A Guide to its Techniques* (JSOTSup, 26; Sheffield: JSOT Press, 1984), pp. 328-32; M.J. Dahood, 'The Breakup of Stereotyped Phrases: Some New Examples', *JANES* 5 (1973), pp. 83-89.

2.   Hebrew זקן also designates the beard. The relationship of the beard to a man's honor, and thus potentially to the office of elder, needs to be explored further.

findings regarding the social location of the נער in early Israel, would
be to assume that the merismus works to indicate the entire *status*
gamut, rather than the spectrum of age, with זקן referring to a man who
has achieved the status of *paterfamilias*, while נער refers to a dependent
male working under the tutelage of someone other than his own father
who thus is unlikely ever to attain the coveted status of 'elder'. Just as
we saw that, in general, a נער was an adult male and not one of the
youngest persons in the community, the זקן has long been recognized to
be a community leader and head of household, but not necessarily
'elderly'.[3]

Not surprisingly, since the use of parallel pairs is principally a device
of poetry, the phrase נער–זקן appears only a few times in prose narrative, in sharp contrast to the distribution of the word נער when not in
combination. The pair appears three times in the Pentateuch, once in the
Former Prophets and once in Esther. The remainder occur in Isaiah,
Jeremiah, Psalms, Proverbs and Lamentations.

Genesis 19.4: 'But before they lay down, the men of the city, the men
of Sodom, both young and old, all the people to the last man, sur-
rounded the house…'

The narrator clearly does not mean to include the very youngest individuals of Sodom, only those who were sexually mature and capable of
assault. No 'boys' are included here, only 'men', but men of rank along
with men with little to lose.

Exodus 10.9: 'Moses said, "We will go with our young and our old;
we will go with our sons and daughters and with our flocks and herds,
because we have the LORD's festival to celebrate."'

Moses declares that the entire Israelite community will go, supposedly to celebrate the festival of Yahweh. 'Youngsters' would be
included as sons and daughters; the phrase here once again indicates the
full range of adults.

Deuteronomy 28.50: 'a grim-faced nation showing no respect to the
old or favor to the young…'

Deuteronomy 28.47-68 threatens the people with hardship, exile,
even return to the captivity in Egypt for failure to obey the stipulations

---

3. For the age, status, prerequisites and functions of the 'elders', see Reviv,
The Elders in Ancient Israel; R. de Vaux, *Ancient Israel. I. Social Institutions* (New
York: McGraw–Hill, 1965); McKenzie, 'Elders in the Old Testament', pp. 522-40;
Matthews and Benjamin, 'The Elder', pp. 170-74; Bendor, *Social Structure of
Ancient Israel*, pp. 256-57.

of Yahweh. Here we may suspect the hand of a late Deuteronomistic redactor. The phrase does, however, express aspects that are consistent with a status range rather than an age range. Those in the position of 'elder' will not be shown the appropriate respect; the grace or patronage (חן) that was expected by the נער would also be wanting.

Joshua 6.21: 'Then they devoted to destruction by the edge of the sword all in the city, both men and women, young and old, oxen, sheep, and donkeys...'

The Israelites, upon capturing the city of Jericho, destroyed all that was in the city, 'from man to woman, from נער to זקן'. That the term as used by this author is not simply indicating the children of Jericho is suggested by the fact that just two verses later (6.23) the Israelite spies who visited the prostitute Rahab and spied out the land, who were surely adult men, are referred to as נערים.

Esther 3.13: 'Letters were sent by couriers to all the king's provinces, giving orders to destroy, to kill, and to annihilate all Jews, young and old, women and children, in one day, the thirteenth day of the twelfth month, which is the month of Adar, and to plunder their goods.'

Esther is clearly a late composition, but in the use of the phrase נער–זקן, as with other occurrences of נער and נערה in Esther, the author uses the word as it is used by earlier writers. The term specifies the range of Jewish males (היהודים) who are to be extirpated. Children are indicated by the term טף, and are included with the women.

By contrast to the rather formulaic use of the phrase by the prose narrators, the poets break up the expression with other intervening descriptions, but the sense seems to remain: to express the totality of the people.

Isaiah 3.4, 5: 'And I will make boys their princes, and babes shall rule over them. The people will be oppressed, everyone by another, and everyone by a neighbor; the youth will be insolent to the elder, and the base to the honorable.'

The prophet, in a description of disaster that sounds very like the Babylonian captivity, describes a world in which everyone with leadership potential (including the זקנים)—anyone with power, with wisdom, with experience, with expertise—will be taken away from Jerusalem and Judah. In that power vacuum, the world will be turned upside down. The נערים will be captains, the young children will rule. The נער will 'lord it over' the זקן, as will the 'lightweights' treat the 'heavyweights'. Although age is clearly a factor here, it is used to express a lack of skill and status. Those from the lower rungs of the society will come out on top when all of those who are important are taken away.[4]

Isaiah 20.4: '…so shall the king of Assyria lead away the Egyptians as captives and the Ethiopians as exiles, both the young and the old, naked and barefoot, with buttocks uncovered, to the shame of Egypt.'

Isaiah describes the fate of Egypt and Cush at the hands of the Assyrians. Whichever end of the status line they occupied before, they will alike be stripped of all modesty and all honor.

Isaiah 65.20: 'No more shall there be in it an infant that lives but a few days, or an old person who does not live out a lifetime; for one who dies at a hundred years will be considered a youth, and one who falls short of a hundred will be considered accursed.'

When the poet describes the New Creation, the motif is one of fullness of life, thus of age. Status seems nowhere to be the issue in this passage, although McKenzie has pointed out that longevity was seen as a sign of Yahweh's favor.[5] Clearly, by the time of this writing, the word no longer carried the significance that it did in the earliest period.[6]

Jeremiah 51.22: '…with you [Israel, as God's instrument] I smash man and woman; with you I smash the old man and the boy; with you I smash the young man and the girl.'

This late oracle from Jeremiah presents an interesting case. In the preceding verses, the objects of destruction have been political entities or military functionaries (vv. 20-21). In v. 23, the targets are the pastoralist and the agriculturist, with their livestock, and finally the leaders (פחות וסגנים, although this last phrase may not belong here, but may have been added from v. 28). Standing between these is v. 22, which designates categories of people: man and woman, נער and זקן, young man and young woman.[7] The middle pairing, since it does not extend to

---

4.   Background on the situation at the time of the writings of First Isaiah is available in M.A. Sweeney, *Isaiah 1–39* (FOTL, 16; Grand Rapids: Eerdmans, 1996); R.E. Clements, *Isaiah 1–39* (NCB; Grand Rapids: Eerdmans, 1980).

5.   J.L. McKenzie, *Second Isaiah* (AB, 20; Garden City, NY: Doubleday, 1968), p. 199.

6.   For more background on the late Isaianic writings, see P.D. Hanson, *Isaiah 40–66* (IBC; Atlanta: John Knox Press, 1995).

7.   These last two terms, בחור and בתולה, have themselves generated a great deal of speculation with regard to social location. They seem to be prime young people from honorable families; they are viewed as ideal marriage prospects. The בחור appears to be someone who will eventually achieve the status of 'elder', but who probably does not yet hold that rank.

the two genders, has been regarded by some as an addition, which is evidenced by the fact that it is missing from the Old Greek. Another possibility is that the translators of LXX, not quite understanding what was meant by the phrase, omitted it even though it was contained in their Hebrew original. Societal station does seem to be at issue here, not age, although the late (exilic or early postexilic) dating of the passage makes specificity in the use of the word נער less likely.

Psalm 37.25: 'I have been young, and now am old, yet I have not see the righteous forsaken or their children begging bread.'

In this instructional psalm, the principal contrast being drawn is between the wicked and the righteous. The נער in the Bible is frequently depicted as in need of instruction, and most of the occurrences of the word among the writings are in wisdom contexts. Although usually translated in terms of age, this verse could equally be translated in terms of status: I have been a נער and now am an elder. In either case, the psalmist suggests that he has seen the world from both sides and wishes to impart to his hearers what he learned in the process of living.

Psalm 148.12: 'Young men and women alike, old and young together!'

This psalm is a hymn of praise whose creation theme suggests a wisdom setting as well. As mentioned in reference to Jer. 51.22, the young men and women (בחורים וגם־בתולות) are male and female young adults with 'good prospects'. The other pair (זקנים עם־נערים) delimits the ends of an entirely different spectrum, whether of age or of status is not possible to determine since the text is principally an enumeration, providing very little context.

Proverbs 22.6: 'Train children in the right way, and when old, they will not stray.'

This is the only proverb that exhibits this merism, but it is only one of many whose concern is the proper training of נערים. The verb used for training here (חנך) is rare in biblical Hebrew. It can mean the dedication of a new house or the consecration of a temple. Only here is it used of instruction or discipline of either children or servants. An adjective derived from this word is used to describe the servants of Abraham, born in his house, who accompanied him when he went to rescue Lot (Gen. 14.14). In light of the evidence from Hebrew narrative, this might more appropriately be translated, 'Commit a "fosterchild" to the right path, and if he becomes an elder, he will not depart from it'.

Lamentations 2.21: 'The young and the old are lying on the ground in the streets; my young women and my young men have fallen by the sword; in the day of your anger you have killed them, slaughtering without mercy.'

In Lamentations, the poet grieves the destruction of Jerusalem.[8] The theme of 2.20-21 is to delineate the victims of this great tragedy. Women and children, priest and prophet are mentioned, followed by נער and זקן, who are lying on the ground in the streets, and the בתולת and בחורים who have fallen by the sword. The acrostic device used to structure ch. 2 suggests that it was liturgical, and in any case it comes clearly from sometime after 586 BCE. The context tells us little about what is intended by the phrase נער–זקן here, but in light of the lateness, the phrase may be a fixed expression simply emphasizing the totality of the destruction. The contemporary hearers might not have made any assumptions about whether age or status were involved.[9]

Lamentations 5.11-14: 'Women are raped in Zion, virgins in the town of Judah. Princes are hung up by their hands; no respect is shown to the elders. Young men are compelled to grind, and boys stagger under loads of wood. The old men have left the city gate, the young men their music.'

In these verses, the poet has done considerable breaking up of stereotyped pairs, creating a complex strophe that covers the full range of the adults of Judah. He begins with the women and 'choice females' (בתלת) of Judah (v. 11) and ends with the 'elders' (זקנים) and 'chosen males' (future elders, בחרים, v. 14). Between he places 'chiefs' and 'elders' (v. 12), 'choice males' and 'disinherited' (נערים, v. 13). Children do not seem to be in view in this passage, but the full range of status does seem to be represented.

The Expressions נער–קטן and נערה–קטנה

Another fixed phrase that appears several times in the Hebrew scriptures is נער–קטן or נערה–קטנה. The noun נער, as we have seen from the

---

8.   See the extensive history of interpretation in Westermann, as well as the background in Hillers: C. Westermann, *Lamentations: Issues and Interpretation* (Philadelphia: Fortress Press, 1994); D.R. Hillers, *Lamentations: Introduction, Translation, and Notes* (AB, 7A; Garden City, NY: Doubleday, 1972).

9.   Contemporary English speakers who use the expressions 'from soup to nuts' or 'from stem to stern' might be hardpressed to state what is being described, precisely, in one or the other expression.

preponderance of Hebrew narratives, does not indicate that the individual so named was necessarily young, but rather indicated something more complex about his social location: namely that he was 'out of the nest', no longer under the protection and guidance of his father. Certainly, the term was rarely applied to persons who were children or even prepubescent, at least not in texts coming to us from the period of the early monarchy or before. The adjective קטן, on the other hand, modifies נער to give it precisely this meaning. This (קטן) is the usual way of expressing 'young' or 'small' in Hebrew, and when used of a person the term virtually always indicates age, not stature. In expressing the comparative or superlative, 'younger' or 'youngest', the term used is *always* קטן. No form of the word נער is found with this meaning. Indeed, the word is never employed indisputably as an adjective, although it sometimes appears as a substantive, usually translated as 'youth'. In the Ugaritic texts, as will be discussed in the next chapter, apart from one possible usage as the substantive, the word *n'r* is unknown as an adjective.

2 Kings 5. The story of the healing of Naaman (2 Kgs 5.1-14) is filled with contrasts in status, from the king and his great and favored commander down to the little servant girl, who was declassed by her age, her gender and her status as נערה.[10] These contrasts are drawn by the use of pairs of words that are drawn from opposite ends of the social spectrum. Particularly significant is the way the author plays with גדול (great, rich, powerful, literally big) and קטן (young, insignificant, powerless, literally small). In this context, the נערה קטנה from Israel (v. 2) probably was a girl, likely of a younger age than was usual for being outside her father's household in domestic service. After Naaman's skin condition has been healed, we are told that it became like that of a נער קטן (v. 14; cf. Job 23.25). Again, probably a boy is meant, not a servant of the usual age. Perhaps the author is drawing our attention to the lack of body hair typical of childhood and eunuchs.

Other Very Young נערים. In a few other citations, the individual seems actually to have been a young boy. In each case, however, his circumstances, not his age, make him a נער. His age is revealed by the adjective.[11] Most of these texts have been treated in the appropriate chapters

10. This narrative was discussed in more detail in Chapter 6.
11. David (1 Sam. 16.11) was הקטן, the youngest of his brothers, but in his ser-

based on what the narrative tells us about their function or situation.

1 Kings 11.17: 'but Hadad fled to Egypt with some Edomites who were servants of his father. He was a young boy at that time.'

The motif of the adult heirs to the throne being slain while a young son escapes and is brought up elsewhere is common. Hadad probably was a boy under the care of regents until he was ready to rule on his own.

2 Kings 2.23: 'He [Elisha] went up from there to Bethel; and while he was going up on the way, some small boys came out of the city and jeered at him, saying, "Go away, baldhead! Go away, baldhead!"'

Probably the taunts of young boys are in view here, boys who are clearly not under supervision and have not been 'well-brought-up'. The נער was thought to be prone to misbehavior at all stages of his life, and much concern is expressed about his training and discipline.

1 Samuel 20.35: 'In the morning Jonathan went out into the field to the appointment with David, and with him was a little boy.'

A young boy, who serves as arrow-fetcher and weapon carrier, but not apparently as armor-bearer quite yet, accompanies Jonathan into the field and unwittingly serves as a distance marker by which Jonathan sends his secret message to David. Presumably, the usual adult military assistant would have been harder to fool.

Isaiah 11.6: 'The wolf shall live with the lamb, the leopard shall lie down with the kid, the calf and the lion and the fatling together, and a little child shall lead them.'

In the 'peaceable kingdom' envisioned by the prophet, domestic livestock will not be attacked by wild animals, but both will be pastured together. As is frequently the case in biblical narratives, the tending of the livestock (and most particularly protection from depredation) is the task of a נער, and a young boy can manage this job in such non-violent times.

Not Young, but Inexperienced, Undeserving.
1 Kings 3.7: 'And now, O LORD my God, you have made your servant king in place of my father David, although I am only a little child; I do not know how to go out or come in.'

---

vice as נער to Saul he was not נער קטן, that is, he was not a young boy, just the last-born.

In this prayer Solomon refers to himself as נער קטן, although he has already married Pharaoh's daughter and has been responsible for several deaths. He has, in fact, lost the protection of his father David and has had to struggle fiercely to hold onto the throne, given his status as a later-born son. The biblical texts frequently stress the need for training and discipline for a נער and depict him as one who lacks wisdom, who doesn't know 'this from that'. The נער of Isa. 7.16, who serves as a sign to Ahaz of the lifting of the siege, does not 'know how to refuse the evil and choose the good'. Although some have suggested that this is the child of the prophet, that is by no means made explicit. That the child is called a נער may reflect the fact that only his mother is mentioned or that the siege represents danger from which even his father cannot protect him. The usage of the term, by Isaiah's time, may also have been less precise than in the earlier narratives. In Isa. 8.4, the נער who is described as the child of the prophet, does not 'know how to call "My father" or "My mother"', perhaps a reference to the need for a fosterling to learn to address the adults in his new home by those titles. Solomon identifies himself as a נער (1 Kgs 3.7), one who does not know what he needs to know in order to rule successfully, and he asks for wisdom.

In Chronicles, the later historian has David describe his son, shortly before his own death, as נער ורך (a נער and inexperienced), and thus not up to the task of building Yahweh's house (1 Chron. 22.5; 29.1). After the death of Solomon, his son Rehoboam, endangered by the rebellion of Jeroboam, is described in the same terms. Josiah, who at the age of 16 had already reigned for 8 years after the assassination of his father Amon, was called נער, possibly because of his status as an orphan. In the listing of the troops who brought David to power at Hebron, Zadok is called נער, which hardly seems a designation for youthfulness, given that he is also a 'valiant warrior' and brings 22 commanders from his 'father's house', in which household he was obviously no longer resident. Curiously, not one of these late references to נערים is a person whose father is living and present. Nevertheless, it is not unlikely that the nuance of the term had been lost by this period.

Jeremiah 1.6, 7. 'Then I said, "Ah, Lord GOD! Truly I do not know how to speak, for I am only a נער." But the LORD said to me, "Do not say, I am only a נער"...'

The prophet Jeremiah identifies himself as a נער (not however as a

נער קטן), although he is an adult at the time of his call.[12] He addresses Yahweh as 'my lord' (אדני, v. 6), which is typical of the way נערים who are servants address their masters. Like the untrained נערים discussed above, who do not know about good and bad, about going in and coming out, about calling Mother and Father, Jeremiah stresses his inexperience: he does not know how (or what perhaps) to speak. He is relying on Yahweh for guidance and training, deliverance and patronage. Jeremiah was 'foreordained' for Yahweh's service before birth (בבטן, v. 5). Clearly, the term נער here has 'more to do with societal status than with age'.[13]

This circumstance of Jeremiah's call is echoed in the situations of other biblical נערים. Samson receives his dedication as a Nazirite before birth (בבטן, Judg. 13.5), as does Samuel (1 Sam. 1.11). Both of these are also נערים, as we have seen. Perhaps girls were dedicated to the service of a god at a shrine or temple from an early age as well. Certainly the knowledge that the נערה קטנה who served the Queen of Aram had about the prophet of Israel could have been acquired from such service. Perhaps she was captured from a shrine rather than from a household.

Poetic and Proverbial Uses

In addition to the use of the word נער in the fixed expressions discussed above, it is found occasionally in other poetic and proverbial settings, as well as a few times in late prose. These lack the narrative context that is so helpful in determining meaning, but in some cases parallelism provides clues. Some of these passages are quite problematic, with various emendations proposed by scholars who have studied them. In most of the other cases, the understanding of the word נער (and נערה) that has been developed by close reading of the early narratives in which the

12.   Both Jeremiah and Solomon identify themselves as נערים (which in itself is unusual, since נערים are spoken about far more than they speak themselves, generally), but neither one of them calls himself נערך, 'your נער'. That identification of the speaker as client and the hearer as patron is common in the Hebrew Bible, but it is everywhere expressed as עבדך, 'your servant'. Equally significant is the fact that a man (or woman) never refers to his offspring as נערי, 'my נער'.

A thorough discussion of the divisions of Jeremiah, along with proposals for their dating, is found in J. Bright, *Jeremiah* (AB, 21; Garden City, NY: Doubleday, 1965).

13.   J.R. Lundbom, 'Rhetorical Structures in Jeremiah 1', *ZAW* 103 (1991), pp. 193-210 [196].

word is used will be shown to fit the context of the poetic or late use of the word quite adequately. Each of these examples will be examined briefly in turn.

Prophets

The prophets used the noun נער infrequently, although the eighth-century prophets used it slightly more often than the later ones.[14] Quite often, they made use of the set pairing נער–זקן in one form or another as illustrated above, or sometimes a variant of this that placed נערים in parallel with בחורים (Isa. 40.30) or with בנים (Isa. 13.18), for instance. That these expressions indicate the totality of the people is obvious. More difficult, in dealing with parallel pairs, is the determination of whether the two terms are synonomous, opposite, or from the same semantic field, but with one exceeding the other in some quality.

In addition to Isa. 7.16 and 8.4 (mentioned in connection with 1 Kgs 3.7 above), Isaiah highlights the lack of training of נערים in his description of a time when the trees will be so few than even a נער can write them down. The implication seems to be that, although a נער might be taught some writing skills for the carrying out of his duties, his literacy was not extensive.[15]

Zechariah, writing after the return from exile, portrays a נער who has been given the task of measuring Jerusalem (Zech. 2.8). He is apparently a servant. Zechariah 11.16 has long represented a challenge to scholars, and the list of proposed emendations for this passage is long. Petersen suggests seeing here a verbal form (נער II) meaning 'to lament', which is quite appropriate in this context.[16] Jeremiah 51.38 is to be understood in a comparable way. Similarly, Isa. 1.31, along with Judg. 16.9, are not the usual reference to a person, but indicate fiber or chaff (tow) from the production of linen.

Early in the history of the classical or writing prophets, Hosea introduced an image of Israel that was to become a standard motif used by the nation's prophets for centuries.[17]

---

14. The single use of נערה in the prophets (Amos 2.7) was discussed in Chapter 6.

15. Cf. the נער who listed the elders of Succoth (Judg. 3.8).

16. See also the background by Petersen and the emendation suggested by Meyers: D.L. Petersen, *Zechariah 9–14 and Malachi* (OTL; Louisville, KY: Westminster/John Knox Press, 1995), p. 203; C.L. Meyers and E.M. Meyers, *Zechariah 9–14* (AB, 25C; New York: Doubleday, 1993), p. 287.

17. For background on the book of Hosea, see H.W. Wolff, *Hosea* (Hermeneia;

Hosea 11.1: 'When Israel was a child [נער], I loved him and out of Egypt I have called my son [לבני, τα τεκνα αυτου].'

Israel indeed understood itself to have served a '*na'ar*ship' in Egypt, performing slave labor, unransomed by her 'father', Yahweh, who seemed to remain behind in the land while the nation did its term of service. The story of the exodus was viewed as the moment in which they were bought back from a time that amounted to debt slavery. The process began when the land of Canaan, their נחלה, their patrimony, was no longer able to feed them. In leaving their land and their God in search of food in Egypt, the nation became a נער (or in some metaphors a נערה). Then a time finally came when the father called their children (reading MT), or his children (reading the Greek), to return to the land of their father.[18]

Hosea was not the only prophet to use this image of the servanthood or '*na'ar*ship' of Israel in Egypt in his writings. Surveying the occurrences of the substantive form of נער, which is usually translated 'youth', produces the interesting result that the substantives occur almost exclusively in the poetic books and legal codes rather than in prose narrative (40 occurrences in poetic books, 3 in legal codes, 6 in prose narratives).[19] In 20 of these cases, the period of Israel's slavery in Egypt is what is being described by the poet in much the same way that Hosea uses the noun.[20]

Other Poetic Writings
The word נער, in the poetic writings, seems most at home in a wisdom setting. Even in the Psalms and Prophets, it appears most often in a

Philadelphia: Fortress Press, 1974); F.I. Andersen and D.N. Freedman, *Hosea: A New Translation with Introduction and Commentary* (AB, 24; Garden City, NY: Doubleday, 1980).

18. Kuhnigk and Dahood already earlier translated נער as 'slave' or 'servant' here. (W. Kuhnigk, *Nordwestsemitische Studien zum Hoseabuch* [BibOr; Rome: Pontifical Biblical Institute, 1974], p. 127; M. Dahood, in *RSP*, II, pp. 82-83.) Andersen suggests that Yahweh 'chooses Israel and confers the status of child on him'. In that way Israel has become 'the senior, the privileged heir' (Andersen and Freedman, *Hosea*, p. 577).

19. The word appears נעורים, נער or נעורות.

20. Isa. 47.12, 15; Jer. 2.2; 3.4, 24, 25; 22.21; 31.19; 32.30; Ezek. 16.22, 43, 60; 23.2, 3, 8, 19, 21; Hos. 2.17 (Eng. 15); Ps. 129.1, 2; Isa. 54.6; Jer. 48.11 represent somewhat different but closely related images.

didactic context. Beyond that, much remains in these passages that is a challenge to the interpreter.

In the book of Job, the uses of נערים in the prose prologue clearly mean 'servants', and Job 29.5 is appropriately translated in the same way. Job 24.5 and 40.29 were discussed in Chapter 5, where the difficulties in understanding these phrases were pointed out. Job 29.8 contains the pairing of נערים (who withdrew from Job's august presence) with ישישים (who rise and stand), a word unknown outside of Job, but which the writer appears to use with roughly the same meaning as זקנים.

Ecclesiastes 10.16: 'Alas for you, O land, when your king is a servant [נער] and your princes feast in the morning. Happy are you, O land, when your king is a nobleman [בן־חורים] and your princes feast at the proper time—for strength, and not for drunkenness!'

Some have seen in this 'upside-down' social order (cf. Eccl. 10.5-7) a reference to Solomon or Josiah or Rehoboam (who were נערים when they began to rule), but the Preacher is probably simply making the point that rulers should be drawn from the upper echelons of society.

The only psalm that uses נער outside of the fixed pair נער–זקן is Psalm 119, the longest of the collection. It is an acrostic wisdom composition on the theme of obedience to the law that asks the question (v. 9), 'How can a נער keep his path pure?' The setting is too stylized to provide much information in identifying how the author understood the term.

In the book of Proverbs, the use of נערה clearly indicates a serving girl in every instance (Prov. 9.3; 27.27; 31.15). For the males, the subject is instruction throughout, beginning with the prologue to the entire work that explains that the purpose of the proverbs, among other things, is to teach 'knowledge and prudence to the נער' (1.4). In explaining the perils of adultery, the teacher indicates having seen 'a נער without sense' in the vicinity of the 'strange woman', and thus vulnerable to danger (7.7). In an ancient version of our saying 'Handsome is as handsome does', we are told that 'even a נער is known by his deeds' (20.11). Proverbs 22.15, 23.13 and 29.15 all urge the use of corporal punishment in the training of a נער, using a 'rod' (שבט). Close readings of the ways the word is used elsewhere suggest that these are servants, probably young adults, and not children. The same treatment is also recommended for slaves (עבדים, 29.19, 21). Nowhere is the use of the 'rod' advocated for ילדים (children), although Prov. 13.24 suggests that a

man is wise to use the rod on בנו (his son), without specifying the age of
the one disciplined in this way.

Late Prose Historical Sources

Chronicles, as we have seen above, uses נער in several settings of the
speech about Solomon's inability to handle, without his father's assistance, the task of temple-building. In this, the historian seems to be using something of a stock phrase.

The book of Esther, which uses both נער and נערה extensively, uses
those terms with precisely the nuance that was developed from reading
the contexts of those words in *early* prose narrative. I have suggested in
Chapter 6 that this may have come from a deliberate modelling of the
Esther story on the brief account of the selection of Abishag the Shunammite.

Nehemiah, too, although clearly a late source, uses the term נער to
designate servants in a way that would be clearly compatible with our
understanding of the נער as one who is away from his father's house,
serving in another man's household or camp. The servants of Nehemiah
and the other returning Judahites are referred to in 4.10, 16, 17 (Eng.
vv. 16, 22, 23) and 5.10 as carrying weapons and working on the construction of the wall. In 13.19, some of the servants guard the gate on
the sabbath. The only remarkable aspect about any of this, potentially,
is Nehemiah's statement (5.10) that he, his brothers and his נערים were
lending money to help people avoid debt slavery. The source and extent
of a servant's money is not clear, unless these נערים were working for
wages. Certainly the social world depicted in Nehemiah is not one in
which every son in Judah remained in the extended family, working the
patrimonial land of the house of his father. Thus, the institution of sending sons out to work for others as נערים is quite likely in this context.[21]
Nehemiah mentions that Sanballat has נערים who served as messengers.
That this was not a position of 'high rank', as some have suggested, is
made clear by the disapproval of the fact that the נערים of the former
governors 'lorded it over' the people (6.5).

---

21. Twentieth-century American Mennonite families practise this sharing of
labor, sending sons whose help is not needed at home to another farm in the community, where they can assist (and be fed by) another householder. (I thank Prof.
Theodore Hiebert for calling my attention to this practice and Lonnie Voth for
sharing his experience of it.)

Abstract Substantive: 'Youth'

In addition to the citations mentioned earlier in conjunction with the discussion of Hosea 11.1, a number of passages remain in which a substantive based on the noun נער is understood to mean 'youth'. The majority of these occur in prophecy or other poetic books. The context of most of the rest is not the blocks of narratives from old sources, but rather redacted speeches and comments as well as legal material (e.g. Lev. 22.13; Num. 30.4, 17).

In certain instances, the individual named has indeed been characterized as a נער at some point in the biblical story, and a translation of 'since my *na'ar*ship' is probably most appropriate. This phrase is used of Samuel (1 Sam. 12.2), Goliath (1 Sam. 17.33), who likely started out as an armor-bearer, David (2 Sam. 19.8), Obadiah (1 Kgs 18.12), in charge of Ahaz's palace, and perhaps even Job (31.18), in light of the expression 'from my mother's womb' and its connection to the *na'ar* ship of Samson and Samuel. The same concept of servanthood is clearly indicated in Lam. 3.27 and Prov. 29.21.

The husband or wife or sons of one's youth are a frequent motif (Joel 1.8; Mal. 2.14; Ps. 127.4; 144.12; Prov. 2.17; 5.18), and it is not impossible that these were marriages or births that occurred during a time of servant status. Sins or evil since 'youth' (Gen. 8.21; Ps. 25.7; Job 13.26; or conversely Ezek 4.14) and the protection or guidance of Yahweh since 'youth' (Ps. 71.5, 17) appear, as do occupations practiced 'since youth' (Gen. 48.34; Zech. 13.5) and the possibility of dying in 'youth' (Job 36.14; Ps. 88.26 [15]). Finally, there is the unique and uplifting image of 'youth renewed as an eagle's' (Ps. 103.5) which reminds us that in the course of time, the nuance of servanthood or risk, of being away from the father's house, was lost and replaced by the concept of 'youngness', based more on the fact that this was the time when such separations most often occurred, and not on any supposed 'root' or 'original' meaning of the word נער.

Chapter 8

RELATED WORDS IN OTHER LANGUAGES

Egyptian

Although the many references to *n'r* in the texts discovered at Ras Shamra would seem to be the logical place to begin a search for cognates to the Hebrew word נער, I hope to show that an erroneous understanding of the Ugaritic term has crept into the literature as a result of a misreading of the Egyptian evidence, and consequently the understanding of the Egyptian context must be set right before an adequate examination of the Ugaritic usage of the term can be carried out. Fortunately, a recent article by Walter Mayer and Ronald Mayer-Opificius has provided a basis for this effort.[1]

An Egyptian word that would seem to bear a relationship to the Hebrew נער appears in a handful of inscriptions. This word is *n'rn* or *n-'-r-na*. The most important sources for our understanding of this Egyptian word, borrowed no doubt from Egypt's Semitic neighbors, are the accounts of the Battle of Kadesh. These accounts are especially useful since the inscriptions appear at several sites, allowing lacunae in one account to be supplied by reference to another. Their very nature, as descriptions of a battle, provides the narrative context that is so necessary in determining the meaning of a word in any language, and the interplay between text and picture provides additional valuable data.

The Battle of Kadesh reflects the efforts of the great empires of the Late Bronze Age to control the flow of men and goods through the Levant. Suppiluliumas (1375–1335 BCE) of the Hittites had begun to expand southward, finally reaching Damascus and taking control of Kadesh, a small city-state on the Orontes River in the process. With its strategic position on one of the main north–south travel routes, the city was an important part of the Hittite defenses against Egyptian north-

---

1. Mayer and Mayer-Opificius, 'Die Schlacht bei Qadeš', pp. 321-68.

ward expansion. When Muwatallis (1306–1282 BCE), the grandson of Suppiluliumas, engaged in battle against Ramesses II (1290–1224 BCE, grandson of Ramesses I, first ruler of the Nineteenth Dynasty), Kadesh was a predictable theater for their encounter. The conduct and outcome of the battle, in which Ramesses II claimed victory, became the subject matter for a whole series of inscriptions in various Egyptian monuments.[2] Our sources for information about the Battle of Kadesh include reliefs plus three bodies of texts, referred to as the *Poem*, the *Bulletin* or *Record* and the *Captions* to the reliefs.[3]

In these records, the *n-'-r-na* are mentioned by name in R 11,[4] a portion of the caption to a scene among the reliefs that depicts the camp of Pharaoh, with an incursion of Hittite troops being fought off by combatants from the camp.[5] Breasted initially labeled these defenders 'recruits'.[6] The poem describes the route and preparations taken by

2.   These include the temples at Karnak, Luxor and Abydos, the Ramesseum and Abu Simbel. To see what these lines of hieratic text look like and how they are placed on the walls of the various Egyptian monuments, see K.A. Kitchen, *Ramesside Inscriptions. II. Historical and Biographical* (Oxford: Basil Blackwell, 1979), pp. 125-33.

3.   Although this 'Bulletin' has been asserted to be some sort of 'official report' of the battle, Gardiner contends that it is simply one more (albeit longer) relief caption (A.H. Gardiner, *The Kadesh Inscriptions of Ramesses II* [Oxford: Griffith Institute, Ashmolean Museum, 1975], pp. 3, 5, 6; J.H. Breasted, *Ancient Records of Egypt: Historical Documents from the Earliest Times to the Persian Conquest*. III. *The Nineteenth Dynasty* [Ancient Records of Egypt, 2nd series; Chicago: University of Chicago Press, 1906], pp. 125-57.)

4.   This entire caption reads, following the translation of Gardiner: 'The coming of the Ne'ārīn of Pharaoh from the land of Amor. They found that the host of the Khatti enemies hemmed in the camp of Pharaoh on its western side, while His Majesty sat alone, his army not with him, the host of the chariots hemming in…his soldiers, while the army of Amūn in which Pharaoh was had not yet ended the pitching of the camp, and the army of Prē' and the army of Ptaḥ were marching and their…had not yet arrived from the wood of Robawi. And the Ne'ārīn broke into the host of the wretched Fallen one of Khatti as they were entering into the camp of Pharaoh, and the servants of His Majesty killed them and did not allow one of them to escape, their hearts being confident of the great strength of Pharaoh their goodly Lord, he being behind them like a mountain of copper and like a wall of iron for ever and ever' (Gardiner, *Kadesh Inscriptions*, p. 37.)

5.   Sketches and photographs of this camp scene, as it is depicted at various of the monuments, can be seen in Yadin, *The Art of Warfare*, pp. 107-109, 236-37.

6.   Breasted, *Ancient Records*, 133, Sect. 302.

Away from the Father's House

Pharaoh before arriving at the camp near Kadesh. Breasted interprets line 18 of this account: 'Marching through Palestine, and along the Phoenician coast road, Ramesses passed into Amor, where he formed his van of picked men, on the shore in the land of Amor.'[7] Originally, he interpreted the relief of the camp scene *without* reference to the account of the trip up the coast road, saying simply, 'These hostile intruders [Hittites breaking into the camp] are quickly dispatched by the household troops of Ramses, who are to be seen on foot poniarding them'.[8] He abandoned this understanding, however, in response to Meyer, who claimed,

> Rameses marched up the Phoenician Coast and dispatched here an elite squadron as a vanguard which would march along the Amorite Coast and penetrate to him at the Eleutheros Valley. Subsequently they were designated by the Semitic term *na'aruna*, 'youthful troops'.[9]

How these came to be understood as 'crack troops' can be understood by the following excerpt from the well-respected scholar Alan Gardiner, in reference to the troops that Breasted referred to as a 'van of picked men' (above):

> It seems to me, however, that this sentence must allude to the force which is depicted in all the temple-scenes as suddenly arriving and, having found the camp of Pharaoh surrounded, attacking the Hittites in the rear; the accompanying legend begins '...The arrival of the youthful troops (*n'rn*, see above under No. 259) of Pharaoh from the land of Amor...,' Kuentz, 366. Various suggestions have been made about these fresh troops: Breasted (*Battle of Kadesh*, 38) thought they might have belonged to the fugitive division of Amūn now returning on finding themselves no longer pursued by the enemy; Burne (*JEA* VII, 194) conjectured that they might have been attached to the rear of the division of Prē'. But Breasted himself (loc. cit.) had seen the objection to both these guesses; why should these troops be spoken of as arriving from the land of Amor? The only possible answer, as Meyer, *Geschichte*, II, 1, 462 has seen, is that they were a special 'battle-force' (*skw tpy* 'first battle-force',

---

7.   Breasted, *Ancient Records*, 127, Sect. 298.
8.   Breasted, *Ancient Records*, 190.
9.   'Ramses rückte an der Küste Phoenikiens (Zahi) von und sonderte hier eine Elitetruppe als Vorhut ab, die an der Küste des Amoriterlandes entlang ziehen und durch das Eleutherostal zu ihm stossen sollte; nachher werden sie mit semitischen Namen als *na'aruna*, "junge Mannschaft", bezeichnet'. (E. Meyer, *Geschichte des Altertums*. II/1. *Die Zeit der ägyptischen Grossmacht* [Stuttgart: J.G. Cotta'sche Buchhandlung, 1929], p. 462).

so to be rendered in place of Breasted's 'first rank', see above) that had
pushed up the coast to beyond Tripolis, whence they struck inland by the
important road that crosses the Eleutherus river (Nahr-el-Kebîr) and
leads to Ḥomṣ or else by another a little further south. It is only natural
that Ramesses II, wishing to make the most of his own exploits, should
have given as few details as possible about the force which proved his
salvation.[10]

If Breasted had followed his own first instincts about this passage,
almost a century of confusion about the meaning of this term might
have been avoided, since 'household servants' may come rather close to
the function of the *n'rn* in the account of the Battle of Kadesh.

In his analysis of the appearance of this word in the Onomasticon of
Amenhotep, Gardiner was less inclined to insist on quite such a strongly
technical military definition:

> *N'ryn* 'Ne'ārīn'; no such people or country appears elsewhere in Egyp-
> tian texts, the only similar word being a Semitic one, Hebr. נְעָרִים
> 'youths', employed in the hieroglyphs to designate some sort of troop in
> the Egyptian army, *Wb.* II, 209, 10. However, Sidney Smith comments
> as follows: 'There is a possibility that this is a true geographical name.
> The Assyrians from the ninth century onwards continually mention the
> *Nairi*-land or -lands; these districts were situated along the Taurus,
> between Miliddu (= Malatia) and Lake Wan, and were sometimes sub-
> ject to Urarṭu but not normally. The name does not occur earlier, so we
> may presume that it is a political term that arose owing to the landslide
> of 1200 B.C.[11]

Inevitably, the notion crept into the lexica that the *n-'-rú-na* were a
particular 'type of Egyptian' military troop, 'eine ägyptische Truppen-
gattung; נערים'.[12] The origin of this notion that the term represented
some sort of *Eliteformation* was based on E. Meyer's conclusion that
Ramesses had left the *n-'-rú-na* behind on the Amorite coast.[13] From
this point, by a process of scholars citing other scholars, this view came

10. *AEO*, p. 188*.
11. *AEO*, p. 177*.
12. A. Erman and H. Grapow, *Aegyptisches Handwörterbuch* (Berlin: Verlag
von Reuther & Reichard, 1921), p. 77; M. Burchardt, *Die altkanaanäischen Fremdworte und Eigennamen im Aegyptischen: I: Die kritische Analyse der Schreibung*
(Leipzig: J.C. Hinrichs, 1909), no. 559.
13. Meyer, *Geschichte des Altertums*, pp. 462-63.

to be accepted as 'common knowledge'.[14] In more recent years, the rejection, by Schulman, of the idea that these were *special* forces of some sort has been largely unheeded. Calling attention not only to the Kadesh inscriptions, but also to Papyrus Anastasi I and the inscription of Merneptah at Karnak, Schulman asserts, 'In none of these occurrences does *n'rn* appear to be the name of a special unit or body of troops, or contain any real technical connotation. It was merely an Asiatic word for soldiers, and was so used by the Egyptians.'[15]

Mayer and Mayer-Opificius survey the long history of literature produced in studying this battle report and suggest that, in all of the changing opinions and shifting consensuses, no solution has managed adequately to explain the contradiction between the allegedly decisive victory of Ramesses II and the subsequent weakness of Egyptian policy in Syria.[16] At the heart of their reinterpretation of this ancient account is a re-evaluation of the Egyptian term *n-'-rú-na*, to which task they have produced an excursus.[17]

After a careful survey of the Ugaritic texts (which come, of course, from close to the time and location in which this battle was fought), these authors come to the conclusion that the term *n'r* in the Ras Shamra texts describes[18]

> ...a subordinate function as apprentice, assistant, underling, or servant, whereby it is a question of a free person not a slave. Clearly this is likewise true in the case where a member of this category of persons serves in a military context: thus, for instance, they can possess a bow, but they

---

14. E.g., Stähli, *Knabe*, 48; de Vaux, *Ancient Israel*, I, p. 221; A.F. Rainey, 'The Military Personnel of Ugarit', *JNES* 24 (1965), pp. 17-27; *idem, The Social Structure of Ugarit: A Study of West Semitic Social Stratification during the Late Bronze Age* (The Social Stratification of Ugarit [Waltham, MA, 1963] copyright dissertation Brandeis University, 1962. Xerox copy made in 1975 by University Microfilms, Ann Arbor, MI, 1967); J. Macdonald, 'Status and Role of the Na'ar', *JNES* 35, (July 1976), pp. 147-70; W.F. Albright, 'Mitannian Maryannu, "Chariot-Warrior", and the Canaanite and Egyptian Equivalents', *AfO* 6 (1930–31), pp. 217-21.

15. A.R. Schulman, 'The N'rn at the Battle of Kadesh', *JARCE* 1 (1962), pp. 47-52.

16. Mayer and Mayer-Opificius, 'Schlacht bei Qadeš', pp. 322-33.

17. Mayer and Mayer-Opificius, 'Schlacht bei Qadeš', pp. 354-59.

18. They bracket any close examination of the cognate Hebrew term, since its semantic domain is clearly similar to that of the Ugaritic word.

are situated on a level with guards and overseers. The *n'r* of a *marjanu* is undoubtedly classed with the servants who are responsible for the horses and wagons. However else one may nuance a particular case, there is no way that it entails some sort or another or 'elite'.[19]

With this in mind, the caption (R 11) is interpreted. The reference to *n-'-rú-na* the second time it is used in the caption stands in parallel to an Egyptian word, *śdm-'š*, which unquestionably means servant. Attention is also called to the fact that the combatants engaging the attacking Hittites are wearing long garments, not the short garb usually worn by the typical Egyptian soldier. Furthermore, the line that Gardiner (for instance) has interpreted as '[t]he coming of the Ne'ārīn of Pharaoh from the land of Amor' can equally well be understood as '[t]he *n-'-rú-na* of Pharaoh came from Amor' signalling the ethnicity of this heroic group of servants, rather than announcing the deployment of a special cadre of the troops.[20] All of this evidence leads Mayer and Mayer-Opificius to suggest that these were not 'crack troops', but rather a ragtag troop of 'servants, handymen, stable boys and assorted camp followers' ('Diener, Handlanger, Pferdeburschen und sonstigen *camp followers*') who had been picked up along the way.[21] Furthermore, in contrast to the Egyptian army regulars who had been spoiled by royal patronage, these Amorite 'youths' had done their duty and saved the life of the Pharaoh, which explains the ironic tone in Ramesses' praise of their role in this mission.[22]

19. '…eine untergeordnete Funktion als Lehrling, Gehilfe, Handlanger oder Diener, wobei es sich aber um Frei und nicht um Sklaven (*'bdm*) handelt. Dies gilt offenbar auch dann, wenn sich Angehörige dieses Personenkreises in militärischem Umfeld befinden: So können sie beispielsweise einen Bogen besitzen, sie befinden sich aber auf einer Stufe mit Wächtern und Bütteln. Der *n'r* eines *marjannu* gehört ohne Zweifel zu den Bediensteten, die für die Pflege der Pferde und des Wagens zuständig waren. Wie auch immer im Einzelfall zu nuancieren sein mag, es führt von hier kein Weg zu einer irgendwie gearteten Elite'. Mayer and Mayer-Opificius, 'Schlacht bei Qadeš', p. 355.

20. Gardiner, *Kadesh Inscriptions*, p. 37; Mayer and Mayer-Opificius, 'Schlacht bei Qadeš', pp. 356, 357.

21. Mayer and Mayer-Opificius, 'Schlacht bei Qadeš', p. 356.

22. Mayer and Mayer-Opificius, 'Schlacht bei Qadeš', p. 357.

In light of this understanding of *n-'-rú-na*, Mayer and Mayer-Opificius discuss the remainder of the limited Egyptian evidence about this
unquestionably Semitic term. The Merneptah Inscription bears the
phrase 'all the veterans of the army and the *n-'-rú-na* carried booty'
(KRI IV.7. 11/2). The suggestion here is that the quantity of booty
which Merneptah carried away from Libya was so great as to require
even the army veterans to function as porters alongside the *n-'-rú-na*,
whose task this ordinarily would have been.[23] Papyrus Anastasi I (from
Egypt, end of the thirteenth century) contains a letter, long recognized
as satirical, in which the sender Hori addresses his recipient, the scribe
Amen-em-opet, in an extravagance of mocking praise: 'Thou art sent
on a mission to *Djahan* at the head of the victorious army, to crush
those rebels called *Nearin*.'[24] Apparently, the scribe has been sent to
quell a rebellion of porters and horse grooms, not to meet the advance
of a powerful army. In a similarly scathing vein, Hori suggests that
Amen-em-opet is the general of an army of *n-'-rú-na*: 'O Who-is-it,
thou choice scribe, *mahir* who knows (how to use) his hand, foremost
of the *nearin*, first of the army host...'[25] The scribe is general of an
army of stable boys!

Pritchard quite rightly makes the comparison of this letter to 1 Kgs
20.13-22 in which the battle to free the city of Ahab from the siege
being carried out by Ben-hadad of Aram is begun and accomplished by
the נערים of the district governors, as promised by the prophet. In this
narrative, as in the Kadesh inscriptions, the victory of the inexperienced
servants signals an upset in the usual power dynamics in favor of the
powerless, the underdog. Clearly, the task of the prophet is not to give
strategic advice on which body of skilled fighters should begin the
battle, but rather to suggest that Yahweh has promised victory, even
though the Israelites have only the provincial governors' servants for
troops. The irony in both of these narratives has been overlooked by
commentators, whose assumption seems to be that the fact of victory
must indicate exceptional skill and training of the troops. Thus Montgomery suggests, 'The first noun (Heb. primarily 'youths', Eng. 'young

---

23. Mayer and Mayer-Opificius, 'Schlacht bei Qadeš', p. 358.
24. P. Anast. I, 17, 3/4 (*ANET*, 2nd edn, p. 476).
25. I.e., 'What's-your-name'; P. Anast. I, 26, 9-27, 1 (*ANET*, 2nd edn, p. 478;
Mayer and Mayer-Opificius, 'Schlacht bei Qadeš', p. 358).

men') is a technical military term…' Gray goes somewhat further and postulates 'the usage of *neʻārīm* as a mobile force of professional soldiers…a picked body of striking troops'. DeVries calls them a 'special elite guard' and 'elite corpsmen'.[26] These overreadings suggest the importance of the use of literary analysis of texts to detect the use, by the author, of such rhetorical devices as irony. In any case, the Egyptian evidence *in toto* supports the notion that the *n-ʻ-rú-na* were men who had attached themselves to the Egyptian army as porters, weapons bearers and perhaps even camp cooks, hewers of wood and fetchers of water. It is likely that these were young men who had left their fathers' houses in search of employment or of some other means of making their way as a result of familial poverty and indebtedness perhaps or of being later-born sons.

Ugaritic

Both Cyrus Gordon and Mitchell Dahood suggested the usual nuances of the Hebrew word נער (i.e. youth or servant) for the Ugaritic equivalent when it began to turn up in the texts from Ras Shamra.[27] Aistleitner proposes 'member of a servant class' (*Mitglied e. dienenden Berufsklasse*) and for the feminine 'maidservant' (*Dienerinnen*).[28] Nevertheless, very soon the Egyptian evidence discussed above was called upon to assert Meyer's 'elite corps' (*Eliteformation*) as the definition of the Ugaritic word as well. Rainey's thorough cataloguing of the various military subsets follows this pattern. Because the *nʻrn* were 'able fighting men in Canaan' (for which his evidence includes Erman and Grapow's *WAS*, Gardiner's *AEO* and the Merneptah Stele), he con-

---

26. In support of his analysis, Gray cites de Vaux, who in turn refers back to the Egyptian evidence in addition to 1 Kgs 20, as well as other scriptural occurrences which have been discussed in prior chapters. (Montgomery, *Kings*, p. 323; Gray, *I & II Kings*, pp. 376-77; DeVries, *1 Kings*, p. 249; de Vaux, *Social Institutions*, p. 220).

27. Gordon's *UT* glossary entry 1666 suggests boy, child, unmarried son. He points out that the texts distinguish between *bn* and *nʻr* 'so that *nʻr* has some other meaning such as "servant"…members of a certain guild, perhaps "servitors" or "soldiers"'. For this last possibility he cites the New Egyptian evidence discussed above (*UT*, p. 445; *RSP*, p. 82).

28. J. Aistleitner, *Wörterbuch der ugaritischen Sprache* (Berlin: Akademie Verlag, 1967), p. 208, entry 1808.

cludes that 'the *n'rm* of Ugarit were first-class, experienced fighting-men'.[29] How this correlates with the presence of נערים in the household lists is not clarified.

Certainly the evidence from Ugaritic texts must be used with care for the identification of the נער in ancient Israel, as also the Egyptian texts must be considered indicative but not definitive in interpreting the Ugaritic. The importance of interpreting a word from within the social world in which it is used is especially compelling in the case of a word like נער, which describes an individual's social location, since such words would be particularly dependent on the social features of lan-guage, features that are dependent on the social structure in which they are used.

Still, although without doubt the final decision about the meaning of a word must come from its use by native speakers, the Ugaritic vocabu-lary and social system represent the most closely related antecedents for early Israel. Ugarit is undoubtedly an important contributor to the stock—genetic, linguistic and social—from which ancient Israel drew its roots. The Ugaritic texts come to us, as it were, frozen in time, not having been subjected to the most recent millennia of transmission (and perhaps tendentious editing) that the biblical Hebrew texts have under-gone. Their contribution to the discussion has the potential to be en-lightening, although I will be careful to eliminate any contamination from erroneous reading of Egyptian records as I give an extremely cur-sory examination to those documents from Ras Shamra in which the words appear. Because our examination of these texts will be very brief, the main issue to be resolved in each case will be whether the social location which I have proposed for the נער in biblical Hebrew makes sense for the word's usage in particular instances in cognate languages.

Lists

A number of the texts in Ugaritic that have been discovered consist entirely of lists whose extent and condition of preservation vary widely. Beyond serving an obvious function for some sort of record-keeping, our understanding of the purposes of these lists is somewhat specula-tive. One of the more complete and more thoroughly studied, KTU 4.68, has an Akkadian syllabic colophon on one margin. Unfortunately,

29. Rainey, 'Military Personnel', p. 21.

even that helpful information has not finally answered the question whether each of the listed entities was to *receive* or to *provide* a bow, nor whether the bow itself designates the weapon or the personnel who used it.[30] The uncertainties involved are compounded by the fact that words in a list have a context only slightly more explicit than does a word in isolation. Such words have no syntax, they are neither subject nor object of verbs. The best one can hope to glean from such documents is a sense of semantic domain (what sorts of things are listed together) and perhaps some hierarchical ordering, although whether such ordering is along an axis of importance, chronology, proximity or any other variable is not always immediately apparent. While interesting results have come from research into biblical lists, those lists have not yielded their treasures willingly. Nevertheless, some information can be gathered from the lists in which the word *n'r* is found, which appear to fall into two types: accountings of military personnel and of household members.

Military. Three Ugaritic texts yield *n'rm* in lists of occupations, presumed to be military: KTU 4.126, 4.68 and 4.179. The latter text is clearly a list of occupations, probably all military, with some sort of numerical notation associated with each, although to what end is not entirely clear. The third entry is *n'r mrynm*, '*na'ar* of the Maryannu'. Wright *inter alios*, has proposed the Maryannu as 'chariot warriors', to whom quite likely was attached a servant to do the heavy work of tending stock, chariot and weapons.[31] KTU 4.68 is a list of cities followed,

---

30. In fact, the ideogram for 'bow' is scarcely readable, although probably correct (Ch. Virolleaud, 'Les villes et les corporations du Royaume d'Ugarit', *Syria: Revue d'Art Oriental et d'Archéologie* 21 (1940), pp. 123-51 [137]).

31. Macdonald, who insists that the *n'r* held an 'eminent place', places them as commanders of the Maryannu rather than their servants. In the course of his argument, he himself points out that sons and land grants are both mentioned with respect to the Maryannu, but not the *n'r*. Certainly in Israel, sons and land were two of the things conferring the highest status, clearly undercutting Macdonald's argument here. On land grants, see also Gray. Reviv has more recently published observations on the Maryannu (J. Macdonald, 'The Unique Ugaritic Personnel Text KTU 4.102', *UF* 10 [1978], pp. 161-73; J. Gray, *The Legacy of Canaan: The Ras Shamra Texts and their Relevance to the Old Testament* [VTSup, 5; Leiden: E.J. Brill, 1957], pp. 167-69; Albright, 'Maryannu'; H. Reviv, 'More about the "Maryannu" in Syria and Palestine', in B. Ooled *et al.* (eds.), *Studies in the History of the Jewish People and the Land of Israel*, II Haifa: University of Haifa, 1972]; H. Reviv,

after a clear demarcation, by a list of associations or occupations.[32] After each entry or group of entries is a numerical notation. The right side of the tablet is blank, perhaps for future notations. The first entry in the occupation list is *n'rm*, followed by other terms that seem to be military functions. A marginal note in Akkadian indicates that these groups are to be furnishers or recipients of 'bows'. A similar text is KTU 4.126, which has city names and occupations or associations commingled, although it lacks both the Akkadian colophon and the numeric notations. Some of these entries are grouped together as in KTU 4.68.

Very little can be understood about the relative status of these nouns: the definitions of many of them are not clear, nor has their ranking within Ugarit's social system been demonstrated. The *n'rm* appear as the first entry (KTU 4.68), third entry (KTU 4.179), and twelfth entry (KTU 4.126), although even a *consistent* position in these lists might be difficult to interpret. Across the three lists there appear to be somewhat fluid groupings that seem to bear some relationship to each other. For instance, *ṯnnm, 'šr, n'r mrynm* in 4.179 resembles *mrynm, mrum, 'šrm, ṯnnm* (4.126) and *'šrm, mrum, ṯnnm* (4.68); likewise *nqdm, khnm, qdšm, pslm, mkrm* (4.126) and *nqdm, khnm, qdšm, nsk.ksp, mkrm* (4.68), although the significance of these associative groupings is far from clear. More interesting, perhaps, is the fact that in 4.68 are juxtaposed *n'rm, mdrġlm, kzym* compared to *n'rm, 'bdm, kzym* in 4.126. Since the last term in each of these refers to a horse groom, and clearly *'bdm* are servants or slaves, perhaps these soldiers (which Gray called 'arm-ourers') are either bearers of some sort of heavy weapon or warriors who have need for such support personnel.[33] In any case, the principle of association suggested here is physical labor, not elite status. This is consistent with the idea of men who have left their fathers' houses and signed on in heavy manual service with the fighting troops.

'Some Comments on the Maryannu', *IEJ* 22.4 [1972], pp. 218-28).

32. Principally by analogy to medieval Europe this list has given rise to litera-ture suggesting 'guilds' in ancient Ugarit. The reader is invited to evaluate this evi-dence in, for instance, Macdonald, 'Unique Ugaritic Personnel Text'; Gray, *Legacy of Canaan*, p. 166; Gordon, *Ugaritic Literature*.

33. See the discussions by Gordon, Gray and Macdonald (*UT*, §§19.436, 1535; Macdonald, 'Unique Ugaritic Personnel Text', p. 17; Gray, *The Legacy of Canaan*, p. 169).

Households. The exact purpose for which the household censuses were prepared is also open to a variety of interpretations. One possibility is that these were 'excess' personnel dedicated to the king or to the temple either to provide labor or to be provided for as part of the 'social safety net'.[34] Whether this dedication was the result of piety or the inability of the *paterfamilias* to provide adequately for all family members is not clear. Tax rosters, ration lists or enrollments of captives have all been suggested as the identity of these documents.[35] KTU 4.339 is a list of households belonging to U[]t(?)šb and those belonging to the king, each cited by the name of the householder with various numbers of persons in various relationships to him, in the format PN and his wife, or PN and his wife and his son. The very first person named is Kš(r)n and his wife and his *n'r*. Among the king's personnel are Annmn and his three *n'*[r] (curiously using the singular, if the reconstruction is accurate). KTU 4.367 is a brief text listing royal personnel in which a lacuna has been reconstructed to read 'two sons of Iwrḫzs [n]*'rm*' followed by an entry for 2 individuals (*bnš*) of Iytlm and 20 yoke of oxen. Whether these sons of Iwrḫz are to serve as *n'rm* or perhaps are being turned over to the king after living away from their father's house in service to some other lord is not clear. KTU 4.419 is a very broken text that mentions a wife (l. 3) and 3 wives (l. 6); the fourth line reads 'and 4 *n'r...*', leaving little evidence on which to base any conclusion. KTU 4.360 appears to be a census of several households, making note of which sons in each family are 'able-bodied' or 'workers' (*b'lm*).[36] The family of Yrḫm includes his two sons, workers and three *n'rm* and one daughter.

The most studied of these household texts, KTU 4.102, is comprised of lists of various numbers of particular types of household members, each group said to be 'in the house of PN'. The relationships include *aṯṯ*

34. Macdonald, 'Unique Ugaritic Personnel Text', pp. 171-72, and references cited therein.

35. Indeed the lists of military personnel could also, in some cases, be lists of captives.

36. So Virolleaud (PRU V.80; PRU II.2, 11) in Claude F.-A. Virolleaud, 'Textes en cunéiformes alphabetiques des archives sud, sud-ouest et du petit palais', in *Le palais royal d'Ugarit* (Mission de Ras Shamra; Paris: Imprimerie Nationale, 1965), pp. 105-106; see also Rainey, 'The Social Stratification of Ugarit', p. 97; Contra Stähli, *Knabe*, pp. 49-50.

'wife', *aṭt adrt* 'noble wife', *bn, bt, pǵt, and gzr*.[37] The exact identity of these last two terms is not clearly established. Only one or the other type of wife is mentioned in each 'house', although there may be more than one wife. In those entries in which more than one of the other terms are included (all on the reverse side of the tablet), *pǵt* is mentioned before *gzr*, but *bn* precedes either of them. Two 'houses', one on each side of the tablet, contain *n'rm*: the household of Ilsk(?) has two, following a single wife; that of Sk[] has three noble wives, three *gǵrm*, and five *n'rt*.[38] The only secure conclusion about the word in these texts is that a *n'r* could be a part of a household. The simplest explanation is that these particular individuals were household servants, potentially serving the roles that sons or daughters would ordinarily fill since they appear more frequently when other offspring are lacking.[39] Situations as permanent slave, debt slave, hired servant or 'foster child' are all conceivable, and would dovetail with the evidence from the Hebrew scriptures.

Epistolary and Mythologic Texts

Letters and narratives, of course, hold the promise of providing more context from which to gain clues about the social institution that was indicated by the Ugaritic words *n'r* and *n'rt*. The only extant letter in Ugaritic in which the word *n'r* appears is KTU 2.33, which comes from the Royal Archives. It is a message to the king, using the Lady of Ugarit as intermediary, from one Ewršrm, who is encircled by the enemy and wishes to withdraw to the side of Mount *Amn*. Apparently the king has assigned him a levy of 2000 horses, which he says that he is unable to deliver, owing to the press of the enemy. Although much is unclear about his entreaty, he asserts, 'I will not expose my wife (or) *n'ry* to the face of the enemy' (ll. 28-29). Clearly *n'r* here is a dependent of the

37. On these terms, see J.C. de Moor, *An Anthology of Religious Texts from Ugarit* (Religious Texts Translation Series, 16; Leiden: E.J. Brill, 1987), pp. 76, 95, 96, 108; A. van Selms, *Marriage and Family Life in Ugaritic Literature* (Pretoria Oriental Series; London: Luzac, 1954), pp. 95, 96, 107.

38. As in the Hebrew texts, the feminine form appears far less commonly than the masculine.

39. Stähli has come to nearly this same understanding, at least for KTU 4.108. The story of Aqhat enumerates the duties of a son (which include setting up the 'Ancestor's stela', fixing the roof, and leading his father home when he is drunk, KTU 1.17. I.42-48) and also those of a daughter (fetching water and leading the donkey, KTU 1.17. II.1-5) (Stähli, *Knabe*, p. 49; Parker, *Ugaritic Narrative Poetry*, p. 69).

named individual, one for whom Ewršrm has both affection and responsibility. A 'foster son' employed in the household or in some other way
functioning in the roles of a son would obviously be compatible with
this letter.

In the mythologic texts, we find $n'r$ as both noun and verb exclusively in texts relating to 'antidotes' or healing, either from snake
venom or from drunkenness. KTU 1.100 is a mythological/apotropaic
text in three sections: an account of 12 incantations (each addressed by
Špš to a different god) against snake bite, a mythical account of how
Ḥrn neutralized the venom of the snake, and a ritual involving a bride
and groom and the magic powers of a snake. Line 65, which reads
$'r'rm.yn'rnh$ is rendered by most translators as a verbal form meaning
'to shake', although Virolleaud indicates that the verb fails to present
'aucun sens acceptable' ('any acceptable meaning').[40] Tsevat, likewise,
while identifying the text as mythological and not merely an
incantation, admits difficulty with this line.[41] Assuredly, however, this
is part of a ritual designed to bring healing.

In the account of the Feast of El (KTU 1.114), the first side of the
tablet contains the narrative account of the banquet, while the reverse,
which unfortunately is not in good condition, explains the prescription
needed to cure the hangover that Ilu suffers as a result of drinking to
excess at his feast.[42] The third line of the reverse (which is l. 28), reads
$kmtrpa.hn.n'r$, which Virolleaud read as 'Voici l'enfant' ('Here is the
child'), leaving open the meaning of the first word.[43] More recently
Pope proposed that this form is the particle k- with enclitic emphatic
$-m\bar{a}$, followed by a verb form that involves healing. He suggests that $n'r$

40. J. Nougayrol, *et al.* (eds.), *Ugaritica*. V/2. *Les nouveaux textes mythologiques et liturgiques de Ras Shamra* (Mission Ras Shamra, 16; Paris: Imprimerie
Nationale, 1968), p. 571. For additional background on this text, see de Moor, *Religious Texts from Ugarit*, pp. 146-56.

41. M. Tsevat, 'Der Schlangentext von Ugarit: UT 607-KTU 1.100-Ug V,
564ff.-RS 24.244', *UF* 11 (1979), pp. 759-78 [765].

42. On the *mrzḥ (marzaḥ* feast), see: J.L. McLaughlin, 'The Marzaḥ at Ugarit:
A Textual and Contextual Study', *UF* 23 (1991), pp. 265-81. For background on
this text, see M.H. Pope, 'A Divine Banquet at Ugarit', in M.S. Smith (ed.), *Probative Pontificating in Ugaritic and Biblical Literature* (Munster: Ugarit-Verlag,
1994), pp. 175-77; de Moor, *Religious Texts from Ugarit*, pp.134-37.

43. Nougayrol *et al.* (eds.), *Ugaritica*, V, p. 551.

might refer to El's malady or to his recovery from it.[44] Margalit reads, 'If you would cure (him?), here is the remedy'.[45] Dietrich, Loretz and Sanmartín render the phrase, 'Wenn du heilst, das ist die Mischung' ('If you would heal, this is the mixture'), assuming a relationship to the root נער II, 'to shake'.[46] The translation of ll. 2-5 (27-30) by de Moor is perhaps the most compelling: 'And with these they restored the strength of his hands. When they had healed (him), look, he awoke. What should one put on the brow of the unconscious patient?' What follows is an herbal prescription with instructions for its application.[47]

Inevitably, these suggestions call to mind Job 33.25 and 2 Kgs 5.14, both of which contain the Hebrew word נער and which involve healing Job and Naaman, respectively, of skin diseases. These have been understood as returning to the smooth skin of a child, but these Ugaritic texts leave open the possibility that a verb, not a noun, should be understood in these texts. The implications of all this for the present study of נער in Hebrew are obvious. If the word forms from the root *n'r* in these texts are, in the end, determined to be verbs, they are probably not relevant to the task at hand. If they are nouns, Virolleaud's suggestion, 'Behold, the *n'r*' is consistent with what has been demonstrated in the Hebrew text, if the word is understood to be within the semantic domain of service personnel. That a servant should be found at hand, presumably bearing the prescribed materials, would be a reasonable understanding of this line in view of the Hebrew. What is less appropriate is to understand this to refer to an infant or even a child, in light of the fact that the overwhelming impression of the ages of נערים in Hebrew *and* of *n'rm* in Ugaritic are young men of at least sufficient age to serve in military and domestic service. Very young נערים are quite special cases, often designated by the adjective קטן, as seen in Chapter 7.

Related issues are raised by KTU 1.107, another mythological/apotropaic text, also involving the god Špš and snake venom, in this instance used to banish the clouds that cover the earth. The badly damaged text reads, beginning at l. 37:

44. Pope, *Ugaritic and Biblical Literature*, pp. 175-76.

45. B. Margalit, 'The Ugaritic Feat of the Drunken Gods: Another Look at RS 24.258 (KTU 1.114)', *Maarav* 2.1 (1979–80), pp. 65-120 [72].

46. M. Dietrich, O. Loretz and J. Sanmartín, 'Der Stichometrische Aufbau von RS 24.258 (= UG 5, s. 545 NR. 1)', *UF* 7 (1975), pp. 109-14 [110, 113].

47. De Moor, *Religious Texts from Ugarit*, p. 136.

ġr.šrġzz.ybky.km.n'r
[wydm'.k]m..ṣġr.špš.bšmm.tqru
]plt.y[ ].md.nplt.bṣr
].wtpky.k[m.]n'r.tdm'.km

The translation seems obvious: 'He [or emended to you] cried like a
נער', which is understood by most translators to be 'like a child', since
the word appears to be in a parallel construction with ṣġr, a word meaning 'small'. The 'crier' is assumed to be *Ql-bl*, son of *Špš*, but the progress of the narrative is difficult to follow because of the numerous
lacunae. Clearly, this text is concerned with the same motifs as those
discussed above. Once again, the question arises of whether to consider
this a child. Given the cultic context, we may think here of an individual who becomes a *n'r* by being devoted by his parents to the service of
a deity or a temple, as Samuel was. In such a case, he may have been of
far more tender years than those נערים who were sent from their fathers'
houses to serve military roles or even domestic labor. Such separation
from family would, no doubt, produce weeping from a young child.
Indeed, a related understanding has been suggested for the crux in
1 Sam. 1.24: in place of the rather pointless translation, 'And the lad
was young' (or worse, 'and the lad was a lad', or indeed even the only
slightly more informative 'and the נער began his service as a נער')
Frolov has suggested that young Samuel roared or growled, as a sign of
God's spirit being with him.[48] In any case, this incantation text has too
many unanswered questions to yield a definitive answer, but it is at
least potentially compatible with the understanding of the social location of the נער as derived from the biblical materials.

Foodstuffs or Textiles
A few economic texts mention *n'r* in very fragmentary contexts that
suggest quantities of flour or of tow (perhaps as fuel for the fire) or even
of textiles. In every case, the substance appears in connection with a
word *dd*, which appears to indicate a quantity or even a container. These
texts (KTU 4.60; 4.362; 4.402; 4.426; 4.663; 4.789) would seem to
suggest a material 'shaken out' or 'beaten out', and are thus likely to be
from an entirely different semantic field than is biblical נער.[49]

---

48. Indeed, a variant of this idea was already suggested by Althann (R. Althann,
'Some Texts in 1 Samuel', pp. 27-28; see also S. Frolov and V. Orel, 'Was the Lad
a Lad?', pp. 5-7).
49. Except perhaps for Judg. 16.6 and Isa. 1.31.

Personal Names

Two texts, KTU 4.12 and KTU 3.7, appear to use *n'r* as part of a personal name. The former text is a list of persons designated as *bn* X. The final entry in the list is one *bn n'r!(?) il*. Perhaps this represents a theophoric name, designating 'servant of Ilu' as the patronym. An intriguing possibility suggests itself. Perhaps the young person who became a *n'r* by being dedicated by his parents to a deity or temple took on such an appelation as his name. The second text contains a list of individuals for whom one *Mṣry* 'vouches'. The reverse side of the tablet appears to continue the list, and the final entry, at what is clearly the bottom of the tablet, is *n'r.b.ulm*, N'r from Ulm, or perhaps better *a n'r* from Ulm. We can only speculate, but clearly these names are not inconsistent with the notion of service developed for Hebrew נער.

Seals, Ostraca and Other Inscriptions

A number of seals as well as impressions of seals have been found by archaeologists in the Levant that are inscribed with a personal name followed by נער or עבד and then another personal name.[50] At least one Ammonite and one Phoenician seal bearing the same inscription have been found as well.[51] Obviously, the person who bore such a seal used it in service to the other named individual, although the exact rank or function of such persons is not specified. The discovery of these *na'ar* and *'ebed* seals in conjunction with *lmlk* jar handles suggests that these servants bore responsibility for managing agricultural estates and vineyards, probably seeing to the distribution of commodities for trade, collecting commodities from those who actually worked the land, and paying taxes.[52] That a few servants were in positions as stewards that required them to possess such a seal should not be taken as evidence

50. N. Avigad, 'New Light on the Na'ar Seals', in F.M. Cross, W.E. Lemke and P.D. Miller, Jr (eds.), *Magnalia Dei: The Mighty Acts of God: Essays on the Bible and Archaeology in Memory of G. Ernest Wright* (Garden City, NY: Doubleday, 1976), pp. 294-300.

51. J. Naveh, 'Unpublished Phoenician Inscriptions from Palestine', *IEJ* 37 (1987), pp. 25-30; W.E. Aufrecht, *A Corpus of Ammonite Inscriptions* (Ancient Near Eastern Texts Studies, 4; Lewiston, NY: Edwin Mellen Press, 1989), pp. 137-38.

52. D. Ussishkin, 'Royal Judean Storage Jars and Private Seal Impressions', *BASOR* 223 (1976), pp. 1-14.

that all members of either group (נער or עבד) had positions of custodianship. Ordinary servants, who did not possess such tangible evidence of their position, have simply vanished without a trace. We will never know what fraction of נערים had managerial responsibilities, but they were probably the exception.[53]

Although those scholars who have been influenced by the traditional reading of the Egyptian evidence have asserted that the נער was of 'high rank', especially compared to the position of an עבד, Avigad has suggested quite the opposite: "*'Ebed* is known to have been the title of high-ranking officers of the royal court, whereas the title *na'ar* is never mentioned in the texts among the highest officials of the realm.'[54] Obviously, without an examination of the values of the society and the attributes that bestowed status, the question of 'highness' cannot be finally decided. Although their attendance on powerful people may have given them a great deal of influence and indirect power, both of these categories of workers were in service to others, engaged in building up the 'house' of another instead of their own. We should be cautious in exporting our own values to ancient Israel. While we may see an administrative position on the behalf of a royal or noble household ('inside work, no heavy lifting') as a superior status, particularly compared with agricultural labor, for instance, the individuals involved might have preferred to be working a piece of land of their own, siring sons of their own, gaining respect and authority in the village of their fathers.

Albright's original analysis of the first of the seal impressions that bore the inscription *l'lyqm n'r ywkn* asserted that this was the stamp of Eliakim, Steward of Jehoiachin, king of Judah, which placed it in the time frame 597–586 BCE.[55] This decision caused some difficulties in establishing the chronology of strata immediately above and below the level in which the impression was found, and more recently scholars have proposed the destruction layers of Sennacherib's campaign, 701 BCE.[56] This has not only solved problems for archaeologists, but it accords well with the time frame for the provenance of the Hebrew

53. Avigad, 'Na'ar Seals', p. 295.
54. Avigad, 'Na'ar Seals', p. 294.
55. W.F. Albright, 'The Seal of Eliakim and the Latest Preexilic History of Judah, with Some Observations on Ezekiel', *JBL* 51 (1932), pp. 77-106.
56. Y. Garfinkel, 'The Eliakim Na'ar Yokan Seal Impressions: Sixty Years of Confusion in Biblical Archaeology Research', *BA* 53 (1990), pp. 74-79.

texts, or at least the source materials for those narratives, in which נער
appears with the greatest frequency.

Phoenician, Aramaic, Akkadian and Greek Evidence

Phoenician

In addition to the seals and seal impressions mentioned above, two
other inscriptions, which come from Phoenician sources, employ a cognate of Hebrew נער. The first, the so-called Kilamuwa Inscription, is a
palace dedication from the second half of the ninth century BCE, found
in northwest Syria (KAI 24).[57] In it, King Kilamuwa recounts the suc-
cesses of his reign. On the second side, he says,

> Him who had never seen the face of a sheep, I made the possessor of a
> flock. Him who had never seen the face of an ox, I made the possessor of
> a herd of cattle and a possessor of silver and a possessor of gold. He who
> had not (even) seen linen since his youth, in my days he was covered
> with byssus.[58]

The word appears as למנערי. Since the other situations that Kilamuwa
lists indicate poverty and lack of status rather than ages or stages of life,
an understanding of this phrase as 'since his servanthood' or '*na'ar*ship'
or perhaps 'since his departure from his father's house' is quite tenable.

The other text (KAI 37) is a marble tablet coming from Cyprus
(Kition), and dating from the fourth–third century BCE.[59] For background on Cyprus as a Phoenician city, see the recent article by Marguerite Yon.[60] The text is a listing of obligations due to the priests of
the Temple of Astarte.[61] The form of the word (A.8, 12 and B.11) is
לנערם קפא followed by a number, so, for instance 'for the two servants,

---

57. H. Donner and W. Röllig, *Kanaanäische und aramäische Inschriften*, I
(Wiesbaden: Otto Harrassowitz, 1962), pp. 4-5; *idem, Kanaanäische und aramäische Inschriften*, II (Wiesbaden: Otto Harrassowitz, 1964), pp. 30-34.

58. *ANET*, pp. 654-55.

59. Donner and Röllig, *Kanaanäische und aramäische Inschriften*, I, p. 8; *idem,
Kanaanäische und aramäische Inschriften*, II, pp. 54-55.

60. M. Yon, 'Kition in the Tenth to Fourth Centuries B.C.' (trans. W.A.P.
Childs), *BASOR* 308 (1997), pp. 1-17.

61. M. Delcor, 'Le personnel du Temple d'Astarté à Kition d'après une tablette
Phonicienne (CIS 86 A et B)', *UF* 11 (1979), pp. 147-64.

two *qp'* , indicating some measure of which the identity is uncertain.[62] The resemblances between this text and the various personnel lists from Ugarit are obvious, and suggest the same sort of social location, namely, a נער dedicated to the temple.

Aramaic

From the Aramaic-speaking Jewish garrison stationed at Elephantine in Egypt has come a collection of papyri of various sorts from the fifth century BCE.[63] One of those is the *Wisdom of Ahiqar*, 11 sheets of papyrus whose first 78 lines are devoted to telling the story of Ahiqar, while the remainder preserve his proverbs or teachings. Long before this copy of *Ahiqar* in Aramaic was discovered, versions of the story and proverbs were known in Syriac, Armenian and Greek, among other languages, as well as references to it in the book of Tobit.[64] The first line of the aphorisms contains the word נער, although its meaning is far from clear. The Aramaic of the first two lines, and Cowley's translation of most of Column vi are:

Col. vi, lines 79-80:

מ[זה] חסין הו מן חמר נער בנ[ג]תא

ברא זי יתאלף ויתסר ויתשים ארחא ברגלוהי...

Col. vi, lines 79-94

What is stronger than wine foaming in the press? The son who is trained and taught, and on whose feet the fetter is put shall prosper. Withhold not thy son from the rod, if thou canst not keep him from wickedness. If I smite thee, my son,[65] thou wilt not die, and if I

---

62. R.S. Tomback, *A Comparative Semitic Lexicon of the Phoenician and Punic Languages* (SBLDS, 32; Missoula, MT: Scholars Press, 1978), p. 217.

63. For background on this Jewish community, see B. Porten, *Archives from Elephantine: The Life of an Ancient Jewish Military Colony* (Berkeley: University of California Press, 1960).

64. For an excellent (and brief) survey of the various recensions of Ahiqar and their relationships to each other, see J.C. Greenfield, 'The Wisdom of Ahiqar', in J.P. Day, R.P. Gordon and H.G.M. Williamson (eds.), *Wisdom in Ancient Israel: Essays in Honour of J.A. Emerton* (Cambridge: Cambridge University Press, 1995), pp. 43-52.

65. 'My son' here probably refers to the student for whom Ahiqar's instruction is offerred, not necessarily biological offspring. Day points out that the Egyptian wisdom tradition never uses 'my son' in instructions, while the book of Proverbs makes liberal use of the expression, as do Babylonian and Sumerian wisdom texts, along with Ahiqar. This, he suggests, is evidence of the fact that Israel's wisdom

leave (thee) to thine own heart thou wilt not live. A blow for a slave, rebuke for a maid, and for all thy servants discipline. A man who buys a licentious slave (or) a thievish maid brings anxiety into his house, and disgraces the name of his father and his offspring with the reputation of his wantonness. [Lines 86-91 deal in animal analogies.] Two things are a merit (?), and of three there is pleasure to Shamash: one who drinks wine and gives it (to others), one who restrains (?) wisdom...and he hears a word and does not reveal (it). Behold, this is precious before Shamash. But one who drinks wine and does not give it to others and his wisdom goes astray...who sees?... Thou hast placed...the peoples their wisdom the gods... (l 94)'[66]

Among the other suggestions for translations of these two words are 'braying ass', or 'fermenting wine', which presumably would froth or 'shake' in some manner.[67] None of the previous suggestions has won over the field, and they are obviously not germane to the discussion of נער as some sort of personage. Clearly, however, this entire section of sayings is concerned with slaves or servants of one sort or another, for which a variety of Aramaic terms are employed. Furthermore, the column ends by returning to the topic of drinking wine. In light of those facts, I would like to propose the translation,

What is stronger than an ass? A נער at the winepress.

This translation stays within the semantic domain of 'servanthood', alludes to the tendency of נערים to be troublesome,[68] and forms a loose *inclusio* with the final discussion of wine-drinking. Such a translation would dovetail nicely with the understanding of נער developed from biblical narratives. The other proposals do not undermine that understanding, they simply make this text irrelevant.

The word נער does not occur in biblical Aramaic. The Targumim avoid the use of נער and נערה, preferring instead עולימא and עולימתא. The Talmudim and Midrashim have moved well beyond the time frame

tradition is more influenced by Semitic than by Egyptian conventions (J. Day, 'Foreign Semitic Influence on the Wisdom of Israel', in Day, Gordon and Williamson (eds.), *Wisdom in Ancient Israel*, pp. 55-70 [66]).

66. A. Cowley, *Aramaic Papyri of the Fifth Century B.C.: Edited, with Translation and Notes* (Oxford: Clarendon Press, 1923), pp. 222-23.

67. Cowley, *Aramaic Papyri*, p. 233; J. Hoftijzer and K. Jongeling, *Dictionary of the North-West Semitic Inscriptions with Appendices by R.C. Steiner, A. Mosak Moshavi and B. Porten*. II. *M–T* (Leiden: E.J. Brill, 1995), p. 739.

68. See Chapter 6 above.

of the narratives in which the word appears in Hebrew, and the Rabbis developed a fairly specialized notion of the meanings of the words, but those discussions clearly reflect a later attempt to recover the nuance of the word and will not be pursued in the current discussion.[69]

Akkadian

Because of the failure of Akkadian to retain proto-Semitic *'ayin*, establishing cognates in the Akkadian literature is inconclusive, and so will be treated only briefly here. The likely candidate as a parallel to Hebrew נער is Akkadian *nâru*, a loan word meaning 'singer', which of course refers to temple musicians.[70] This is a far more specialized usage than the Hebrew, but several intriguing texts suggest that the social location of these singers may be similar to that of the נערים and נערות in Israel, that is, dependent servants, vulnerable, perhaps captives. For instance:

> 'I took as booty his courtiers' LU.NAR.MEŠ SAL.NAR MEŠ (OIP 2 52.32).
> 'I removed male and female musicians and counted them as spoil' (Asb. 70 vi 28).
> 'He will give the price of the slave girl and of the musician to PN' (HSS 19 114.11).[71]

While these are tantalizing, the connection to the Hebrew is too inconclusive to sustain the weight of any conclusions based on them.

Greek

The LXX uses several words in its translation of נער and נערה with no obvious pattern, thus: παῖς, παιδίσκος, παιδίσκη, παιδάριον, νεανίσκος, παρθένος.[72] These exhibit the same range of meanings as the

---

69. Bamberger, for example, cites evidence that the rabbis classified a girl as *na'arah* from the age of 12 years and one day (if by then she had pubic hair) until six months later, when she became a *bogereth*. That this construct has no bearing on the biblical texts needs no elaboration! (B.J. Bamberger, 'Qetanah, Na'arah, Bogereth', *HUCA* 32 [1961], pp. 281-94).

70. Gelb suggests that this is a Semitic loan word; *CAD* indicates it was borrowed from Sumerian (I.J. Gelb, *Glossary of Old Akkadian* [Materials for the Assyrian Dictionary; Chicago: University of Chicago Press, 1957], p. 193).

71. J.A. Brinkman (ed,), *The Assyrian Dictionary of the Oriental Institute of the University of Chicago*. XI. *N, Part 1* (Chicago: University of Chicago Press, 1980), pp. 376-78.

72. Also represented, with somewhat less frequency: νέος, νήπιος, κοράσιον, θεράπων, δοῦλος, διάκονος.

English words by which the Hebrew is translated. They cover, in some instances, both slave and free, child and young adult. Apparently, by the Hellenistic period, the particular connotations of the Hebrew words had been lost and only a general sense remained. Thus the Hebrew term was translated opportunistically and eclectically. This is certainly consistent with our finding that, in later biblical texts, the words no longer functioned to indicate such a specific social location as in the premonarchic and early monarchic narratives.

The Futile Search for a Root Meaning

The basic methodology of this study has been to examine the use of the Hebrew words נער and נערה in the context of narratives, which is the only appropriate approach for determining the social location that the words denoted. Language is, after all, a product of the social world in which it is used, and as such is totally dependent on the understanding of native speakers to give it meaning. No field more than biblical studies has suffered from the excesses of those who seek to distill pure meaning, untainted by context, by endeavoring to discover the oldest usage of words and to give them an etymology. The dangers of this are made clear by Barr:

> The main point is that the etymology of a word is not a statement about its meaning but about its history; it is only as a historical statement that it can be responsibly asserted, and it is quite wrong to suppose that the etymology of a word is necessarily a guide either to its 'proper' meaning in a later period or to its actual meaning in that period.[73]

Therefore, only with an understanding that an etymology merely tells us an *earlier* meaning, which cannot be privileged as the supposed *real* meaning, can we speculate about a vector along which the word has traveled through time, arriving at the period under consideration with a particular denotation. Nevertheless, the temptation to such speculation is too great to resist, although any hypothesis must remain unproven.

Since both Hebrew and Ugaritic have other perfectly functional ways to express the concept 'young', I will reject at the outset the notion that the 'root' meaning of נער is 'young'.[74] The vast majority of the persons referred to as *n'rm* in both languages are adults. Biblical נערים are very

---

73. Barr, *The Semantics of Biblical Language*, p. 109.
74. Hebrew צעיר, קטן, Ugaritic *ṣġr*, for instance.

rarely children, and what we view as 'early adulthood' scarcely seems 'young' in a world where hard work and marriage started early and where life was very likely to be over by the age of 40.[75] With that in view, a majority of our נערים were probably middle-aged! It seems that the direction of semantic shift over time moved *toward* a connotation of youthfulness, not the other way around.

The proposed etymologies that rely on some connection to the braying of a donkey and the breaking voice of an adolescent male are simply too strained for further consideration. Buxdorf long ago proposed that the 'root' meaning of נער was '*puer, puerulus, infans*', because the child is '*excusus ex utero materno*', and he thus imagined the word to be derived from *n'r* II, 'to shake'.[76] This creative image lacks credibility, since the נערים were almost never babies or small boys (and virtually never spoken of at the *moment* in which they were 'shaken' from their mothers' wombs). Nevertheless the word, as found in the narratives of early Israel, does seem to indicate an individual who has been 'shaken from the nest' as it were, stripped from his father's house. Unless a great many new and unexpected documents are discovered and deciphered, this fanciful reconstruction comes as near to a root or an etymology as I intend to go.

75. Stager, 'Archaeology of the Family', pp. 18-21; Carney, *The Shape of the Past*, p. 88.
76. *ThWAT*, V, p. 508.

Chapter 9

CONCLUSIONS

Social Location of the נער and נערה in Ancient Israel

Power, Status, Role

After examining so many biblical texts, what have we discovered about
the meaning of the Hebrew words נער and נערה? Consistently, the individuals so named in pre-exilic prose narratives are in some way sepa-
rated from the בית אב into which they had been born. Most often, they
are attached to another בית, the house of their master, and they perform
service of a variety of types. Meyers observes that 'military captives,
transients (sojourners), and supplementary workers, indentured from
other families may also have been included in the compound family'.[1]
This is a good description of the sorts of individuals who might find
themselves as נערים. Sometimes the 'household' to which they were
attached and in which they served was a shrine or temple or military
encampment. In any case, the head of the house or camp served as their
patron and surrogate father.

Many of the נערים were unremarkable, performing the most mundane
(and sometimes arduous) of tasks. A few were in intimate attendance on
powerful persons in the stories and were able to exercise considerable
influence. Influence, however, is only indirect power, and as such is
'feminized'. It is the sort of power that women were able to exercise,
and therefore less valued, less honorable than direct power, which is a
masculine value. In addition, this power was generally the power to
accomplish the master's goals, not one's own. A נער might be in a
position of considerable responsibility, but it was responsibility to build
up the house of his master, not of himself or of his own father. With
only one exception, men whose status was as נער did not own land, did

---

1.   Meyers, 'The Family in Early Israel', p. 17.

not marry, did not have sons. Their labors did not advance their own honor, but the honor of their masters. Thus we found that only in terms of our own contemporary values could we consider the נערים to hold 'high positions' or to be of 'high status'

This description of the נער which we derived from pre-exilic prose texts was also applicable to the use of the designation in postexilic prose writings as well, for the most part, although the frequency of use in later sources diminished substantially. In poetic sources, these words gradually lost this precise nuance and took on a more generalized sense of 'youth'.

Becoming a נער

For the נערים who function as servants, the biblical texts almost never provide direct information about the circumstances that led individuals to leave the 'family farm' and attach themselves to other households. In a few cases capture is specified or alluded to. In most cases, economic circumstances probably caused individuals to be hired out, indentured or sold, and mounting adversity probably often led from the temporary forms of service to the more permanent types of servitude. Our evidence for these institutions comes principally from the prophets and the law codes, however, and its exact relationship to the נער must be by implication only. Probably the נער was at least nominally a free citizen.

Much of the confusion that has arisen about the meaning of נער and נערה has come from those texts in which persons are not functioning as servants and are sometimes not physically away from home. We have seen that these are נערים for whom the tie to the בית אב, the bond to the father, has been severed by extraordinary circumstances. Even while physically 'at home' they have become disembedded from the household, seen as a protective and controling sphere.

Other Words in the Same Semantic Domain

The relationship of נער and נערה to other Hebrew words for disadvantaged persons must await studies that determine, as precisely as the evidence will allow, the social locations for those terms. Nevertheless a few preliminary observations can be made. Occasionally, a נער is also called עבד, but the latter were probably permanent slaves. Analysis of servitude has been complicated by the fact that persons seeking to ingratiate themselves with those more powerful than themselves (that is seeking patronage) refer to themselves as עבדך or שפחך. The widow

(אלמנה) and the נער or נערה seem to occupy similar social locations, with dislocation striking the female characters even more harshly than the males. There is not sufficient overlap in the texts to say much about the relationship of נער to גר, although possibly the גר is one who finds himself outside the bounds of his ethnic group or nation for reasons similar to the ones which cast the נער outside the bounds of the household.

How then shall we translate נער? No single English word seems to capture the implications of the social location of the נער. Servant, fledgling, outcast, apprentice, fosterling—each capture a portion of the sense of the word. In anthropological language 'client' is perhaps the most accurate term, but the associations of that word with modern professions makes it inappropriate in translating נער in the stories in which the נערים appear.[2]

Were the נערים the *'apiru?*

David's followers were at times called נערים, and they also fit the model of 'social banditry' associated with the term *'apiru* in the Amarna letters. The question must then be asked whether the נערים and the *'apiru* represent the same sociological phenomenon. The debates over this term have been extensive and vigorous, and this is not the time to enter into an extended analysis of the El Amarna evidence. Nevertheless, a few observations can be made based on what is generally agreed about the *'apiru*. The controversy over whether it represents an ethnic designation has no bearing on how it might relate to Hebrew נערים: most of our characters have been Israelite, although individuals of a few other ethnic groups are also called נערים. The social location of the *'apiru* is generally one of marginalization, living in groups at the fringes of settled communities by raiding or by hiring out as mercenaries. In this respect, very few of the נערים could be categorized with the *'apiru*. Despite the easy identification with the individuals who were gathered around David, most נערים are not found in 'bands' and do not live by 'social banditry.' Most are attached, individually or in small numbers, to settled households. Although thought to be 'troublesome',

---

2. Paula Hiebert translates גר by the word 'client', which is wonderfully apt, although it would be appropriate in most cases to add that a גר is a 'client in search of a patron', whereas a נער is a client who has already established such a relationship (Hiebert, ' "Whence Shall Help Come to Me?", p. 126.)

they are not presented in the narratives as living 'outside the law'. That having been said, however, the clear possibility existed for movement between one status and the other in any time and place in which both groups coexisted. Both groups had limited prospects within the existing social order. A נער who lost his patron (or was unable to find one) might well have joined a band of *'apiru*. One of the *'apiru* might have left the band for a position of service in a household or military camp. Beyond this sort of fluidity, no identification can be securely made between the two groups.[3]

Implications

The most apparent implication of these findings about the social location of the נער and נערה in ancient Israel is that understanding their social location will allow us to better understand the social world of the biblical texts in general, and the realities of the narratives in which the word is found in particular. The reader is left to explore the extent of that implication, but two specific cases will be mentioned briefly.

The text of Proverbs (22.15; 23.13; 29.15) suggests (or so we have long understood), 'Spare the rod, spoil the child'. This has been interpreted as a biblical mandate for spanking children. Understanding that these verses refer not to children but to household servants of adult years may come as a great surprise to some (and a great relief to others!).

A more serious point of contact with the social location of the נער comes from Luke's parable of the Prodigal Son. In a recent article, Harrill has pointed out that the prodigal has been forced, by squandering his resources, to hire himself out as 'dependent labor', submitting to an institution called in Greek *paramonē*, which shares many similarities

---

3. For overviews of this phenomenon, see: Chaney, 'Ancient Palestinian Peasant Movements', esp. pp. 72-83; A.F. Rainey, 'Unruly Elements in Late Bronze Canaanite Society', in D.P. Wright, D.N. Freedman and A. Hurvitz (eds.), *Pomegranates and Golden Bells: Studies in Biblical, Jewish, and Near Eastern Ritual, Law, and Literature in Honor of Jacob Milgrom* (Winona Lake, IN: Eisenbrauns, 1995) pp. 481-96; R.A. Horsley, 'Àpiru and Cossacks: A Comparative Analysis of Social Form and Historical Role', in Jacob Neusner *et al.* (eds.), *Religion, Literature, and Society in Ancient Israel, Formative Christianity and Judiasm* (New Perspectives on Ancient Judaism, 2; Lanham, MD, University Press of America, 1987), pp. 3-26.

with the social location of the נער.[4] Our study of the נער can deepen our understanding of this parable, and further study of this first-century indentured status can suggest more about the social location of the Hebrew נער. In this way, we can increase our understanding of the realities of life for 'second-class citizens' of the worlds of both the First and the Second Testaments.

4.   J.A. Harrill, 'The Indentured Labor of the Prodigal Son (Luke 15.15)', *JBL* 115 (1996), pp. 714-17.

APPENDIX

Named נערים

Abijah 1 Kgs 14.3, 17
Abishag 1 Kgs 1.2-4
Absalom 2 Sam. 13.32; 14.21; 18.5,
    12, 29, 32

Benjamin Gen. 43.8; 44.22, 30, 31,
    32, 33, 34

David 1 Sam. 17.33, 42, 55, 58
    (16.11)

Ephraim and Manesseh Gen. 48.16
Esther

Gehazi 2 Kgs 4.12, 22, 24, 25, 38;
    5.20, 22, 23; 6.15, 17; 8.4 (2 Kgs
    9.4?)

Hadad 1 Kgs 11.17

Ichabod 1 Sam. 4.21
Isaac Gen. 22.12
Ishmael Gen. 21.12, 17, 18, 19, 20

Jacob and Esau Gen. 25.27
Jeremiah Jer. 1.6, 7
Jeroboam 1 Kgs 11.28; 2 Chron.13.7
Jether Judg. 8.20
Joseph Gen. 37.2; 41.12
Joshua Exod. 33.11
Josiah 2 Chron. 34.3

Moses Exod. 2.6

Purah Judg. 7.10, 11

Ruth

Samson Judg. 13.5, 7, 8, 12, 25
Samuel 1 Sam. 1.22, 24, 25, 27; 2.11,
    18, 21, 26; 3.1, 8
Shechem Gen. 34.19
Solomon 1 Kgs 3.7; 1 Chron. 22.5;
    29.1

Zadok 1 Chron. 12.28
Zechariah Zech. 2.8
Ziba 2 Sam. 9.9; 16.1, 2; 19.18

BIBLIOGRAPHY

Aistleitner, Joseph, *Wörterbuch der Ugaritischen Sprache* (Wörterbuch; Berlin: Akademie Verlag, 1967).

Albright, William F., 'Mitannian Maryannu, "Chariot-Warrior", and the Canaanite and Egyptian Equivalents', *AfO* 6 (Spring 1930–31), pp. 217-21.

—'The Seal of Eliakim and the Latest Preexilic History of Judah, with Some Observations on Ezekiel', *JBL* 51 (1932), pp. 77-106.

Alter, Robert, *The Art of Biblical Narrative* (New York: Basic Books, 1981).

Althann, Robert, 'Northwest Semitic Notes on Some Texts in 1 Samuel', *JNSL* 12 (1984), pp. 27-34.

Andersen, Francis I., and David Noel Freedman, *Amos: A New Translation with Introduction and Commentary* (AB, 24A; New York: Doubleday, 1989).

—*Hosea: A New Translation with Introduction and Commentary* (AB, 24; Garden City, NY: Doubleday, 1980).

Anderson, A.A., *2 Samuel* (ed. David A. Hubbard and Glenn W. Barker; WBC; Dallas: Word Books, 1989).

Aufrecht, Walter E., *A Corpus of Ammonite Inscriptions* (Ancient Near Eastern Texts and Studies, 4; Lewiston: Edwin Mellen Press, 1989).

Avigad, Nachman, 'New Light on the Na'Ar Seals', in Frank Moore Cross, Werner E. Lemke and Patrick D. Miller, Jr (eds.), *Magnalia Dei: The Mighty Acts of God: Essays on the Bible and Archaeology in Memory of G. Ernest Wright* (Garden City, NY: Doubleday, 1976), pp. 294-300.

Baltzer, Klaus, 'Liberation from Debt Slavery After the Exile in Second Isaiah and Nehemiah', in Miller, Jr, Hanson and McBride (eds.), *Ancient Israelite Religion*, pp. 477-84.

Bamberger, B.J., 'Qetanah, Na'arah, Bogareth', *HUCA* 32 (1961), pp. 281-94.

Barr, James, *The Semantics of Biblical Language* (Oxford: Oxford University Press, 1961).

Barrick, W. Boyd, 'The Word BMH in the Old Testament' (PhD dissertation; Chicago: University of Chicago, 1977).

Barstad, Hans M., *The Religious Polemics of Amos: Studies in the Preaching of Amos 2,7b-8; 4,1-13; 5,1-27; 6,4-7; 8,14* (Leiden: E.J. Brill, 1984).

Bendor, S., *The Social Structure of Ancient Israel: The Institution of the Family (Beit 'Ab) from the Settlement to the End of the Monarchy* (ed. Emunah Katzenstein; Jerusalem Biblical Series; Jerusalem: Simor, 1996).

Berlin, Adele, *Poetics and Interpretation of Biblical Narrative* (Sheffield: Almond Press, 1983).

Bird, Phyllis, ' "To Play the Harlot": An Inquiry Into an Old Testament Metaphor', in Peggy L. Day (ed.), *Gender and Difference in Ancient Israel* (Philadelphia: Fortress Press, 1989), pp. 75-94.

Boling, Robert G., *Judges: Introduction, Translation and Commentary* (AB, 6A; Garden City, NY: Doubleday, 1975).

—'Judges: Notes', in Wayne A. Meeks (ed.), *The HarperCollins Study Bible: New Revised Standard Version* (New York: HarperCollins, 1993), pp. 367-407.

Borowski, Oded, *Agriculture in Iron Age Israel* (Winona Lake, IN: Eisenbrauns, 1987).

Breasted, J.H., *Ancient Records of Egypt: Historical Documents from the Earliest Times to the Persian Conquest.* III. *The Nineteenth Dynasty* (Ancient Records of Egypt, 2nd series; Chicago: University of Chicago Press, 1906).

Bright, John, *Jeremiah* (AB, 21 Garden City, NY: Doubleday, 1965).

Brinkman, J.A. (ed.), *The Assyrian Dictionary of the Oriental Institute of the University of Chicago.* XI. *N, Part I* (Chicago: University of Chicago Press, 1980).

Brueggemann, Walter, *First and Second Samuel* (ed. James Luther Mays; IBC; Louisville, KY: Westminster/John Knox Press, 1990).

Burchardt, Max, *Die altkanaanäischen Fremdworte und Eigennamen im Aegyptischen: Erster Teil: die kritische Analyse der Schreibung* (Leipzig: J.C. Hinrichs, 1909).

Campbell, Antony F., SJ, *Of Prophets and Kings: A Late Ninth-Century Document (1 Samuel 1–2 Kings 10)* (CBQMS, 17; Washington, DC: Catholic Biblical Association, 1986).

Campbell, Edward F., *Ruth* (AB, 7; Garden City, NY: Doubleday, 1975).

Campbell, John K., *Honour, Family and Patronage: A Study of Institutions and Moral Values in a Greek Mountain Community* (Oxford: Clarendon Press, 1964).

Carasik, Michael, 'Ruth 2,7: Why the Overseer Was Embarrassed', *ZAW* 107 (1995), pp. 493-94.

Carlson, R.A., *David, the Chosen King: A Traditio-Historical Approach to the Second Book of Samuel* (trans. Eric J. Sharpe and Stanley Rudman; Uppsala: Almqvist & Wiksell, 1964).

Carney, Thomas F., *The Shape of the Past: Models and Antiquity* (Lawrence, KS: Coronado Press, 1975).

Caspari, D. Wilhelm, *Die Samuelbücher* (KAT; Leipzig: Deichert, 1926).

Caspari, Wilhelm, 'The Literary Type and Historical Value of 2 Samuel 15–20', in David M. Gunn (ed.), *Narrative and Novella in Samuel: Studies by Hugo Gressmann and Other Scholars 1906–1923* (trans. David E. Orton; JSOTSup, 116; Sheffield: Almond Press, 1991), pp. 59-88.

Chaney, Marvin L., 'Ancient Palestinian Peasant Movements and the Formation of Premonarchic Israel', in David Noel Freedman and David Frank Graf (eds.), *Palestine in Transition: The Emergence of Ancient Israel* (SWBA, 2; Sheffield: Almond Press, 1983).

—'Latifundialization and Prophetic Diction in Eighth-Century Israel and Judah' (Unpublished paper, Colloquium on Reformed Faith and Economics, Ghost Ranch, 1987).

Chinchen, Delbert, 'The Patron-Client System: A Model of Indigenous Discipleship', *Evangelical Missions Quarterly* 31 (October 1995), pp. 446-51.

Chirichigno, Gregory, *Debt-Slavery in Israel and the Ancient Near East* (JSOTSup, 141; Sheffield: JSOT Press, 1993).

Chow, John K., *Patronage and Power: A Study of Social Networks in Corinth* (JSNTSup, 75; Sheffield: JSOT Press, 1992).

Clements, Ronald E., *Isaiah 1–39* (NCB; Grand Rapids: Eerdmans, 1980).

Clines, David J.A., *Ezra, Nehemiah, Esther* (NCB; Grand Rapids: Eerdmans, 1984).

—*Job 1–20* (WBC; Dallas: Word Books, 1989).

Conroy, Charles, *Absalom Absalom! Narrative and Language in 2 Sam 13–20* (AnBib, 8; Rome: Pontifical Biblical Institute, 1978).

Coogan, Michael David, 'Job's Children', in Tzvi Abusch, John Huehnergard and Piotr Steinkeller (eds.), *Lingering Over Words: Studies in Ancient Near Eastern Literature in Honor of William L. Moran* (Atlanta: Scholars Press, 1990).

Coote, Robert B., *Amos Among the Prophets: Composition and Theology* (Philadelphia: Fortress Press, 1981).

Cowley, A., *Aramaic Papyri of the Fifth Century B.C.: Edited, with Translation and Notes* (Oxford: Clarendon Press, 1923).

Cross, Frank Moore, *Canaanite Myth and Hebrew Epic* (Cambridge, MA: Harvard University Press, 1973).

Crüsemann, Frank, *The Torah: Theology and Social History of Old Testament Law* (trans. Allan W. Mahnke; Minneapolis: Fortress Press, 1996).

Cutler, B. (in collaboration with John Macdonald), 'Identification of the Na'Ar in the Ugaritic Texts', *UF* 8 (1976), pp. 27-36.

Dahood, Mitchell, 'The Breakup of Stereotyped Phrases: Some New Examples.' *JANES* 5 (1973), pp. 83-89.

—*Psalms III: 101-150: Introduction, Translation, and Notes with an Appendix, the Grammar of the Psalter* (AB, 17A; New York: Doubleday, 1970).

—*Ras Shamra Parallels: The Text from Ugarit and the Hebrew Bible*, I (AnOr, 49; Rome: Pontifical Biblical Institute, 1972).

Darr, Katheryn Pfisterer, 'Literary Perspectives on Prophetic Literature', in James Luther Mays, David L. Petersen and Kent Harold Richards (eds.), *Old Testament Interpretation: Past, Present, Future: Essays in Honor of Gene M. Tucker* (Nashville: Abingdon Press, 1995), pp. 127-43.

Davis, John, *The People of the Mediterranean: An Essay in Comparative Social Anthropology* (London: Routledge & Kegan Paul, 1977).

Day, J., 'Foreign Semitic Influence on the Wisdom of Israel', in J.P. Day, R.P. Gordon and H.G.M. Williamson (eds.), *Wisdom in Ancient Israel: Essays in Honour of J.A. Emerton* (Cambridge: Cambridge University Press, 1995), pp. 55-70.

Delcor, M., 'Le personnel du Temple d'Astarté à Kition d'après une tablette Phonicienne (CIS 86 A et B)', *UF* 11 (1979), pp. 147-64.

DeVries, Simon J., *1 Kings* (eds. David A. Hubbard and Glenn W. Barker; WBC; Waco, TX: Word Books, 1985).

Dhorme, E., *A Commentary on the Book of Job* (trans. Harold Knight; London: Thomas Nelson, 1967).

Dietrich, Manfried, Oswald Loretz and J. Sanmartin, *Die keilalphabetischen Texte aus Ugarit* (AOAT, 24; Neukirchen–Vluyn: Neukirchener Verlag, 1976).

Dietrich, W., *Prophetie und Geschichte: Eine redaktionsgeschichtliche Untersuchung zum Deuteronomistischen Geschichtswerk* (FRLANT; Göttingen: Vandenhoeck & Ruprecht, 1972).

Donner, H., and W. Röllig, *Kanaanäische und aramäische Inschriften* (2 vols.; Wiesbaden: Otto Harrassowitz, 1962, 1964).

Driver, Samuel R., and George B. Gray, *A Critical and Exegetical Commentary on the Book of Job: Together with a New Translation* (ICC; New York: Charles Scribner's Sons, 1921).

Eisenstadt, S.N., and Louis Roniger, 'Patron–Client Relations as a Model of Structuring Social Exchange', *Comparative Studies in Society and History* 22 (1980), pp. 42-77.

Elliott, John H., 'Patronage and Clientism in Early Christian Society: A Short Reading Guide', *FF* 3.4 (December 1987), pp. 39-48.

Erman, Adolf, and Hermann Grapow, *Aegyptisches Handwörterbuch* (Berlin: Verlag von Reuther & Reichard, 1921).

Eskenazi, Tamara Cohn, 'Torah as Narrative and Narrative as Torah', in James Luther Mays, David L. Petersen and Kent Harold Richards (eds.), *Old Testament Interpretation: Past, Present, and Future: Essays in Honor of Gene M. Tucker* (Nashville: Abingdon Press, 1995), pp. 13-30.

Fewell, Danna Nolan, and David M. Gunn, 'Tipping the Balance: Sternberg's Reader and the Rape of Dinah', *JBL* 110.2 (1991), pp. 193-211.

Fokkelman, Jan P., *Narrative Art and Poetry in the Books of Samuel: A Full Interpretation Based on Stylistic and Structural Analyses* (Assen: Van Gorcum, 1981).

Fox, Nili, 'Royal Officials and Court Families: A New Look at the yĕlādîmin in 1 Kings 2', *BA* 59 (1996), pp. 225-32.

Frick, Frank S., *The Formation of the State in Ancient Israel: A Survey of Models and Theories* (SWBA, 4; Sheffield: Almond Press, 1985).

Frolov, Serge, and Vladimir Orel, 'Was the Lad a Lad? On the Interpretation of I Sam 1.24', *BN* 81 (1996), pp. 5-7.

Frymer-Kensky, Tikva, *In the Wake of the Goddesses: Women, Culture, and the Biblical Transformation of Pagan Myth* (New York: Fawcett Columbine, 1992).

—'Law and Philosophy: The Case of Sex in the Bible', *Semeia* 45 (1988), pp. 89-102.

Gardiner, Alan H., *Ancient Egyptian Onomastica*. I. *Text* (London: Oxford University Press, 1947).

—*The Kadesh Inscriptions of Ramesses II* (Oxford: Grifffith Institute, Ashmolean Museum, 1960).

Garfinkel, Yosef, 'The Eliakim Na'Ar Yokan Seal Impressions: Sixty Years of Confusion in Biblical Archaeology Research', *BA* 53 (1990), pp. 74-79.

Garnsey, Peter, and Richard Saller. *The Roman Empire: Economy, Society and Culture* (Berkeley: University of California Press, 1987).

Gelb, I.J., *Glossary of Old Akkadian* (Materials for the Assyrian Dictionary; Chicago: University of Chicago Press, 1957).

Gordis, Robert, *The Book of Job: Commentary New Translation and Special Studies* (New York: Jewish Theological Seminary of America, 1978).

Gordon, Cyrus H., *Ugaritic Literature: A Comprehensive Translation of the Poetic and Prose Text* (Rome: Pontifical Biblical Institute, 1949).

—*UT* (AnOr, 38; Rome: Pontifical Biblical Institute, 1965).

Gottwald, Norman K., *The Hebrew Bible: A Socio-Literary Introduction* (Philadelphia: Fortress Press, 1985).

—*The Tribes of Yahweh: A Sociology of the Religion of Liberated Israel, 1250–1050 B.C.* (Maryknoll, NY: Orbis Books, 1979).

Gray, John, *I & II Kings: A Commentary* (OTL; Philadelphia: Westminster Press, 1963).

—*The Legacy of Canaan: The Ras Shamra Texts and Their Relevance to the Old Testament* (VTSup, 5; Leiden: E.J. Brill, 1957).

—*The New Century Bible Commentary: Joshua, Judges, Ruth* (NCB; Grand Rapids: Eerdmans, 1986).

Greenfield, J.C., 'The Wisdom of Ahiqar', in J.P. Day, R.P. Gordon and H.G.M. Williamson (eds.), *Wisdom in Ancient Israel: Essays in Honour of J.A. Emerton* (Cambridge: Cambridge University Press, 1995), pp. 43-52.

Gressmann, Hugo, *Die älteste Geschichtsschreibung und Prophetie Israels* (SAT, 2.1; Göttingen: Vandenhoeck & Ruprecht, 1921).
—'The Oldest History Writing in Israel', in David M. Gunn (ed.), *Narrative and Novella in Samuel: Studies by Hugo Gressmann and Other Scholars, 1906–1923* (trans. David E. Orton; JSOTSup, 9; Sheffield: Almond Press, 1991).
Habel, Norman C., *The Book of Job: A Commentary* (OTL; Philadelphia: Westminster Press, 1985).
Hamilton, Victor P., *The Book of Genesis: Chapters 18–50* (NICOT; Grand Rapids: Eerdmans, 1995).
Hanson, K.C., 'BTB's Reader's Guide to Kinship', *BTB* 24 (1994), pp. 183-94.
Hanson, Paul D., *Isaiah 40–66* (IBC; Louisville, KY: Westminster/John Knox Press, 1995).
Harrisell, J.A., 'The Indentured Labor of the Prodigal Son (Luke 15.15)', *JBL* 115 (1996), pp. 714-17.
Heltzer, Michael, 'The New-Assyrian Sakintu and the Biblical Sōkenet (1 Reg 1,4)', In *La femme dans le Proche-Orient antique: XXXIIIe Rencontre assyriologique internationale* (Paris: Recherches sur les Civilisations, 1987).
Hertzberg, Hans Wilhelm, *I and II Samuel* (OTL; London: SCM Press, 1964).
Hiebert, Paula S., ' "Whence Shall Help Come to Me?": The Biblical Widow', in Peggy L. Day (ed.), *Gender and Difference in Ancient Israel* (Philadelphia: Fortress Press, 1989).
Hiebert, Robert J.V., 'Deuteronomy 22.28-29 and Its Premishnaic Interpretations', *CBQ* 56 (April 1994), pp. 203-20.
Hillers, Delbert R., *Lamentations: Introduction, Translation, and Notes* (AB, 7A; Garden City, NY: Doubleday, 1972).
Hobsbawm, Eric J., *Bandits* (New York: Pantheon, rev. edn, 1981).
—'Social Banditry', in H.A. Handsberger (ed.), *Rural Protest* (New York: Barnes & Noble, 1973).
Hoftijzer, J., and K. Jongeling, *Dictionary of the North-West Semitic Inscriptions with Appendices by R.C. Steiner, A. Mosak Moshavi and B. Porten. II. M–T* (Leiden: E.J. Brill, 1995).
Hollister, C. Warren, 'Knights and Knight Service', in Joseph R. Strayer (ed.), *Dictionary of the Middle Ages. VII. Italian Renaissance-Mabinogi* (New York: Charles Scribner's Sons, 1986), pp. 276-79.
Hopkins, David C., *The Highlands of Canaan: Agricultural Life in the Early Iron Age* (SWBA, 3; Sheffield: Almond Press, 1985).
Horsley, R.A., 'Àpiru and Cossacks: A Comparative Analysis of Social Form and Historical Role', in Jacob Neusner (ed.), *Religion, Literature, and Society in Ancient Israel, Formative Christianity and Judaism* (New Perspectives in Ancient Judaism, 2; Lanham, MD: University Press of America, 1987), pp. 3-26.
Hubbard, Robert L., *The Book of Ruth* (NICOT; Grand Rapids: Eerdmans, 1988).
Janzen, J. Gerald, *Job* (IBC; Atlanta: John Knox Press, 1985).
Jastrow, Morris, Jr, *The Book of Job: Its Origin, Growth and Interpretation Together with a New Translation Based on a Revised Test* (London: J.B. Lippincott, 1920).
Kitchen, K.A., *Ramesside Inscriptions. II. Historical and Biographical* (Oxford: Basil Blackwell, 1979).

Klein, Lillian R., 'Honor and Shame in Esther', in Athalya Brenner (ed.), *A Feminist Companion to Esther, Judith, and Susanna* (Feminist Companion to the Bible, 7; Sheffield: Sheffield Academic Press, 1995), pp. 149-75.

Klein, Ralph W., *1 Samuel* (WBC; Waco, TX: Word Books, 1983).

—'Israel/Today's Believers and the Nations: Three Test Cases', *CurTM* 24.3 (1997), pp. 232-37.

Koehler, Ludwig, and Walter Baumgartner, *The Hebrew and Aramaic Lexicon of the Old Testament* (rev. Walter Baumgartner and Johann Jakob Stamm; Leiden: E.J. Brill, 1995).

Kooij, Arie van der, 'The Story of David and Goliath: The Early History of its Text', *ETL* 68.1 (April 1992), pp. 118-31.

Kuhnigk, W., *Nordwestsemitische Studien zum Hoseabuch* (BibOr, 27; Rome: Pontifical Biblical Institute, 1974).

Labov, William, *Language in the Inner City: Studies in the Black English Vernacular* (Philadelphia: University of Pennsylvania Press, 1972).

Laniak, Tim, 'Esther—A Tale of Honor and Shame' (Paper presented at SBL Annual Meeting, Chicago, Illinois, 1994).

Lasine, Stuart, 'Judicial Narratives and the Ethics of Reading: The Reader as Judge of the Dispute between Mephibosheth and Ziba', *HS* 30 (1989), pp. 49-69.

Lenski, Gerhard, and Jean Lenski, *Human Societies: An Introduction to Macrosociology* (New York: McGraw–Hill, 1978).

Levenson, Jon D., *Esther: A Commentary* (OTL; Louisville, KY: Westminster/John Knox Press, 1997).

Liddell, H.G. (ed.), *An Intermediate Greek–English Lexicon Founded Upon the Seventh Edition of Liddell and Scott's Greek–English Lexicon* (Oxford: Clarendon Press, 1889).

Linton, Ralph, *The Study of Man* (New York: Appleton–Century–Crofts, 1936).

Lipiński, Edward, 'Skn et Sgn dans le sémitique occidental du nord', *UF* 5 (1973), pp. 191-207.

Long, Burke O., *1 Kings with an Introduction to Historical Literature* (FOTL, 9; Grand Rapids: Eerdmans, 1984).

—*2 Kings* (FOTL, 10; Grand Rapids: Eerdmans, 1991).

Loretz, Oswald, 'Ugaritisch Skn-Skt und hebräisch Skn-Sknt', *ZAW* 94 (1982), pp. 126-27.

Lundbom, Jack R., 'Rhetorical Structures in Jeremiah 1', *ZAW* 103 (1991), pp. 193-210.

Lyke, Larry L., 'Where Does "the Boy" Belong? Compositional Strategy in Genesis 21.14', *CBQ* 56.4 (1994), pp. 637-48.

Macdonald, John, 'The Role and Status of the Suharu in the Mari Correspondence.' *JAOS* 96.1 (1976), pp. 57-68.

—'The Status and Role of the Na'Ar in Israelite Society', *JNES* 35.3 (July 1976), pp. 147-70.

—'The Unique Ugaritic Personnel Text KTU 4.102', *UF* 10 (1978), pp. 161-73.

Mace, David R., *Hebrew Marriage: A Sociological Study* (New York: Philosophical Library, 1953).

Malina, Bruce J., *The New Testament World: Insights from Cultural Anthropology* (Louisville, KY: Westminster/John Knox Press, rev. edn, 1993).

—'Patron and Client: The Analogy Behind Synoptic Theology', *FF* 4.1 (March 1988), pp. 2-31.

Malina, Bruce, and Richard Rohrbaugh, *Social-Science Commentary on the Synoptic Gospels* (Minneapolis: Fortress Press, 1992).

Margalit, Baruch, 'The Ugaritic Feat of the Drunken Gods: Another Look at RS 24.258 (KTU 1.114)', *Maarav* 2.1 (1979–80), pp. 65-120.

Matthews, Victor H., and Don C. Benjamin, 'The Elder', *Bible Today* 30 (1992), pp. 170-74.

—'Social Sciences and Biblical Studies', in *Honor and Shame in the World of the Bible* (Semeia, 68; Atlanta: Scholars Press, 1996), pp. 7-21.

—*Social World of Ancient Israel: 1250–587 BCE* (Peabody, MA: Hendrickson, 1993).

Mayer, Walter, and Ronald Mayer-Opificius. 'Die Schlacht bei Qadeš: Der Versuch einer neuen Rekonstruktion', *UF* 26 (1994), pp. 321-68.

Mayes, A.D.H. *Deuteronomy* (NCB; Grand Rapids: Eerdmans, 1981).

Mays, James Luther, *Amos: A Commentary* (OTL; Philadelphia: Westminster Press, 1969).

McCarter, P. Kyle, Jr, *I Samuel: A New Translation with Introduction, Notes, and Commentary* (AB, 9; Garden City, NY: Doubleday, 1980).

—*II Samuel: A New Translation with Introduction, Notes and Commentary* (AB, 9; Garden City, NY: Doubleday, 1984).

—'1 Samuel: Notes', in Wayne A. Meeks (ed.), *The HarperCollins Study Bible: New Revised Standard Version* (New York: HarperCollins, 1993).

McKenzie, John L., 'The Elders in the Old Testament', *Bib* 40 (1959), pp. 522-40.

—*Second Isaiah* (AB, 20; Garden City, NY: Doubleday, 1968).

McLaughlin, John L., 'The Marzaat Ugarit: A Textual and Contextual Study', *UF* 23 (1991), pp. 265-81.

McNutt, Paula M., *The Forging of Israel: Iron Technology, Symbolism, and Tradition in Ancient Society* (JSOTSup, 108; Sheffield: Almond Press, 1990).

Mendenhall, George E., *The Tenth Generation: The Origins of the Biblical Tradition* (Baltimore: The Johns Hopkins University Press, 1973).

Meyer, Eduard, *Geschichte des Altertums*. II/1. *Die Zeit der ägyptischen Grossmacht* (Berlin: J.G. Cotta'sche Buchhandlung, 1929).

Meyers, Carol L., *Discovering Eve: Ancient Israelite Women in Context* (New York: Oxford University Press, 1988).

—'The Family in Early Israel', in Leo G. Perdue, Joseph Blenkinsopp, John J. Collins and Carol Meyers (eds.), *Families in Ancient Israel* (Family, Religion, and Culture; Louisville, KY: Westminster/John Knox Press, 1997), pp. 1-47.

—' "To Her Mother's House": Considering a Counterpart to the Israelite Bêt 'ab', in David Jobling (ed.), *The Bible and the Politics of Exegesis: Essays in Honor of Norman K. Gottwald on His Sixty-Fifth Birthday* (Cleveland: Pilgrim, 1991), pp. 39-52.

—'Procreation, Production, and Protection: Male–Female Balance in Early Israel', *JAAR* 51.4 (1983), pp. 569-93.

Meyers, Carol L., and Eric M. Meyers, *Zechariah 9–14* (AB, 25C; New York: Doubleday, 1993).

Miller, P.D., Jr, P.D. Hanson and S.D. McBride (eds.), *Ancient Israelite Religion: Essays in Honor of Frank Moore Cross* (Philadelphia: Fortress Press, 1987).

Montgomery, James A., *A Critical and Exegetical Commentary on the Books of Kings* (ICC; New York: Charles Scribner's Sons, 1951).

Moor, Johannes C. de, *An Anthology of Religious Texts from Ugarit* (Religious Texts Translation Series, 16; Leiden: E.J. Brill, 1987).

Moore, Carey A., *Esther: Introduction, Translation, and Notes* (AB, 7B; Garden City, NY: Doubleday, 1971).

Moxnes, Halvor, 'Honor and Shame' (BTB Readers Guide) *BTB* 23, pp. 167-76.

—'Patron–Client Relations and the New Community in Luke–Acts', in J.H. Neyrey (ed.), *Social World of Luke–Acts* (Peabody, MA: Hendrickson, 1991), pp. 241-68.

Mulder, Martin Jan, 'Versuch zur Deutung von Sokènèt in 1 Kön 1:2,4', *VT* 22 (1972), pp. 43-54.

Naveh, Joseph, 'Unpublished Phoenician Inscriptions from Palestine', *IEJ* 37 (1987), pp. 25-30.

Niditch, Susan. 'The "Sodomite" Theme in Judges 19–20: Family, Community, and Social Disintegration', *CBQ* 44 (1982), pp. 365-78.

Naveh, J., 'Unpublished Phoenican Inscriptions from Palestine', *IEJ* 37 (1987), pp. 25-30.

Noth, Martin, *The Deuteronomistic History* (JSOTSup, 14; Sheffield: JSOT Press, 1981).

—*The History of Israel* (New York: Harper & Row, 1958).

—*A History of Pentateuchal Traditions* (trans. Bernhard W. Anderson; Chico, CA: Scholars Press, 1981).

Nougayrol, Jean, E. Laroche, Charles Virolleaud and Claude F.A. Schaeffer, *Ugaritica. V/2. Les nouveaux textes mythologiques et liturgiques de Ras Shamra* (Mission Ras Shamra XVI; Paris: Imprimerie National, 1968), pp. 545-606.

O'Connor, M., *Hebrew Verse Structure* (Winona Lake, IN: Eisenbrauns, 1980).

Parker, Simon B. (ed.), *Ugaritic Narrative Poetry* (Writings from the Ancient World, 9; Atlanta: Scholars Press, 1997).

Paul, Shalom M., *Amos* (Hermeneia; Minneapolis: Fortress Press, 1991).

Perdue, Leo, Joseph Blenkinsopp, John J. Collins and Carol Meyers (eds.), *Families in Ancient Israel* (Family, Religion, and Culture; Louisville, KY: Westminster/John Knox Press, 1997).

Peristiany, J.G. (ed.), *Honour and Shame: The Values of Mediterranean Society* (London: Weidenfeld & Nicolson, 1965).

Petersen, David L., *Zechariah 9–14 and Malachi* (OTL; Louisville, KY: Westminster/John Knox Press, 1995).

Phillips, Anthony, 'Another Look at Adultery', *JSOT* 20 (1981), pp. 3-25.

Pilch, John J., and Bruce J. Malina, *Biblical Social Values and their Meaning: A Handbook* (Peabody, MA: Hendrickson, 1993).

Pitt-Rivers, Julian, *The Fate of Shechem, or The Politics of Sex: Essays in the Anthropology of the Mediterranean* (Cambridge Studies in Social Anthropology; Cambridge: Cambridge University Press, 1977).

Pope, Marvin H., 'A Divine Banquet at Ugarit', in Mark S. Smith (ed.), in *Probative Pontificating in Ugaritic and Biblical Literature* (Munster: Ugarit-Verlag, 1994), pp. 175-77.

—*Job* (AB, 15; Garden City, NY: Doubleday, 1965).

—*Probative Pontificating in Ugaritic and Biblical Literature* (Munster: Ugarit-Verlag, 1994).

Porten, B., *Archives from Elephantine: The Life of an Ancient Jewish Military Colony* (Berkeley: University of California Press, 1960).

Pressler, Carolyn, *The View of Women Found in the Deuteronomic Family Laws* (BZAW, 2/6; Berlin: W. de Gruyter, 1993).

Rad, Gerhard von, *Deuteronomy: A Commentary. Genesis: A Commentary* (trans. John H. Marks; OTL; Philadelphia: Westminster Press, rev. edn, 1972 [1951]).

Rainey, Anson F., 'The Military Personnel of Ugarit', *JNES* 24 (1965), pp. 17-27.

—'The Social Stratification of Ugarit' (PhD dissertation, Brandeis University, 1962).

—'Unruly Elements in Late Bronze Canaanite Society', in D.P. Wright, D.N. Freedman and A. Hurvitz (eds.), *Pomegranates and Golden Bells: Studies in Biblical, Jewish, and Near Eastern Ritual, Law and Literature in Honor of Jacob Milgrom* (Winona Lake, IN: Eisenbrauns, 1995), pp. 481-96.

Ramsey, George W., *The Quest for the Historical Israel* (Atlanta: John Knox Press, 1981).

Ratner, Robert, ''Three Bulls or One?': A Reappraisal of 1 Samuel 1.24', *Bib* 68.1 (1987), pp. 98-102.

Reviv, Hanoch, *The Elders in Ancient Israel: A Study of a Biblical Institution* (trans. Lucy Plitmann; Jerusalem: Magnes Press, 1989).

—'More About the "Maryannu" in Syria and Palestine', in Bustanay Oded, *et al.* (eds.), *Studies in the History of the Jewish People and the Land of Israel*, II (Haifa: University of Haifa Press, 1972).

—'Some Comments on the Maryannu', *IEJ* 22.4 (1972), pp. 218-28.

Rofé, Alexander, 'The Battle of David and Goliath: Folklore, Theology, Eschatology', in Jacob Neusner, *et al.* (eds.), *Judaic Perspectives on Ancient Israel* (1987).

—'The Classification of the Prophetical Stories', *JBL* 89 (1970), pp. 427-40.

—'Family and Sex Laws in Deuteronomy and the Book of Covenant', *Henoch* 9.2 (1987), pp. 131-59.

Rohrbaugh, Richard (ed.), *The Social Sciences and New Testament Interpretation* (Peabody, MA: Hendrickson, 1996).

Roniger, Luis, 'Modern Patron–Client Relations and Historical Clientelism: Some Clues from Ancient Republican Rome', *Archives of European Sociology* 24 (1983), pp. 63-95.

Rook, John, 'When Is a Widow Not a Widow? Guardianship Provides an Answer', *BTB* 28 (1998), pp. 4-6.

Rost, Leonhard, *The Succession to the Throne of David* (Historic Texts & Interpreters, 1; Sheffield: Almond Press, 1982).

Sakenfeld, Katharine Doob, *The Meaning of Hesed in the Hebrew Bible: A New Inquiry* (HSM, 17; Missoula, MT: Scholars Press, 1978).

Saller, Richard P., *Imperial Patronage under the Early Empire* (Cambridge: Cambridge University Press, 1982).

Sasson, Jack, *Ruth: A New Translation with a Philological Commentary and a Formalist-Folklorist Interpretation* (Baltimore: The Johns Hopkins University Press, 1979).

Schulman, Alan R., 'The N'rn at the Battle of Kadesh', *JARCE* 1 (1962), pp. 47-52.

Selms, A. van, *Marriage and Family Life in Ugaritic Literature* (Pretoria Oriental Series; London: Luzac, 1954).

Shiloh, Yigael., 'The Four-Room House: Its Situation and Function in the Israelite City', *IEJ* 20 (1970), pp. 180-90.

Simkins, Ronald, ' "Return to Yahweh": Honor and Shame in Joel', *Semeia* 68 (1996), pp. 41-54.

Skinner, John, *A Critical and Exegetical Commentary on Genesis* (ICC; New York: Charles Scribner's Sons, rev. edn, 1910).

Smith, Henry Preserved, *A Critical and Exegetical Commentary on the Books of Samuel* (ICC; New York: Charles Scribner's Sons, 1899).

Soggin, J. Alberto, *Judges: A Commentary* (OTL; Philadelphia: Westminster Press, 1981).

Speiser, E.A., *Genesis: Introduction, Translation and Notes* (AB, 1, Garden City, NY: Doubleday, 1964).

Stager, Lawrence E., 'The Archaeology of the Family in Ancient Israel', *BASOR* 260 (1985), pp. 1-35.

Stansell, Gary, 'Honor and Shame in the David Narratives', in Frank Crüsemann, Christof Hardmeier and Rainer Kessler (eds.), *'Was ist der Mensch?' Beiträge zur Anthropologie des Alten Testaments* (Tübingen: Chr. Kaiser Verlag, 1992), pp. 94-114.

Stähli, Hans-Peter, *Knabe-Jüngling-Knecht: Untersuchungen zum Begriff Na'ar im Alten Testament* (BBET, 7; Frankfurt: Peter Lang, 1978).

Steinberg, Naomi, 'The Deuteronomic Law Code and the Politics of State Centralization', in David Jobling, *et al.* (eds.), *The Bible and the Politics of Exegesis: Essays in Honor of Norman K. Gottwald on his Sixty-Fifth Birthday* (Cleveland: Pilgrim, 1991), pp. 161-70, 336-38.

Sternberg, Meir, 'Biblical Poetics and Sexual Politics: From Reading to Counterreading', *JBL* 111.3 (1992), pp. 463-88.

—*The Poetics of Biblical Narrative* (Bloomington: Indiana University Press, 1985).

Stone, Kenneth Alan, 'Gender and Homosexuality in Judges 19: Subject–Honor, Object–Shame?', *JSOT* 67 (Spring 1995), pp. 87-107.

—*Sex, Honor, and Power in the Deuteronomistic History* (JSOTSup, 234; Sheffield: Sheffield Academic Press, 1996).

Stulman, Louis, 'Encroachment in Deuteronomy: An Analysis of the Social World of the D Code', *JBL* 109 (1990), pp. 613-32.

Sweeney, Marvin A. *Isaiah 1–39* (FOTL, 16; Grand Rapids: Eerdmans, 1996).

Thompson, William E., and Joseph V. Hickey, *Society in Focus: An Introduction to Sociology* (New York: Harper Collins College Publishers, 1994).

Tomback, R.S., in H.C. Kee and D.A. Knight (eds.), *A Comparative Semitic Lexicon of the Phoenician and Punic Languages* (SBLDS; Missoula, MT: Scholars Press, 1978), p. 117.

Trebolle, Julio C., 'The Story of David and Goliath (1 Sam 17–18): Textual Variants and Literary Composition', *BIOSCS* 23 (Fall 1990), pp. 16-30.

Trible, Phyllis, 'The Other Woman: A Literary and Theological Study of the Hagar Narratives', in J. Butler, E Conrad and B. Ollenburger (eds.), *Understanding the Word: Essays in Honour of Bernhard W. Anderson* (JSOTSup, 37; Sheffield: JSOT Press, 1985), pp. 221-46.

—*Rhetorical Criticism: Context, Method, and the Book of Jonah* (Minneapolis: Fortress Press, 1994).

—*Texts of Terror: Literary-Feminist Readings of Biblical Narratives* (OBT; Philadelphia: Fortress Press, 1984).

—'Woman in the OT (sic)', in *Interpreters Dictionary of the Bible: An Illustrated Encyclopedia* (Supplementary Volume; Keith Crim gen. ed.; Nashville: Abingdon Press, 1976), pp. 963-66.

Tsevat, Matitiahu, 'Der Schangentext von Ugarit: UT 607-KTU 1.100-Ug V, 564ff.-RS 24.244', *UF* 11 (1979), pp. 759-78.

Ussishkin, David, 'Royal Judean Storage Jars and Private Seal Impressions', *BASOR* 223 (1976), pp. 1-14.

Vaux, Roland de, *Ancient Israel. I. Social Institutions* (New York: McGraw–Hill, 1965).

Veijola, Timo, *Annales Academiae Scientiarum Fennicae B* (Helsinki: Suomalainen Tiede-akatemia, 1975).

—*David: Gesammelte Studien zu den David Uberlieferungen des Alten Testaments* (Schriften der Finnischen Exegetischen Gesellschaft, 52; Helsinki: Finnische Exegetische Gesellschaft, Vandenhoeck & Ruprecht, 1990).

Virolleaud, Claude F.-A., *Le palais royal d'Ugarit* (Mission de Ras Shamra; Paris: Imprimerie Nationale, 1965).

Wadsworth, Tom, 'Is there a Hebrew Word for Virgin? Bethulah in the Old Testament', *ResQ* 23.3 (1980), pp. 161-71.

Waldbaum, Jane C., *From Bronze to Iron: The Transition from the Bronze Age to the Iron Age in the Eastern Mediterranean* (Studies in Mediterranean Archaeology, 5.54; Gothenburg: Paul Aström, 1978).

Wallace-Hadrill, A. (ed.), *Patronage in Ancient Society* (London: Routledge, 1989), p. 157.

Watson, W.G.E., *Classical Hebrew Poetry: A Guide to its Techniques* (JSOTSup, 170; Sheffield: JSOT Press, 1984).

Wenham, Gordon J., 'Betulah, "A Girl of Marriageable Age" ', *VT* 22 (July 1972), pp. 326-48.

Westermann, Claus, *Genesis 12–36: A Commentary* (trans. John J. Scullion, SJ; Minneapolis: Augsburg, 1985).

—*Genesis 37–50: A Commentary* (trans. John J. Scullion, SJ; Minneapolis: Augsburg, 1986).

—*Lamentations: Issues and Interpretation* (Minneapolis: Fortress Press, 1994).

Wolff, Hans Walter, *Hosea: A Commentary on the Book of the Prophet Hosea* (Hermeneia; Philadelphia: Fortress Press, 1974).

—*Joel and Amos: A Commentary on the Books of the Prophets Joel and Amos* (Hermeneia; Philadelphia: Fortress Press, 1977).

Wright, Christopher J.H., 'Family', *ABD*, II, pp. 761-69.

Wright, G. Ernest, *Biblical Archaeology* (Philadelphia: Westminster Press, rev. edn, 1962).

Yadin, Yigael, *The Art of Warfare in Biblical Lands in the Light of Archaeological Study* (2 vols.; New York: McGraw–Hill, 1963).

Yon, Marguerite, 'Kition in the Tenth to Fourth Centuries B.C.' (trans. William A.P. Childs), *BASOR* 308 (1997), pp. 1-17.

INDEXES

INDEX OF REFERENCES

BIBLE

INDEX OF AUTHORS

JOURNAL FOR THE STUDY OF THE OLD TESTAMENT
SUPPLEMENT SERIES